Crimes of Peace

Crimes of Peace

Mediterranean Migrations
at the World's Deadliest Border

Maurizio Albahari

PENN

UNIVERSITY OF PENNSYLVANIA PRESS

PHILADELPHIA

Published by
University of Pennsylvania Press
Philadelphia, Pennsylvania 19104-4112
www.upenn.edu/pennpress

Printed in the United States of America
on acid-free paper

1 3 5 7 9 10 8 6 4 2

Library of Congress Cataloging-in-Publication Data

ISBN 978-0-8122-4747-3

To our grandparents,
travelers
before the invention of immigration.
To the life of the drowned. To whom they loved.

Ai nostri nonni,
viaggiatori
prima che l'immigrazione fosse inventata

Našim precima,
putnicima
pre nego što je izmišljena imigracija

Then again, you don't divide up an empire with a
handshake.
You have to cut it with a knife.

—Roberto Saviano, *Gomorrah*

Contents

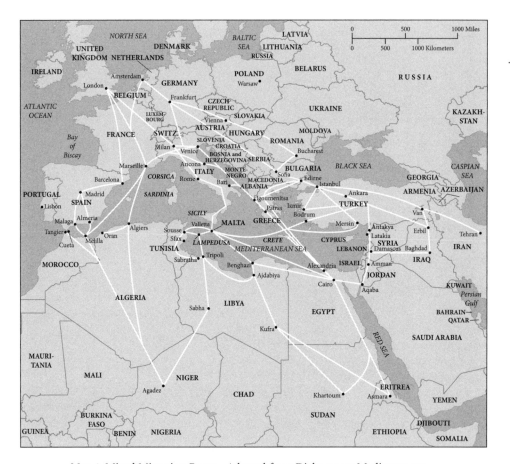

Map 1. Mixed Migration Routes. Adapted from Dialogue on Mediterranean
Transit Migration 2014 i-Map (interactive map) on Mixed Migration Routes

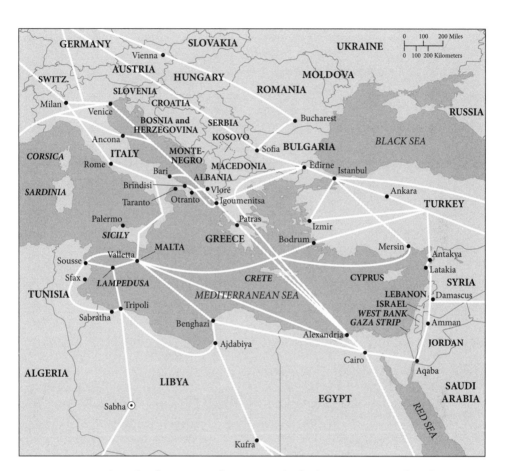

Map 2. Central and Eastern Mediterranean Mixed Migration Routes. Adapted from Dialogue on Mediterranean Transit Migration 2014 i-Map (interactive map) on Mixed Migration Routes

PART I

JOURNEYS

On the Threshold of Liberty

> The current amazement that the things we are
> experiencing are "still" possible . . . is not philosophical.
> This amazement is *not* the beginning of knowledge—
> unless it is the knowledge that the view of history which
> gives rise to it is untenable.
> —Walter Benjamin, "Theses on the Philosophy of History"
> in *Illuminations*

Safe Ports

The cannon is surrounded by a variety of intricate fences. It aims at the bare torso, or perhaps at the bluish horizon beyond the steel bars, the wide-open window, and the raging flames. Agents, rescuers, and hesitant bystanders might be peeking through the airy curtains. Observers are haunted by preemptive angst.

René Magritte's surrealist painting *On the Threshold of Liberty* (1929) uncannily foreshadows recurrent anxieties over security, rights, and democracy. Its eerie suspense resonates with the condition of maritime migrants skirting the edge of the abyss. Set in the vicinity of an Italian port, in 2014, the painting's window would be open onto a procession of gray warships. They are directed to Augusta, Pozzallo, Catania, Porto Empedocle, Trapani, Ragusa, and Palermo, in Sicily; to Brindisi, Taranto, Crotone, Salerno, and Naples, on the southern Italian coast. On the warships' decks stand Italian navy sailors, police agents, doctors, and Red Cross staff wearing paper-thin, white-hooded overalls, gloves, and surgical masks. Agents carry their batons, and a gun strapped to their legs. People in their charge sit on the deck in orderly fashion. Most also wear masks. Some women wear a veil and sunglasses; others show sunburned faces. Small children are nursing; older ones look with curiosity toward the city lights. Several teenagers are alone. Among them, some are pioneers, buying into a better future for the families they left behind. Others have been sent to safety by their distressed parents. Still others hope to reunite with families in northern Europe, or have become orphans. A man holds a baby intent on grabbing his glasses. Others have nothing and no one. Their eyes speak of excruciating exploitation and of physical distress. Everyone is sitting with their backs turned to the white blankets, barely covering the bodies of those who could not be rescued in time. As they climb down the boarding ladder, debilitated passengers are patiently assisted by navy sailors. Some have numbers stapled on their shirt. Wheelchairs and ambulances are waiting. The police prefect and the mayor are busy on their cell phones, as they allocate new arrivals into local facilities. Catholic clergy and local volunteer residents are also busy with preparations—hospitality will need to be extended.

On the outskirts of Tripoli, the smugglers Abdel, Tesfay,[1] and the rest of their transnational syndicate are busy with a new endeavor. The black dinghy, manufactured in China, needs to be taken out of the sand, where it is kept hidden. Dollars will need to be counted, at the end of the day. Guns will be kept at arm's reach. Regional militias, transnational terrorist groups, and governmental forces vie for power. Farther to the west they clash for the control of the Mellitah refinery and of the Greenstream submarine gas pipeline to Italy. They make unstable Libya decidedly unsafe for everyone, from Sabratha to Benghazi. They add to the vulnerability of displaced nonnationals, and engender postcolonial, economic, and national security preoccupations of Italian institutional partners.[2] Far from southern Italy, on the twenty-third floor of a postmodern building in Warsaw, European Union (EU) border (Frontex) agents busily keep track of all the green dots on their flat screens.[3] Each dot represents a group of migrants. The green dots "are small and sparse" between the coast of West Africa and the Canary Islands. They become "more dense" between Turkey and Greece, in the Aegean Sea. The maritime route between Libya and Italy,[4] Africa and Europe, "is almost entirely green." Frontex agents observe with disquiet the insurgency of such "risk regions" and "storm on the borders."[5] For each dot is the messenger of a breach in the EU's preemptive approach to the containment of unregulated migration. From its command center in Rome, not far from the famous Cinecittà movie studios, the Italian state police is overseeing the arrival of the navy warship in the southern port. Huge flat screens visualize in real time the Mediterranean basin and the alerts launched by overcrowded migrant boats, the coast guard, armed forces, or commercial vessels spotting boats in distress. Here, the dots are red. This police facility is networked with Warsaw's Frontex headquarters, thus contributing to the infrastructure of Eurosur, the technological platform intended to fight cross-border crime and possibly save lives at sea.[6] From this fifth-floor room, the Italian police also coordinates the deployment of several Italian navy vessels, including two submarines, and a police plane. This constitutes the bulk of what the Italian government has termed the "military-humanitarian mission 'Mare Nostrum.'"[7] Critics in Italy and the EU disparage it as a state-owned ferry line for unauthorized immigrants and as an insurance policy for traffickers. Supporters hail it as a systematic search-and-rescue endeavor with a scope unprecedented in world history.

The 2011 Arab (Spring) Uprisings have dethroned Europe's emigration gatekeepers in Egypt, Tunisia, and Libya (Chapters 2 and 5). The Iron Curtain, long blocking the gaze and the movement of most Europeans, seems to be a distant memory (Chapter 1). And yet the Mediterranean continues to be a trafficked, heavily militarized, and perilous maritime frontier (Chapters 2, 3, and 5). Adding to traditional layers of anti-immigrant political rhetoric and of gendered labor exploitation,[7] in austere Europe a mood of global apprehension is coalescing around the arrival of Ebola[8] and the looming proximity of "Islamic State" terrorists. Dust, debris, and a toxic smoke that never settles weigh on the daily existence of people in the Gaza Strip, in northern Iraq, in Libya, in Egypt, in Somalia, in Nigeria, in Mali, in the Central African Republic, in Eritrea, and in Syria.[9]

Since its inception in mid-October 2013, following two major shipwrecks (Chapter 5), Mare Nostrum has enabled many migrants in the central Mediterranean to survive the maritime leg of their journey. In eleven months of activity, vessels participating in the operation have brought to safety in Italian ports about 142,000 persons.[10] Almost every one of them has been helped to transship to a navy vessel, a most difficult procedure, while at sea between Libya (or more rarely Egypt) and Sicily. For the most part, migrants in this stretch of the Mediterranean originate from Syria and Eritrea, followed by citizens of Mali, Nigeria, Gambia, Somalia, Pakistan, Senegal, and Egypt. At least 25,500 people are known to have died trying to reach Europe since 2000.[11] In the first nine months of 2014, at least

3,072 people died or were missing in the Mediterranean, making 2014 the deadliest year on record.[12] *Crimes of Peace* traces this record.

Back in the southern Italian port, volunteers are blowing soap bubbles, if only to give children a moment of distraction. The scirocco, the southeasterly Mediterranean wind—sirocco, shlūq, xlokk, jugo, ghibli—makes your face sticky. Locals will tell you in dialect, "lu sciaroccu te trase intra ll'ossa," it gets everywhere, it corrodes baroque buildings and one's bones. Today it brings seawater droplets right onto the news camera's lens. Haze dampens my faux-Moleskine notepad.

Ali's Journey

Ali is a Hazara Afghan now in his late twenties. His journey began in 1995. One of eight siblings, he left Afghanistan when he was ten, ready to face the risks of a perilous and expensive journey, rather than the certainty of coerced Taliban recruitment. One leaves, he explains, not only because one suffers, but because of seeing others suffering. He worked for three years in Iran, where "nobody ever asks who you are."[13] After he paid $2,500, smugglers helped him cross into Turkey, walking for ten days on difficult mountainous terrain, on the same snowy paths routinely taken by thousands of people from Tehran, Baghdad, and Kabul. Some get lost; others lose limbs to the cold. Ali worked in Turkey for two and a half years in conditions "worse than in Iran," with neither identification documents nor the recognition of his refugee condition. Heavy patrolling made venturing alone across the land border with Greece impossible. Markets in Izmir and western Anatolia display a variety of life vests, targeting the hundreds of people intent on reaching Greece. Ali crossed into Greece on a speedboat, but was beaten and sent back to Turkey. In a second attempt, again the police at a Greek port caught and beat him, sending him back. Ali did make it to Greece the third time, sneaking onto a ferry by hiding in a commercial truck. One of his fellow travelers died of asphyxiation. Often, others attempting to cross this way are crushed by the freight. Like them, Ali did not fear death, but rather being discovered by the truck driver or the police. In Greece, he worked in the fields for a year and a half. After several failed attempts, in the port of Patras he hid himself under the air spoiler of a truck without the driver noticing. He made it by ferry to "an Italian port," which he later understood was Bari, on the southeastern coast. When the

Figure 1. Fragments in the "boats' cemetery," Lampedusa. Fishermen's inscriptions often invoke God's protection, shelter, and salvation. Photo: Maurizio Albahari.

carabinieri (army police force) found him, it was impossible to communicate. Though he could speak English, no agent was able or willing to listen
to the story of a journey that took eight years.

In the Adriatic ports of Bari, Brindisi, Ancona, and Venice, many
Afghan teenagers like Ali might not even be allowed out of the ship's hold.
Along with fellow stowaways, including Syrians, Somalis, Iranians, Paki-
stanis, and Kurds, they are summarily returned to Patras or Igoumenitsa in
Greece.[14] Often they are not interviewed individually, nor given the opportunity to apply for asylum in Italy.[15] The decision is not made by an asylum
committee, but by border police or finance guard[16] agents. To the officials'
discretionary gaze, some of these teenagers don't look like minors. Alternatively, the "truth" is expected to emerge "from their body," to quote Fassin
and D'Halluin's work with refugees in France (2005).[17] Their left-hand
bones might or might not be the bones of a minor—x-ray screenings and
mathematical algorithms speak on these travelers' behalf.[18] To use the institutional vocabulary, agents may "reject" them from the national territory
and, without any written document, "entrust" them to the ferries' captains
for their "readmission" journey to Greece, often locked in the hold's baggage compartment.[19] These migrants go back to a struggling life on the
geographic and socioeconomic margins of austere Greek cities.[20] There,
they might be targeted by local supremacist groups—with exclusionary discourses and with makeshift bombs. One October morning in 2008, hundreds of asylum seekers were lining up outside Athens's Central Police
Asylum Department. Intent on preserving public order, the police used
force and charged them. One person was killed and several others injured
by agents of the state precisely as they were trying to ask that state to protect
them.[21] When, conversely, they are allowed to lodge an application in
Greece, it is virtually certain they will be unable to obtain asylum.[22]

In Greece, as in Italy, these migrants are also aware they will not be able
to legally travel to other EU countries to apply for asylum. With very few
exceptions,[23] EU Regulation No. 604/2013, known as Dublin III Regulation,[24] suggests that the country where non-EU persons first enter the EU is
responsible for accepting and examining their asylum applications—which
makes Malta, Cyprus, and Greek islands including Crete less than ideal first
destinations. Having survived the perils of a westward journey taking years,
severely indebted, and keen on reaching friends or families elsewhere in
Europe, they do not have the option of going "back home" either, even
when home is a safe place. They again travel to the port cities, hoping to

reach Italy. Greece, like Italy, is considered a "doorstep of Europe" (Cabot 2014), a stage in refugees' journey toward northern European destinations such as Sweden, Germany, and the Netherlands. These countries feature more established ethnic communities, better legal provisions, and a more promising reception. During 2013, some 398,200 asylum applications were filed in the twenty-eight EU countries, including 109,600 in Germany, 60,100 in France, 54,300 in Sweden, and 27,800 in Italy.[25] Using such figures, several European leaders have voiced their concern regarding the Mare Nostrum mission.[26] Leaders use the standard, somewhat abstract vocabulary of sovereignty and human rights. Bavarian interior minister Joachim Herrmann, a Christian conservative, publicly alleged that the Italian police is not implementing the Dublin Regulation: "Italy in many cases intentionally does not take personal data and fingerprints from refugees to enable them to seek asylum in another country." There were no comments from the Interior Ministry in Rome, in charge of "law and order" in the country, except that "the remarks were made by a regional [Bavarian] minister, not a German government minister."[27] But Germany's turn is soon to come. German interior minister Thomas de Mazière, also a conservative, observed that "it's clear to all European ministers that the justified and responsible campaign by the Italians has become a 'pull factor,' as we call it."[28] Socialist Bernard Cazeneuve, French minister of the interior, asserted that "member states need to regain control of the EU's external borders, better implement asylum procedures, and step up efforts to dismantle human smuggling networks."[29] Between January and July 2014, French authorities denied entry to some 3,411 *clandestins* (unauthorized immigrants), including Eritrean and Syrian nationals, transiting from Italy.[30] Austrian guards, too, discretionally enforce the otherwise "open" Schengen border[31] and, during the summer months of 2014, denied entry to some 2,100 non-EU "foreigners" transiting from Italy.[32]

In the first seven months of 2014, some 17,700 minors were registered as arriving in Italy, including 9,700 unaccompanied—especially from Eritrea, Egypt, Bangladesh, and Afghanistan.[33] Many of them flee the facilities charged with their protection, notably in the absence of information about their legal rights and when enticed by friends, extended family, or trafficking networks.[34]

But Ali was "lucky," as he puts it. From the port, he was taken to one of the immigration reception facilities in southern Italy and, soon after, to an orphanage. He applied for political asylum and was told he would get "an answer" in approximately six months. He was recognized as a political refugee after two years. Ali has been living in a small southern Italian town, where I have often met him over a decade, counting on the sustained support of the Catholic priest to whose care he was entrusted. "Don't panic, I'm Muslim!" reads one of Ali's t-shirts. He collaborates with the priest's interfaith organization, including when it hosts refugees, and has completed high school as a *ragioniere* (accountant). Occasionally he is called on by the police to help with translations, as dozens of other Afghans, including children, are apprehended on sailboats headed to the coast of southeastern Italy, and on ferries in the nearby ports of Bari and Brindisi.

Ali is one of those travelers who survive the long journey across exploitative times, criminal spaces, sovereign containment, economic systems, cultural styles, and legal regulations generally defined with the shorthand "migration." His account exemplifies the perils and complexities of these journeys. Trajectories are often fragmented, and time might seem suspended. In the tracing of a meticulous account of migration, the minutiae of time, space, bilateral agreements, search-and-rescue maritime operations, and immigration laws are not accessory background and minor detail, but the very fabric of sovereignty and of the pursuit of life that intersects with it, at the heart of *Crimes of Peace*.

Ali's paradigmatic journey from Afghanistan to Italy and the diverse stories of the people on the decks of Mare Nostrum warships are part of the "mixed migration" characterizing global mobility. People with different motives and origins are literally on the same smuggler boat, directed to Italy, Malta, and Greece. Thus, in these pages my usage of "migrants" points to "voluntary" (economic) migrants and to "forced" migrants—including asylum seekers, recognized refugees, and more broadly internationally displaced persons in need of humanitarian protection.[35] Scare quotes, here, are not a negation of different experiences of violence and vulnerability. On the contrary, they suggest that experienced violence and factual vulnerability might or might not be met with forms of bureaucratic recognition, authorization, and protection. In other words, persons become refugees, undocumented migrants, non-EU migrants, and economic immigrants in state-centered and contingent legal, social, and moral taxonomies. Thus, this work participates in the analysis of how "law"—including the practices and taxonomies of citizenship, nation building, and border enforcement—"produces citizens, illegal aliens, legal permanent residents, legal immigration, illicit travel, and even territories and the state" (Coutin

2000:10). In turn, a focus on "immigration" provides a lens through which the contradictions of national, postnational, and EU membership can be discerned and inspected.

Different forms of motivation and vulnerability bring would-be maritime migrants to rely on smugglers, and afford the latter the opportunity to become traffickers. Smugglers often exploit their clients, economically and otherwise. Their occasional ignorance of the sea, sustained greed, systematic failure to respect the most basic rules of navigation, and their brutal disciplining subject people in their charge to the experience of violence and the risk of death. Nevertheless, "smuggling" implies the noncoerced nature (initially, at least) of migrants' mobility through the services of paid facilitators and unauthorized travel. Thus, my usage of "smuggling" does not refer to forms of coerced mobility including sex slavery or child labor and trafficking.[36] This qualification is extremely important, for the often automatic conflation of smuggling with trafficking, and the media and political emphasis on "traffickers of death" and "new slave drivers," foreclose larger analyses and elicit specific political and humanitarian responses. The fragmented, tentative, and intercontinental journeys of Ali and of the Mare Nostrum passengers evoke the transnational reach and fluid legal scope of borders.[37] They point to the inadequacy of simplistic models that encapsulate the migratory journey in the passage from a country of origin to a country of destination.[38] They exemplify this work's core ethnographic inquiry: what do democracy, rule of law, sovereignty, and human rights look like in the encounter between those chasing the other side of their horizon and those who have the duty to deter, rescue, welcome, categorize, and potentially deport them? How does the task of managing maritime borders and saving lives take shape in actuality, beyond the abstract vocabulary of sovereignty and human rights? *Crimes of Peace* scrutinizes the intersections of the labor of sovereignty with the lives of those who actively seek to trespass its norms.

The electronic, material, legal, and symbolic borders analyzed here migrate from the mass graves at the bottom of the sea to the transcontinental fences of migrant detention and preemption, and into the command rooms and identitarian trenches of national public spheres.[39] What happens at the border is related to what happens within boundaries of socioeconomic inequality and integration.[40] Outsiders navigating and trespassing the geopolitical borders of liberal democracies do not experience simply the new liberties of a networked world: they also encounter the proliferating thresholds of a globally parochial world.

A Twenty-Year Emergency

The *Vlora* left the Albanian port of Durrës improbably crammed with ten tons of Cuban sugar and an estimated twenty thousand refugees (Chapter 1). On August 8, 1991, this "sweet ship"[41] was eventually allowed to land in the port of Bari in Apulia, southeastern Italy[42]—not too far from my high school.[43] It emblematically reshaped southern Italy—an emigrant-sending "periphery" of Europe—into a central region of maritime immigration and "gateway to the West." The *Vlora* reminded local residents, national politicians, and European institutions that Albania and the Balkan Peninsula lie a mere seventy kilometers (forty-five miles) to the east. It opened this Italian "gate to the Orient" to maritime immigration from Albania, from dissolving Yugoslavia, and from Kurdish regions between Iraq, Iran, Syria, and Turkey. And it elicited a cultural-institutional model of military surveillance and humanitarian containment.

This military-humanitarian nexus and its tensions keep resurfacing, from migrants' administrative detention to the "military-humanitarian operation 'Mare Nostrum.'" What forms occupy the gray area between military and humanitarian, patrol and salvation, detention and hospitality, rights and their infringement? How is the "humanitarian" integrated into "the sovereignty of states" (Fassin and Pandolfi 2010b:15) and of the EU? What does the tension between the military and the humanitarian generate in specific applications? How does the relationship change both constitutive elements? Beyond describing the discourse of a legitimizing ideology, I need to map actual interfaces, policies, and events of this military-humanitarian nexus. For it is at this level that travelers are translated into immigrants, and that militarized and humanitarian sovereignty materializes, in the encounter with the people it is charged with managing. It is also in seemingly well-oiled mechanisms, routine practices, and reiterated situations of conflict that internal tensions emerge, and that the political contradictions policing and humanitarianism are charged with resolving risk becoming unmanageable.

Two decades following the *Vlora*, in the first half of 2011, twenty-three thousand Tunisian citizens embody the mobility demanded by *their* Arab uprising, and, along with forty thousand other African persons who escape from war in Libya, reach across the 113 kilometers (70 miles) that separate them from Italy (Chapter 5). Lampedusa, the tiny island of six thousand residents closer to Tunisia than to mainland Italy, is their gateway to the global north. These North African *ḥarrāga* (Maghrebi Arabic for "those who burn") set fire to authoritarian humiliation, bilateral agreements, documents, mattresses, and frontiers in the pursuit of dignity, whatever its toll. Like them, other migrants occasionally slip away from Italian and Frontex patrolling and disembark undetected in Lampedusa, in Sicily, and in the southern regions of Apulia and Calabria.

Small groups of travelers walk from the coast toward larger cities, hoping to catch a train to northern Italy or northern Europe. Local residents might offer them food and drinks, more rarely shelter. Not everyone greets unseaworthy boats that have made it against the odds, carrying people who have defeated multimillion investments in European surveillance by surviving countless stages of peril and exploitation. There is no abundance of good Samaritans. Residents routinely report the presence of newly arrived migrants to police authorities. It is *others*—security and humanitarian agents—who will now take care of these people, in holding centers. An in-depth analysis of the experience and cultural genealogy of migrant administrative detention (Chapters 1 and 4) helps to clarify such significant reconfigurations of what humanitarianism and hospitality mean and entail. Illuminated, in turn, are ongoing reconfigurations of power, and of national and European sovereignty.

Virtually every spring, summer, and fall since 1991, Italian authorities have been seemingly unprepared to deal with what they routinely call and administratively define an "emergency," if not a "biblical exodus." Occasionally the sea is calm during the winter, too—allowing unregulated maritime migration and heightening the risk of death by exposure. Maritime travelers are met by a bureaucratic machinery that develops precisely based on the spectacle of emergency and on structured improvisation. Emergency is not merely a trope that is invoked but "a way of grasping problematic events" and of representing them in their "apparent unpredictability, abnormality, and brevity" (Calhoun 2010: 55). Calhoun notes that "the managerial response to an emergency focuses on restoring the existing order, not on changing it" (55). But is such "order" truly preexisting? Emergencies, in Italy as elsewhere, serve as a political technique that bypasses and makes exceptional what would need to be thoroughly, more deliberately addressed via democratic methods. Emergencies methodically procrastinate to a never attainable future the analysis of the conditions that enable them.

Throughout two decades of such emergencies an assemblage of governmental, regional, municipal, and nongovernmental actors and institutions has profiled and identified, rescued and confined, embraced and deported people, sometimes making a profit and discretionally opening its gates. In this regard, the flexible fabric of sovereignty needs to be mapped in all its vagaries and just-in-time, structurally improvised strategies. How do liberal democracies effect, in practice, their operations of deterrence, interception, detention, identification, and deportation? How do they legitimate forms of border management and surveillance proven to be costly and legally dubious?

Fishermen rescuing fellow seafarers in need, ignoring them, or throwing body parts back into the sea. A Palestinian nurse who escapes Syria under siege only to die on a boat—and to save three southern Italians with her kidneys and liver. Tourists sunbathing as corpses lie on the shore. Citizens helping to rescue migrants as their ship capsizes. Unexpected acts of illegal solidarity. Migrant detainees swallowing razor blades, batteries, or shampoo to escape from administrative confinement. Police agents guarding the gates of detention to keep out activists, in the name of migrants' privacy and rights. Other gates left ajar. Rule of law trapped behind the bars of Kafkaesque administrative detention. Defendants in criminal trials (including unauthorized migrants) enjoying more procedural safeguards than persons accused of violating administrative immigration rules. Italian sovereignty adrift: on ferries, on warships, across the sea. Such puzzles and oxymora of our time are illuminated as I scrutinize the Italian and EU border architecture in the Euro-Mediterranean area. This takes us to reconfigurations of power and sovereignty in an age that plays with and on the many thresholds of justice and compassion, security and rights, legal evidence and discretion, and is always quite unsure what to make of those on the other side.

The establishment and the policing of borders are integral to the rule of law and its ostensible certainties[44] when it turns "aliens" into "legible" subjects.[45] The discretionary and preemptive boundary policing I consider plays with the threshold of evidence (Chapter 4). It enables the law to transcend its structural limits and to evaluate and sanction otherwise inaccessible inner feelings and mental states. Predictive policing assesses travelers' "real intentions," in addition to nationality, age, and wealth. But agents pass the burden of proof to travelers and would-be migrants, turning the presumption of innocence inside out into a presumption of guilt. Travelers find themselves in the position of having to prove a negative, that they are not economic immigrants, while state agents largely enjoy the benefit of assumption. In such situations, national or Frontex agents and their "risk analyses" do not simply "represent" state and supranational sovereignty, but embody and effect it in their encounters with travelers.[46] The illegality and immorality sanctioned at the border are invoked, in all their consequentiality, by the bipartisan refrain that "*we* only welcome *legal* immigrants." This is increasingly heard across the "virtually global *regime*" of deportability (De Genova 2010:34; original emphasis). How does the border become, in practice, a primary marker not only of people's legal or illegal mode of entry but also of their legal and illegal nature and moral worth?

The southern outposts of immigration governance are then central to liberal democratic practices of national and EU self-legitimation.[47] They are also primary loci of state and EU spatialization,[48] rather than spatial margins. Since the early 1990s they have functioned as improvised laboratories for the emerging regime of European surveillance, sovereign humanitarianism, military pushbacks and containment, and policing by charity. They are at the heart of EU concerns over a mobile humanity that, once at sea, is difficult to contain.

I explore the geopolitical fulcrum of a flexible sovereignty that—through Frontex patrols, Eurosur surveillance, bilateral agreements, and EU border assistance missions—reaches unapologetically beyond national and EU boundaries, from Tunisia to Belarus. Immigration governance outposts are at the heart of the many contradictions of a technopolitical vision that seeks to prevent would-be migrants on the southern and eastern Mediterranean shores from becoming migrants or asylum seekers in Europe. This is where discourses, symbols, and technologies of humanitarianism and salvation have been materially put to work to enable national and European attempts to govern immigration. And they are sites of mourning and resistance, where obituaries for the exclusionary nation (Butler 2003) are also being traced.

The surging deployment of (military) technology and automation in border control does not make legal-political decision making redundant. Who is to rescue a boat in distress in international waters (Chapter 5)? Where should passengers be taken? How should they be sheltered? What should be done with the corpses? These are questions shipmasters and institutional actors face as they carry on their work, from Tripoli to Warsaw. Preemption, situational awareness, biometrics, risk analysis, satellites, warships, and drones increasingly characterize border and immigration management. The exclusive ideology of what Carens (2013) labels a "neo-feudal regime" finds its twenty-first-century infrastructure in the optical fiber cables laid on the Mediterranean seabed.

But ultimately, sovereignty affects persons with bodies, under its jurisdiction or actively excluded from it. With this in mind, one has to ask: how much do we really know about migration, borders, confinement, and ultimately, humanity? Would I rescue a stranger in distress at sea? Would I drink seawater, after two days adrift? Would I toss my friend's corpse overboard, after a week? Would I sew my lips shut, after three months in detention? To address these questions, we do not need only introspective knowledge, but an inquiry into relevant relationships and mechanisms, situations and contexts. Situations and contexts *are* the story here, not colorful supplements.

I travel therefore to sites of patrol, detention, identification, charitable assistance, and deportation where crucial boundaries are routinely embodied, maintained, and trespassed. I account for encounters such as those involving Albanian, Libyan, Italian, Tunisian, and Maltese politicians; Italian police agents and Albanian citizens; Lampedusan youth and their Tunisian, digitally networked friends; finance guard sailors and rescued refugees; frustrated psychologists, immigration lawyers, and Bulgarian detainees. The Bulgarian detainees, trusting my work, asked me to send them "the book" one day. They understood their own predicament, existentially and meta-ethnographically. They certainly do not need to be given voice. They do need a readership.

An ethnographic and analytical lens centered on Italy provides a prism through which one can examine the European governance of migration; such focus also provides a solid ground for the discussion of broader modalities of power and resistance. As these pages detail, Italian pioneering agreements with neighbors such as Libya, Tunisia, Egypt, and Albania are the object of much controversy and humanitarian concern. They also represent an emerging feature of national and EU liberal democracies. A lens centered on coastal southern Italy also reveals the broader saliency of ideas of humanitarian rescue and salvation in the management of borders and migration. Finally, within the global cartography of mobility and sovereign power, the Italian case illuminates not only deeply entrenched and shifting forms of belonging but also broader tensions between universal values and particular diversities, moral consensus and pluralist political participation.[49]

In Italy, perhaps more than elsewhere, the Catholic Church consistently claims its "duty-right to intervene on themes of great moral significance

Figure 2. Fences surrounding Manduria's tent city. Photo: Maurizio Albahari.

such as human life, family, justice, and solidarity."[50] Indeed, I met Catholic priests who, working at the forefront of the reception of migrants, assume the ambiguous role of "experts" in the politics of immigration. Conversely, policymakers and smugglers deploy ideas of sacredness and migrant salvation as they grapple respectively with the maintenance and trespassing of borders.[51]

Boundary demarcation, structural socioeconomic inequality, labor migration, and north-south moral disparagement have long been appreciable in Italy as *domestic* issues of citizenship and nation building.[52] In turn, for more than two decades Italy as a whole has been blamed as the EU's "soft underbelly" and "magnet" for its perceived inability to deter and detect undocumented migration. As part of southern and Mediterranean Europe, the country is also reproached for its people's alleged *moral* deficit and ensuing Continental financial crisis. As we focus on maritime migration, are we witnessing yet another mechanism for "Europe" to produce itself as "self-sufficient"[53] through boundary demarcation? Which Europe? Which socioeconomic and localized segments of the citizenry are parts of

Europe's agency? How does the Euro-Mediterranean area fit within Europe? Social and economic disparities in wealth and power, domestically and internationally, are actively spatialized—and possibly sustained—as North-South dichotomies. This is signaled by the fact that Mediterranean straits and safer passages are enforced as frontiers. Whether, how, and where the "North" secures its distinction vis-à-vis a shifting "South" is not merely an Italian curiosity, then, but a crucial part of the EU's geopolitical and moralized self-definition, and of transnational struggles to unravel entrenched inequalities.

Exploring the grandiose sovereign project of managing the mobility of millions of humans, I found myself grappling with the Italian police's lack of funds to even rent a bus to implement deportations. Accounting for horrifying shipwrecks, I saw truly courageous rescue operations and the administrative detention and criminal prosecution of survivors. I have not witnessed a coherence of practices. What I did find, though, is a burgeoning civic engagement with these issues (Chapter 6). An alternative, less official cartography of power exists and needs to be traced.

Situational Thresholds

The threshold, the border architecture, sovereignty, and the border itself: these constructs tend to convey powerful spatial imageries. Indeed the global border system is grounded also in the proliferation of physical and conspicuous walls and fences (see Chapter 5). Sovereignty grounds much of its cultural credibility and commonsensical nature in its spatialization of fundamentally social and economic relationships.[54] It should be clear, though, that the borders under investigation are not merely spatial ones, and that sovereignty is not confined within the boundaries of national sovereignty. A border is constituted by power-laden, morally infused mechanisms that categorize both citizens and migrants, and that discipline their unequal relationships in the Italian and Euro-Mediterranean physical, symbolic, and administrative map of belonging.

The border threshold analyzed here is not a static and confined space. For it extends throughout holding facilities in urban peripheries of Europe; heavily patrolled and virtually fenced Mediterranean straits; North African oases; desert fences; and West African fisheries, dwindling in part because of European trade and fishing interventions.[55] Borders are part of a multivariate sovereign system: physical, legal, or administrative changes at one border entail changes at other borders, in a neighboring country or across the Mediterranean.

And the border threshold is not temporally confined: political authority, law, and administrative discretion morph into a preemptive power that searches into travelers' pasts and also inspects their intentions, in addition to their wallets (Chapter 4). Border thresholds adapt situationally in relation to who is approaching them. Borders are "smart," in institutional parlance. They almost evaporate under the pressure of desirability, as the EU is intent on attracting highly skilled workers to be granted the "blue card" of permanent residency. They evaporate under the pressure of bank statements, as citizenship is commodified (Chapter 5). For others, the threshold becomes an insurmountable obstacle, and I trace it here.

In other words, the Euro-Mediterranean physical map is always a political map. Border enforcement in the geopolitical sense is politically sustainable and epistemologically comprehensible in relation to multiple legal and symbolic thresholds. Logics and mechanisms of border regulation work symbolically as if isolating a spatialized "sacred" from what surrounds it.[56] Here I am not interested in pursuing the sacred origin of sovereignty,[57] but in explicating the logical presupposition behind borders. I note that there is a certain homology with the sacred at work. Borders, whether in the form of concrete-and-steel walls or biometrical checkpoints, have cultural and geopolitical meaning only insofar as they are understood as marking something worth safeguarding in the first place—the EU as an "area of freedom, security, and justice without internal frontiers, and with full respect for fundamental rights";[58] order and security; the nation and its sovereignty;[59] Western values, Christendom, and so forth.[60] But might the opposite also be true? We should also ask whether the apparatus of border enforcement is to be understood as manufacturing legitimation and consecration, producing and reproducing the "essential" values it defends—which in turn call for more border enforcement. Is the EU defending its borders, or is it also the border regime that defends EU polities? And from what, or from whom?

Common (neo-Westphalian) justifications to sovereignty and border regimes invoke territorial exclusivity and the need to foster *citizens*' social and cultural cohesion and welfare. The governmental ambition of migration regulation is often captured under the rallying point of the protection

of citizens' security and common good. Indeed, in line with national security expectations,[61] these are portrayed as attainable through the militarization of the Mediterranean and the surveillance of the national-global public
sphere. After all, as a Maltese police agent puts it, "that's what governments
do: lock people up."[62]

But I also need to examine a more encompassing, seemingly inclusionary moral economy. A caring and safeguarding concern is mirrored in governmental salvation of *migrants'* physical and moral wellness, by providing
food and shelter at the border and by purportedly preventing trafficking,
drowning, and vagrancy. As the same Maltese police agent puts it, holding
centers on the island are necessary as they "provide housing" and "ease
migrants' integration."[63] In other words, the border functions not only as a
classical surveillance and security mechanism but also as a threshold of
salvation. Surveillance is modulated through administrative policing and
humanitarian practices. Geopolitical sovereignty is modulated into moral
sovereignty and responsibility. Interception at sea, militarized deterrence,
detention, and deportation are implemented and legitimized through a
political-theological paradigm that claims citizens' common good and
migrants' humanitarian salvation. A military-humanitarian continuum is
established, sharing a temporality of emergency in its interventions, an
appeal to emergency ethics, and an overarching invocation of morality and
values.[64]

Moral considerations are routinely invoked as new arrivals are sorted
into decipherable categories through asylum adjudication, detention, police
discretion, integration tests, and radiological exams. It is only once their
moral worth has been tested and evaluated that people deserve provisional
admittance into national communities newly articulated as communities of
values—values including the rule of law and human rights (see Chapters 3
and 4). It seems fundamental, then, to propose a scholarship that is able
and willing to critically engage issues of morality: issues that are increasingly represented, lived, and even contested as moral issues and using a
moral register.[65] The stakes are high. In a moralized world, a lexicon of
moral sentiments, as Fassin (2012:6) puts it, replaces inequality with
"exclusion," domination with "misfortune," injustice with "suffering," and
violence with "trauma." Different ways to name the world elicit different
analytical and political responses.[66]

Having researched would-be migrants' exploitation by smugglers and
traffickers, transnational ill treatment, and maritime death, there is an

analytical question I cannot dodge, as an anthropologist and as an Italian citizen who grew up in coastal southern Italy. It is the question of legal and political responsibilities. Thousands of deaths in the Mediterranean, over two decades, are not misfortunate accidents, inevitable fatalities, acts of God or of nature. They are crimes of peace—this is the argument pursued by this book fence after fence, shipwreck after shipwreck.

From *Crimini di Pace* to *Crimes of Peace*

I borrow the phrase "crimes of peace" from Franco Basaglia and Franca Basaglia Ongaro. Franco Basaglia (1924–80), in particular, is remembered as a major psychiatrist and social reformer and as the main architect of the abolition of mental hospitals of confinement in Italy, in 1978.[67] The Basaglias adopted *"crimini di pace"* as the title of an important edited volume of theirs, broadly concerned with the management of lives and of poverty through psychiatric confinement (2013a [1975]). They demonstrate how the very preemption of *potential* threats and acts of crime associated with behavioral deviancy and societal anomaly generates *actual* crimes, exemplified by the institutions delegated to human cure and care (2013b [1975]). They place particular emphasis on the technical, administrative mechanisms of institutional violence, and on the academic disciplines underpinning and legitimizing them. In a direct reference to the title, they write that the concept of *"crimini di pace"* offers an analytical key to "all forms of institutionalized violence that serve as strategies of conservation for our social system" (2013a [1975]:8). I expand on such crucial understandings. The concept of crimes of peace, as I use it, speaks to the ambitious, laborious, and resilient administrative, political, and ideological work of maintaining a "system" that has proven crumbling and volatile and that *keeps proving* unjust, violent, and unequal.

The concept of crimes of peace is not a theoretical abstraction explaining or transcending matter and people, but an analytical key I have apprehended through a decade of ethnographic and documentary research and personal experience. I submit it for your discernment, meticulously enclosing relevant phrases, silences, mechanisms, technicalities, and precedents. Should you find crimes of peace to be an analytical key conducive to understanding, I hope this happens turning the last page of this volume. Crimes of peace are empirical offenses of structural injustice. Conceptually, crimes of peace posit analytical interrogations, not moral certainties.

Rather than unveiling guilt, investigating crimes of peace deals with explicating events, situations, mechanisms, and networks of correlations— possibly conveying legal and political responsibilities. Based on my analysis, mechanisms and correlations are to be researched beyond the immediate spatial and temporal array of events such as shipwrecks. Omissions, laws, ideologies, political choices, criminal and profiteering activities that precede and produce events need to be implicated. "I didn't do it on purpose," children are fond of saying. Crimes of peace do not need intentionality: they may bank on the variable interest of unequally distributed "tragedies."

Crimes of peace are enabled by situations of institutional and structural injustice that might escape neat legal categorizations. They are reproduced by choices people make while failing to consider implications of and alternatives to their specific actions and inactions. They speak of methodical negligence, ill-conceived policies, and well-oiled criminal networks. They demonstrate willful ignorance of the inescapable corporeality of being human, or conversely exclusive attention to physiological necessities as if these were sufficient to the human condition.

Crimes of peace happen routinely, as entrenched asymmetries of power, wealth, and authority are integral to border dynamics. Referring to Mediterranean shipwrecks, European media increasingly speak of a "war bulletin."[68] And yet crimes of peace are not about despicable war criminals expelled from the rules of civility and coexistence. They happen in nonbelligerent liberal democracies and in their proximity, in everyday wars for which "armistices are never envisioned": at sites of the "war of peace" where crimes are perpetuated in the name of the "order of things" and the "protection of man" (Basaglia and Basaglia Ongaro 2013b [1975]:80). Is it, indeed, peace for all? For within and between the jurisdictions of states and international organizations there are people whose life is defined by detention without charges, criminal abuse, hunger, thirst, dependence on discretion, corruption, rape, sovereignty and salvation. "Peace" does not bring an end to the inequalities structurally exposing many to death, injustice, and exploitation. The concept of crimes of peace speaks to structural injustices of deprivation, dispossession, and environmental "disasters,"[69] but such crimes do not necessarily involve big numbers. One convicted criminal on death row—not only that person's execution, whether "botched" or "perfected"—is a crime of peace.[70] In Kosovo-Serbia, the "correlation" between Hodgkin's lymphoma and NATO's 1999 usage of depleted uranium is a crime of peace.[71] In southern Italy, the lung cancer of a single citizen, due to environmental plunder, toxic waste, and criminal-political connivance, is a crime of peace.

Walter Benjamin, in the first part of the fragment quoted above, writes that "the tradition of the oppressed teaches us that the 'state of emergency' in which we live is not the exception but the rule. We must attain to a conception of history that is in keeping with this insight" (1968 [1955]:257). Thousands of people are the experiential historiographers of crimes of peace. Some of them are witnesses stricken from the record of justice, but not all of them are equally "oppressed." Theirs is an anti-teleological social history without redemptive conclusions, being written with journeys, hunger strikes, deaths, judicial and political action, and testimonies. Their stories are not tales of passive victimhood,[72] but of persons with aspirations, delusions, mistakes, siblings, children, and parents. Am I then, at the very least, allowing for the dissemination they demand, so that nobody can ever again say "there are no alternatives" and "I didn't know"? I am not alone in this endeavor. Together with select humanitarian organizations, religious actors, policymakers, prosecutors, investigative reporters, sailors, and coastal residents, the hesitant, wavering citizenry of the early twenty-first century is already asking: in whose name and on whose behalf are crimes of peace perpetrated?

As I make apparent, information is often available about individual shipwrecks and human rights violations. Accounts of the numerous 2014 summer shipwrecks are available through English-language media. But episodic information does not amount to consequential knowledge—knowledge of the institutional mechanisms, criminal and geopolitical networks of correlation, and catalogues of failures that make of these accidents and violations crimes of peace. Which policies suggest—at the very least to their architects and to informed observers—that smuggling, shipwrecks, and systematic violations of human rights are to be expected?

Even my ability to posit this as an empirical question, rather than a moral one, warrants a diachronic perspective. And answering it warrants a diachronic analysis. The passage of time does not explain anything, by itself. But it needs to be traced, for I have discovered that temporary fences are followed by more permanent fences; that tentative bilateral agreements are followed by more demanding bilateral agreements; that emergencies build on emergencies; that ruptures may happen unannounced; and that every shipwreck fails to warn about the next one—for two decades. My finding, which I intend to substantiate beyond reasonable doubt, is that there is nothing inevitable nor fortuitous to the methodical emergencies, deaths, and confinement I trace, nothing that could not have been changed, prevented, redressed, and discussed differently by knowledgeable and often well-informed actors such as European and North African policymakers, police and armed forces, border guards, search-and-rescue authorities, and NATO officers at work in the Mediterranean.

The interrogations posed by and through crimes of peace warrant answers that need to be empirically grounded and situated, then. But in light of the death, detention, deportation, and disparagement that I detail, some readers might develop a sense of moral introspection, or conversely of self-exemption, denunciation, and scandalized outrage. As the ink dries, you appropriate stories and insights in distinctive ways, and rightly so. As for myself, I *am* convinced that a bystander's helpful intervention is preferable to an omission. Nevertheless, as these pages argue, there is more to intervention, or lack thereof, than morality. What I am proposing, then, is *not* a scholarship that judges, sanctions, or excuses anyone, myself included. On the contrary, the book illuminates the global proliferation of morally imbued borders, and brings out layers of complexity: is moral evaluation a fitting tool to analyze the humanitarian-political continuum? Who is to express authoritative moral judgments on Mare Nostrum, for example— the people rescued, the relatives of the drowned, navy sailors, taxpayers, Italian or EU politicians? More fruitfully, these pages help analyze how moral-political dispositions are cultivated, mobilized, and resisted in the tension between emergent pluralism and global parochialism. Every generation likes to think of itself as different and more humane, if not more just, than the prior one. In reality, we are as capable of participating in crimes of peace as of engaging in more just and egalitarian forms of citizenship.

Mobility, sovereignty, and human rights shape the substance of democracy. They are eminently political issues. But as I attend to relevant venues, mechanisms, and actors I find a constellation of discourses and procedures that do the political work of translating such defining issues into bureaucratic technicalities, humanitarian-military operations, and identitarian, legal, and moral facts. As technicalities, operations, and facts, they risk exemption from the public quest for alternatives. And existing alternatives might be more just than this state of affairs, rather than more compassionate.

Artisanal Ethnography for Liquid States

Can an ethnographic journey trace seemingly nonlocatable mechanics of power, and the genealogies and long-term implications of sovereignty? My diachronic effort presupposes a relational epistemology that eschews a focus on entities in isolation—immigrants, smugglers, Muslims, states, police agents, rights, and so forth. It speaks to (and about) processes, situations, and relations, rather than identities; mobility and confinement, rather than immigrants; state mechanisms, rather than structures; the sociality of dignity, rather than the givens of rights. Below I delve in methodological and analytical challenges that, rather than being relegated to a footnote as "quandaries of the fortunate" (Farmer 2005:175), can be translated into sustained tensions generative of consequential knowledge and informed action.

Border carnage is ongoing. As I write, people are traveling and dying in the Mediterranean. In Rome's holding facility, migrants are committing acts of self-mutilation—if you take apart a cigarette lighter, wires are to be found and lips can be sewn up. Sometimes I wish I could write these pages on a gigantic transparent sheet, which I would then hold vertically while you see the immediate, urgent reality through it. I wish an escape from "the sequential straitjacket of the written form," as historian Carlo Ginzburg puts it (2003:9). In reality, though, mechanisms and relationships—life and death, over two decades—do not work in a straightforward and teleological fashion; they do not coalesce around a climax that can be captured and shown. Instead, I intend to offer an opening into the complexities of ongoing situations, minimizing the movement from (my) learning and knowing to the scholarly presentation of knowledge and evidence.[73] In this respect the ethnographic present helps render situations as neither inevitable nor fortuitous. It helps "render the movement of the social visible to the reader" (Latour 2005:128). Rigorous and honest description *is* analysis here, as it traces the practices, contingencies, routines, and social agencies that make possible a state of affairs. As noted by Bateson (1958) and as phrased by Latour (2005:137), good description can make pointing to additional explanations superfluous. I often entrust you with (your own) explanations. By using my voice I take responsibility for what I say and for how I assemble what I have come to know. The rhetorical and authorial power at my disposal is a tool of narration and analysis, not a redundant exercise in self-indulgence.

Staying truthful to my findings, in these pages I need to convey that shipwrecks and maritime journeys are both reiterated and specifically diffracted, in a myriad of deaths. In this sense, I engage you in an empirically grounded "casuistic" debate, in the neutral sense of the term. In other words, resisting the use of "rules as algorithms fitting all cases," this quest is grounded both in analogy and in a "'thick' understanding of particular problems and situations" (Maurer 2005:74). And I seek to strike readers' chords of material resonance, rather than of moral empathy—for example when I evoke the urgent boredom and dissident exasperation behind the often-impenetrable gates of holding facilities.

Informational inflation. I had to find my way through the informational fine dust of "communicative capitalism" (Dean 2009:17): a thick, vocal, and often confounding maze of documents, laws, human rights reports, news releases, news articles, e-mail communications, public statements, and declarations proliferating at multiple scales, from city councils to regional and national governments and the EU Commission.[74] These need to be understood as sources of information to be verified and as cultural artifacts[75] to be analyzed. Building on my ethnographic expertise and personal experience, I have taken advantage of such abundance to selectively deploy an "open-source intelligence" anthropological approach (see Chapter 3). This approach cross-checks, unpacks, spells out, and relates people, places, policies, and events often "known" at some point, but kept isolated or conversely lumped as aggregate data. My concern, then, is not only to map the "meanings" of information, documents and discourses under scrutiny but also to understand the cultural and material work they do in producing (or challenging) larger ideologies and categories of people.

As an Italian citizen, as a fieldworker, and as an anthropologist who has produced op-ed columns and media discourse about migration, I also appear among the makers of the informational maze. More generally, I am part of the field, in pursuing fieldwork and knowledge production.[76] I might attend the same conferences, write in the same venues, sail in the same vessels, and work in the same ports as the people in these pages. I might share a regional accent with some, and root for the same soccer team with others. With ears and eyes always wide open, I might dream using the same smell and color palette. I might share a vision of public citizenship, and the occasional longing engendered by the memory of place making, displacement, and places' dismemberment.

In extricating such a vortex of people, documents, and information, an "anthropology of public reasoning" (Bowen 2007) constitutes a valuable approach. An anthropology of public reasoning scrutinizes social actors' rhetorical tool kits and their ideological frameworks of legitimation, including liberalism, humanitarianism, and the rule of law. I move through personal encounters, semi-structured interviews, legal documents, eyewitness accounts, and a variety of investigative and media reports. The latter, in particular, are salient also as they co-constitute the circuit of public discourse in which national and EU decision makers and citizens participate.

The fact that many sources, including official state and EU documents, are increasingly publicly available poses broad questions on democracy and citizens' accountability: is the public retrievability of executive decisions a sign of the democratic nature of those decisions, and of the decision-making process? What is happening to the balance between public debate, legislative lawmaking, and executive provisions?[77] Am I, as an Italian citizen with voting rights, part of the Italian government and the EU Commission which I scrutinize here? Could it be that *I* am "sovereignty," after all?

Are human rights for migrants? How are migrants included in "human rights"? This is, we will see, a crucial question. For humanitarianism is implicated in migrants' physical confinement and in their liberation; in restrictive policies and in rescue operations. The conjunction between state reason and humanitarian reason is increasingly complicated,[78] and in some of its facets humanitarianism is a governmental discourse and technique, if not a global political regime.[79] With such complications and innovations in the post–Cold War humanitarian regime,[80] how is Arendt's post–World War II call for the right to have rights relevant (1958 [1951])? Are human rights a scarce luxury in a renewable decade of austerity, a foundational practice of liberal democracy, an ongoing struggle in the pursuit of emancipation, a tool of national and EU statecraft, or the inherent right of every person to belong to humanity? Are human rights, for migrants and for others in minoritarian positions, institutional "permissions" masked as inherent human rights (Žižek 2009:59)? Conversely, do supranational entities such as the European Court of Human Rights (ECHR) and the United Nations (UN) make political, administrative, and bureaucratic membership unnecessary, and the citizen-migrant distinction less relevant?[81] Many scholars and practitioners understand human rights as "moral claims that states are obliged to respect in their legal systems" (Carens 2013:97). But

Dembour and Kelly (2011) ask: are human rights—the right to life, the right not to be detained arbitrarily—for migrants? How can the rights of (forced) migrants, in the interstices of liberal democracies, be protected?[82] What are, in practice, (unauthorized) travelers' human rights? What do rights do? What is done with them, to whom, and by whom?

Is hospitality for migrants? Hospitality, often in a nexus with charity and solidarity, is invoked and extended by governmental actors and by activists critical of governmental action, by religious organizations and by secular ones.[83] The hospitality-detention complex is particularly relevant here. "Guesthood" may "morph . . . into imprisonment," sharply writes Herzfeld in a different context (2012:211), and such a hypothesis literally applies to border trespassers. The relationship between hospitality and sovereignty and "the crucial role of *alterity* and *externality*" are fundamental in the "formation of political theologies," write Candea and Da Col (2012:7; original emphasis). "Hospitality assemblages figure as means to establish the sovereignty of social groups," argues Shryock (2012:24). Is then "hospitality" a sign of active sovereign "adjustments, accommodations, and relocations" (Honig 2009:126), or rather a sign of defensive sovereign retrenchment (Benhabib 2006:47)? I explore and understand hospitality as a cultural and institutional invocation, and in the ambivalent materiality of sovereign humanitarianism.

In the administration and narration of hospitality, "scaling up and down" is also particularly relevant (Shryock 2012:24). In other words, hospitality extended in the neighborhood is magnified as a national and civilizational trait. *Immigrati*, undesired or welcome "guests" of the nation in some remote parish or holding facility, become guests *a casa nostra*, in the private and national home. Different modalities of hospitality and impossible reciprocity (see Chapters 1, 4, and 5) generate different entanglements, tensions, inequalities, and conflicts to be traced.

A liquid site—with sea depths and moral high grounds. These pages are grounded in time spent in coastal southern Italy and Lampedusa; in maritime travel; and in shorter trips to Malta, coastal Libya, Tunisia, Greece, Montenegro, and to Serbia. The Mediterranean Sea, the people crossing it, and the flexible sovereignty regulating that passage make my "site" fluid, if not liquid, exposed to winds, currents, radars, electronic sensors and satellite assemblages; a site of both disciplining and uncontainable human agency. I mean "liquid" in a rather literal sense, then, unrelated to Bauman's somewhat ambivalent "liquid modernity" (2000). My site sits in the situational interstices between national and supranational jurisdictions. It spans from the recent past to the futures envisioned by migrants and by sovereign preemption. It relates to reterritorialization and to "nongeographic border capabilities operating both transnationally and subnationally" (Sassen 2006:417). Additionally, understanding my site as liquid is instrumental to a social inquiry that sticks to a "flat" social domain (Latour 2005:170). This is fundamental. For sticking to a flat social domain allows analysts to avoid the unwarranted "scaling" noted above, especially when the focus of analysis comprises both Mediterranean depths and the moral high grounds of European sovereign aspirations.

As it examines a liquid, uncontainable, and long-term site of personal experience, *Crimes of Peace* builds upon recent, complementary scholarship with similar stakes and comparable regional-global focus. Feldman (2012:180–98) maps the policy and technological infrastructure of the EU's external borders, and calls his practice "nonlocal ethnography." Andersson, tracing West Africans' undocumented migration to Ceuta and Melilla, speaks of his multifaceted approach as of an "extended field site" (2014:284). Lucht follows a group of young men from a small fishing village in Ghana to the socioeconomic margins of life in Naples (2012). Bernal, with particular emphasis on the Eritrean diaspora, scrutinizes global cyberspace as a "national" public sphere materializing outside the confines of that authoritarian country (2014). Nordstrom focuses on "placeless hyperplaced global flows" (2007:xi), and crafts an "experiential" ethnography that navigates the ethical, methodological, and authorial quandaries of research involving smugglers and other actors of the legal/illegal gray area. Waterston (2014) traces a personal and familial journey to map the global and the political, summoning a social history of the present via what I see as an existential anthropology. Indeed, seemingly more localized ethnographies offer an indispensable understanding of global realities. Cabot (2014) interrogates governance, rights discourse, humanitarian practice, and their theatricality through close scrutiny of policing and of nongovernmental aid in Athens. Muehlebach (2012), tracing the moralizing lives of Milan residents and social workers, maps the neoliberal work of compassionate and voluntary labor, and how this is contrasted with the "material" labor of migrants. From the public squares of Cairo and Tehran, Bayat (2013) is able to apprehend everyday life as politics. From a gentrifying neighborhood in Rome, Herzfeld (2009) illuminates the global restructuring of cultural intimacy.

Upon close scrutiny, the invisible hand of neoliberal global restructuring is not at all invisible (e.g., Tsing 2005). At times, it emerges as supported by the muscular arms of governmental intervention. One might argue that the market itself becomes "the regulative principle underlying the state" (Dean 2009:51), although the existing tension between statecraft and *neoliberal* statecraft always needs to be ethnographically attended to, rather than foreclosed. More broadly, the state—its networked institutional actors, competing political and bureaucratic mechanisms, economic interests, territorialized and exclusive claims, loyalties and monopolies it aspires to—intersects with other regimes of power, to be accounted for as they also reconfigure "territory, authority, and rights," to borrow Sassen's (2006) assemblage. For example, we might consider the intergovernmental and supranational infrastructure of the EU and the multiplication of local and regional bureaucracies, armed forces, and nongovernmental organizations (NGOs). Still other regimes of power become eminently visible when smuggling in drugs, tobacco, and weapons—including across the same Ionian routes used by migrants—intersects with organized crime that is *both* local and transnational.

Indeed, thinking with seemingly traditional Italian organized crime in mind is helpful in understanding, if not anticipating, state and supranational sovereignty in the twenty-first century. Consider especially the Camorra and the Sacra Corona Unita (see Chapter 3): their qualities as "mechanisms," rather than "structures" (Saviano 2007:38); their bilateral agreements and transnational collaborations; the alliances, tolerations, and conflicts between new and emerging bosses and clans; their resilient pragmatism and ideological fluidity; their increasingly horizontal segmentation and practical connectivity; their real-time surveillance; their pretense to control spaces, when in reality they seek to profitably shape socioeconomic relationships and bodies in space; their military and benevolent power; the salvific and protective moralizing with which they anoint themselves.

These fluid objects of analysis and the existing scholarly architecture warrant my artisanal approach to ethnography. The qualifier "artisanal" here is to be understood quite plainly. One might consider the importance of gaining artisanal (and ethnographic) skill; the many tools at our disposal; the material, embodied, and gritty texture of production; the distinctiveness of every ethnography. Unique variations are due to our skills and epistemologies, to the volatile nature of our objects of analysis, to the agonistic mechanics of what we do, and to the dissident and yet empirical creativity with which we imbue our work. As in the case of Cretan artisans and apprentices (Herzfeld 2004), an artisanal ethnography works in the crevices of power-laden structures and neoliberal agency, at the intersections of individual resistance and global hierarchies of power. It acknowledges the collective and yet idiosyncratic tradition that enables it. It is constituted not only by words and conspicuous gestures but also by silences, handshakes, and glances of critical scrutiny or mutual understanding. It is an everyday practice, situated in the same world as its readers and interlocutors, well aware of the inequalities at play. It brings words and people together, but it is also interested in disaggregating the symbolic, ideological, and material "glue" holding together different normative orders (Sassen 2006:422; Latour 1999). It pays attention to its own functional aesthetics, and to the aesthetic facet of what it scrutinizes—from the moral and material aesthetics of gaze and surveillance, to Otranto's and Lampedusa's possibly emancipatory public aesthetics (Chapter 6).[84] A relational epistemology and an artisanal ethnography deploy both precedent and casuistry. The structured improvisations of artisanal ethnography parallel the structured improvisations of fluid statecraft, flexible sovereignty, migrant trajectories, and situated rights.

Artisanal ethnography resonates with the similarly never-definitive dimension of justice and equality. Rather than providing prefabricated solutions that "work for everybody,"[85] artisanal ethnography urges selective adaptation of the existing tools it draws attention to, and unauthorized occupation of the spaces it traces. More than to readers, it speaks to users and discerning citizens, including those whose rights and membership are not state recognized.

Exit Strategies

Italy continues to cope with the search-and-rescue obligations of any maritime country, coordinating the interventions of commercial, coast guard, navy, finance guard, and Frontex vessels, in its area of responsibility and beyond. But Mare Nostrum is not to celebrate a second anniversary, in October 2015 (see Chapters 3 and 6). Italian governmental authorities have publicly and repeatedly declared that its costs, at least 9 million euros per month of activity, are unsustainable for a single country. As EU Commissioner for Home Affairs Cecilia Malmström puts it, a new Frontex endeavor named Triton is to "substitute, take over 'Mare Nostrum,' even if it will not be to the same extent. 'Mare Nostrum' has been very ambitious and we don't know if we can find the means to do exactly what Italy has done," Malmström admits.[86] Humanitarian organizations, while welcoming Triton as a more "European" maritime enterprise, are concerned that the border enforcement approach is to become fully dominant at the expense of the humanitarian one.[87] Mare Nostrum dispatched large vessels, equipped with medical facilities, to the vicinity of the Libyan coast. The geographic scope of Triton, at least officially, is confined within territorial waters immediately south of Sicily, Calabria, and Lampedusa. Starting in November 2014 a small fleet of Frontex Triton vessels is expected to defend the border and to rescue maritime migrants, at a third of Mare Nostrum's monthly costs.

Triton, and Frontex more generally, are part of an emerging "integrated" EU approach that seeks to "better manage . . . migration in all its aspects."[88] This approach features a preferential option for temporary and skilled migration;[89] it intends to deal "more robustly with irregular migration," in part through better "cooperation" with non-EU countries; it seeks to protect "those in need through a strong asylum policy"; and it is enabled by a "strengthened, modern management of the Union's external borders."[90] Eurosur, with its networked technology and bureaucratic efficiency, is expected to help in real time "detecting, preventing and combating illegal immigration and cross-border crime and contributing to ensuring the protection and saving the lives of migrants."[91] One has to ask whether such an ambitious approach can be implemented. What does the EU's "strong asylum policy" look like? How does a patrol boat defend the border and rescue people at the same time? Can interception at sea, detention, and removal be effected with "full respect for fundamental rights," as all EU documents stipulate? Is sovereign salvation an actually existing, functioning utopia?

Reactions are diverse. In Lampedusa, the café regulars in Liberty Square are asking: Europe? Where is it? What is it for? In the celluloid world of hypothetical, twenty-first-century Neorealism, segments of the public burst out in sonorous laughter; first rows applaud; those in the back veil their timid sobs. Dozens of people are lingering in the foyer, as the premiere of the border spectacle is by invitation only. A young, unemployed man is sleeping in a greasy cardboard box, right around the corner. On the flat screen world of situational awareness, the not-so-occasional colored dot is an inconvenient breach of "pre-frontier" screening, and a victim in need of salvation. As the sun sets, people on North African shores are rubbing

Figure 3. Piazza Libertà (Liberty Square), Lampedusa. Photo: Maurizio Albahari.

their hands. Travelers are cold; smugglers anticipate heightened profits. In Valletta, search-and-rescue sailors are dining before their night shift, just like their coast guard colleagues in Lampedusa. Farther from the Mediterranean coastline, in the accountant's waiting room, law-abiding taxpayers are disgruntled. In humanitarian, religious, and activist circles, people are crafting short-term provisions and long term decalogues reforming immigration and asylum. In a world of sovereign polities, aggregate data, and so-called burden sharing, the lives of 25,500 people who have perished in fourteen years are shockingly high collateral damage. In a moralizing world of secular redemption, the faces and voices of the 142,000 saved override the silences of the drowned.[92] These faces and voices constitute an abundant credit in the European balance of sovereign salvation, and offset both past dramas and the "tragedies" that "inevitably" are to come. In Antoine de Saint-Exupéry's not-so alien world, stateless little princesses are asking: "Your Majesty, it's such a small planet. Why do *you* need borders?"[93] In a world of liberal democracies, the question is not why others need borders, but for whose benefit we need them in their current form. In a world of persons, and such is ethnography's world, there is evidence of crimes of peace, and of rescue. One expected death is too many. Saving a life is saving the whole humanity, but two lives are never interchangeable. We are brought to ask: costly emergencies and a high-tech fix, or radically different policies for emerging polities?

At 7:29 on a chilly November morning, the sun is rising above the twinkling sea of the Strait of Otranto. From the rocky cliff of Punta Palascìa, the easternmost promontory of the Italian peninsula, you may enjoy a hazy view of the Albanian mountains behind the Greek island of Corfu. Fishermen appreciate the silence. There are no cars and no intruders, save for an anthropologist. No maritime travelers either, at least for now. At 7:30 A.M. sharp, screeching megaphones broadcast the cheerful notes of the Italian national anthem. They come from the nearby radar station of the Italian navy and NATO. One is aurally reminded of how space is materially, legally, and symbolically invested with the sovereignty of state and supra-state institutions. Even when seemingly idyllic, space is traversed by various agendas, techniques, and mechanisms of the political to be investigated.

In Otranto, in Lampedusa, in Valletta the jagged cliffs of the Mediterranean trap discolored dolls, torn photo albums, unnecessary dinars, broken sandals, and crumpled space blankets. There seems to be a crowded fishing boat on the horizon. Will it make it to the coast? Will it be allowed to land? Who are the people on board? How will they be received? With every boat, the claustrophobically airy room evoked in Magritte's *On the Threshold of Liberty* is reinhabited by the people and situations at the center of this book. What are their stories? What kind of encounter will they have with humanitarian personnel and armed forces? What will bystanders do? Will travelers be made to fall into the fault lines of Euro-Mediterranean inequality and injustice? Will they engender subversion and emancipation, for themselves and for those kept on the other side of their horizon?

Chapter 1

Genealogies of Care and Confinement

Brothers Beyond the Sea

About eight hundred political dissidents are seeking refuge and political asylum in the Italian embassy in Tirana, capital of the People's Socialist Republic of Albania.[1] Thousands of people also trespass the gates and fences of another seventeen embassies, including those of France, West Germany, and newly postcommunist countries such as Poland and Bulgaria. It is the warm July of 1990. Italian cities across the Adriatic are hosting the soccer World Cup, and it really looks like Italy might beat Argentina and make it to the final. In Albania, citizens increasingly resent the claustrophobic, militarized, and isolationist regime that clings to the legacy of authoritarian leader Enver Hoxha, who died in 1985. Trying to leave Albania without authorization amounts to treason, and is punished accordingly. But under pressure from the UN, Albanian authorities eventually grant passports to the dissidents, allowing them to leave the country. Italy wins only the third-place match, with England.

The Italian government organizes and facilitates the passage of some dissidents into Italy.[2] On July 13, 1990, a commercial ferry brings them to the Italian port of Brindisi, in the region of Apulia across the Strait of Otranto. Both in Brindisi and in the national public sphere every person on board is greeted as a hero of anticommunism.[3] Local institutions such as municipalities offer hospitality, and mass media wax enthusiastic for these *profughi* (political refugees), as everyone calls them, fleeing a dictatorial regime. Albanian arrivals express uncontainable celebration and joy, and among Italians it is not uncommon to hear that these are brothers who for too long have been kept brutally segregated from the rest of the world.

Indeed, Albanians embody a little-known neighbor. Conversely, Italy and the Italian language have entered Albanian homes on a daily basis: while foreign radio and television channels were not allowed, hidden and creatively improvised antennas bypassed governmental censorship. Italian mass media helped provide Albania (and Italy) with a glossy, celebratory, consumerist version of "Italy." By the late 1980s they contributed to the creation of Italy as the closest "America" for Albanians.[4] In relatively recent times, trans-Adriatic relationships had been pioneered by Apulian fishing boats (up to the 1930s) reaching the Albanian coast.[5] Trans-Adriatic relationships had been also colonized by Fascist Italy's invasion of Albania (1939–43), and navigated by Italian tobacco smugglers covertly conducting business with Albanian communist authorities from the 1970s to 1990.[6]

Enver Hoxha's statue is brought down in Tirana's Scanderbeg Square on February 20, 1991, following student-led political demonstrations. A few days later, in early March, soldiers guarding the port of Durrës shoot in the air but are unable to stop a crowd from boarding several cargo vessels. A few hours later, more than a thousand profughi disembark, unexpectedly, in Brindisi. These are the earliest instances of conspicuous unauthorized maritime migration in the contemporary history of Italy.[7] Another seven or eight thousand people are approaching this southeastern coast of Italy. Cargo ships and fishing boats such as the *Lirija* (Liberty), *Apollonia, Kavaja, Legend, Tirana, Alba, Fadil Daun, Milos, A. Kondi, Partizani, Kallmi, Panajat Papa,* and *Illyria* are allowed to land in the Apulian port cities of Monopoli, Otranto, Brindisi, Bari, and Gallipoli. The police grant the new arrivals work residence permits and transfer them to different shelters throughout Italy. Some commentators speculate that the Albanian authorities, by at least allowing so many people to leave, are blackmailing Italian counterparts in order to obtain urgently needed financial aid.

I remember those days. All my friends and I could talk about was the arrival of "the Albanians," just a short drive from our high school in Gallipoli. Clothes were collected; many profughi were hosted in local parishes and hotels. In what were chilly nights, in Brindisi and elsewhere in coastal Apulia local families went to beaches and docks with pots of warm food and clean clothes, and extended hospitality to Albanian families. Newspapers and television shows organized fund-raisers to help the new arrivals, and employers made a point of offering jobs. Medical and police personnel worked after hours or voluntarily.

Those maritime arrivals elicited sovereign responses that extend into the present. Early experiences of physical confinement were institutionalized into the immigrant holding centers eventually dotting the Italian peninsula and the EU's borders. Catholic ideas and influential members of the clergy also assumed a fundamental role in the humanitarian confinement that defines the Italian and EU liberal-democratic approach to unauthorized migrants.[8]

Don Giuseppe, a Catholic priest, was at the forefront of the effort to accommodate the 1991 Albanian arrivals to Apulia. His blue eyes, contrasting with the gray and black clothes he customarily wears, betray the emotion with which he remembers those days. In the coastal town of Otranto he was the director of the diocesan branch of Caritas, the large international relief, development, and social services organization inspired by Catholic social teachings. In that capacity, he provided assistance to some twelve hundred refugees kept in the tourist camping ground of nearby Frassanito, under the authority of the police prefect.[9] Particularly concerned about two hundred children who were in the camp, he arranged for the local Juvenile Court to temporarily entrust them to Caritas's care. These children, continues Don Giuseppe, were accommodated in parishes and Caritas branches, and local families were also involved in welcoming them into their homes.[10] Don Giuseppe's recollections raise questions on the potentially arbitrary if not authoritarian nature of humanitarian decision making. Were these children unaccompanied? Had they lost contact with their relatives during disembarkation? Had they been separated from their families? But rather than just problematizing Caritas's concern and care for these children, these questions point to the early emergence of a policing-humanitarian nexus, later magnified and institutionalized. For over two decades, police prefects, and more broadly the Italian government that they represent at the local level, have needed to provide food and shelter to new arrivals, to bureaucratically identify them, and to secure their "orderly" distribution on Italian territory. In 1991, prefects are dealing with the inexperience and improvisation of the various actors involved, including volunteers, medical personnel, police agents, and their own bureaucracy.

It is policing that soon preoccupies institutional actors. In March 1991, Apulian authorities and police forces receive a vague directive from government officials in Rome to "stop the influx" of maritime arrivals.[11] A few Albanian boats are temporarily prevented from landing in Apulian ports. Italian authorities soon recognize the practice as impossible to implement and sustain, but the idea resonates with a number of opinion makers in national media. Shortly following the end of the 1990–91 Gulf War, they articulate unsubstantiated concerns with the "Islamic danger" inherent in such migration. Still others raise the threat to the body of the nation after a few cases of scabies are reported among Albanian persons.

A Sweet Ship with Twenty Thousand Passengers

The warm morning of August 7, 1991, the *Vlora* is docked in the Albanian port of Durrës, where it is registered. Moored at quay 5, it is unloading Cuban sugar. The Italian-made transatlantic cargo ship stands out among all other vessels for its impressive size. Among Durrës residents there is word that the military is not guarding the port. Incredibly, the port is open: it is possible to depart. Arben, like other local youth, is playing on the beach, and decides to follow his curiosity and the surging crowd. Word of mouth is contagious; the scene grows hectic. People in the region, especially in the capital, Tirana, catch a ride with strangers or hop on a truck headed to the port. Many are driven by a sense of adventure, others by poverty. Most people have never been on a boat. Adelina, just graduated from college and with no financial concerns, is curious to see what's happening and goes to the port without telling her parents and siblings. Some are frustrated with former communist elites who are clinging to their privileges, and more broadly with the lack of substance in President Ramiz Alia's promises of political and social change. Others heading to the port are known criminals. But what unites most people is that there is no planned decision to emigrate, no ticket to purchase, no luggage to pack, no lunch to bring, and no passport to show on either side of the Strait of Otranto. Police and army agents in the port of Durrës cannot do much about the imposing crowd. They eventually join it. When all these people arrive to quay 5, they see hundreds of others already on the *Vlora*. Many fall in the water as they try to climb the mooring lines. Once on board, they recognize a cousin, a friend, a coworker, and even their own parents.

Halim Milaqi,[12] the *Vlora*'s captain, has never before been in charge of a human cargo ship. He is concerned. And the main engine needs repairs. But he is stabbed in the leg with a screwdriver, and threatened. He is asked to leave the port and head the *Vlora* to the Netherlands, Germany, or Italy—anywhere but Albania. He does not have a choice. The engineers on board manage to fix the engine, but fresh water for the cooling system and for drinking is already scarce.

Around 3 P.M. Milaqi is heading toward the closest destination he can think of, the port of Brindisi across the Strait of Otranto. People on board occupy every imaginable space. They sit quietly as the night approaches. A sense of solidarity and community pervades the passengers. Some find condensed milk and sardines on board; others eat some of the Cuban sugar, only to augment their dehydration and unquenchable thirst. People fall asleep as the night goes on quietly. Things are not easy for Milaqi. The Brindisi coast guard and a hovering Italian finance guard helicopter ask him by radio to change course and return to Albania. But early in the morning of August 8, people on board can already see the lights of Brindisi. Somebody begins to shout "Itali! Itali!"—to be echoed by the estimated twenty thousand people on board.

There is disappointment as the *Vlora* changes course. Soon people realize that the vessel is sailing north, along the Italian coast. It has been allowed to land in Bari, the Apulia region's capital. It is an unbearably warm morning in Bari. Port authorities, curious citizens, and military personnel begin to wonder whether the announced biblical proportions of the imminent arrival have been exaggerated. But the *Vlora* is finally visible on the horizon, around 10 A.M. It is eventually allowed to dock and salutes the city with its sirens. Every square inch of the dock, still soiled with coal unloaded a few days earlier, is crowded with people who have disembarked. And every square inch of the *Vlora* still seems occupied—its deck, its railings, its antennas and radar. From the deck, some passengers take the risk and jump in the water, losing their clothes in the impact. Still, everyone flashes the victory sign with their fingers. Nderim, a child, says he left because in Albania there is only bread and water. No fruits like the one he has just been given.

Locked in the Stadium: Milk, Coffee, and Tear Gas

The *Vlora* travelers' first encounter with "Italy" is with its state police and army. Agents try to enforce a semblance of public order at Bari's docks. The Red Cross arrives only hours later. Several police agents are on summer vacation, and they have to be called back on duty too. Bari's mayor, Enrico Dalfino, is among the first to reach the port because he intends to welcome the refugees in person. Visibly moved, for almost twenty-four hours he coordinates the work of his city's civilian police agents and volunteers. But there is no system in place to distribute food and water to people who have been on the boat for more than twenty-four hours. There is a cacophony of sirens, surgical masks, gloves, stretchers, batons, and tear gas. Police agents work shifts of thirty-six hours. Local residents bring milk and coffee thermoses, water bottles, and pots of food. Some Albanian youth manage to find refuge in nearby shops, some of them only to be reported to the police. Others are given a ride—a local resident skillfully loses the police patrol following him.

Dalfino, the mayor, would like to create a temporary humanitarian tent city in the vicinity of the port. This is not compatible with the decisions being made by the government in Rome, though. His proposal of a tent city is not considered. Orange buses of the local public transportation authority start arriving. Albanians are eager to leave the port—many are fainting, others are pretending to, just to be taken somewhere else, by ambulance if need be. Anything is better than the dock, and the city's orange buses seem to offer a way out. The new arrivals can finally glimpse the imposing Norman-Swabian castle, Romanic churches, textile shops, and the tall apartments, small cars, and billboards of Bari. Virtually all of them have already seen Italy, on television. Many are able to understand and speak Italian. Their journey in Bari is short, though. The orange buses enter the old soccer stadium, Stadio della Vittoria, and everyone has to step off. The Ministry of the Interior has decided that Albanian citizens are to be confined there. The ministry, essentially in charge of "law and order" in the country, is guided by Christian Democrat Vincenzo Scotti (1990–92). Between August 8 and 14, most of the persons who arrived on the *Vlora* are brought into the stadium, with the exception of the ones who had managed to escape and of select women and children. In light of the growing tension, utility workers who should assist with waste management and even police agents leave the stadium. Albanian citizens are locked in. Army trucks have to physically block the stadium's gates from the outside.

Helicopters and cranes drop food rations and water bottles. In the stadium there is no trace of the comradery and solidarity that had characterized the *Vlora*'s journey. Well-known criminals, from Tirana and Durrës, stock and control the food. Some of them act as spokespersons and demand from Italian authorities the guarantee of residence permits for everyone.

There are incidents and riots. The police allow some women and children out in the city; but everyone else is locked in the stadium, under the scorching sun and without adequate washrooms for days.

The national chief of police, Vincenzo Parisi, visits his agents serving in Bari. The president of the Italian Republic, Christian Democrat Francesco Cossiga (1985–92), also lands in Bari. Local administrators expect him to express national solidarity and gratefulness for Bari's generosity in dealing with such unprecedented arrivals. President Cossiga does set up a news conference. But his tone is akin to the military severity with which he dealt with student protests in the late 1970s, as minister of the interior. In that unusual news conference in Bari, he criticizes with violent and disparaging words Mayor Dalfino, a fellow Christian Democrat, for his humanitarian stance on the Albanian matter. Cossiga goes as far as to promise he will do his best to strip Dalfino of his civic function. For President Cossiga, Interior Minister Scotti, and Chief of Police Parisi have decided, upon the *Vlora*'s arrival, the *respingimento* (pushback) against the Albanians. They are to be collectively repatriated without even being identified individually. Mayor Dalfino opposes such collective summary removal. But the police's point of view is that these Albanians have never entered Italy—they have not presented a passport, and were never allowed entry officially. Authorities in Bari, the port of entry, may simply "push them back."

An Albanian family manages to entrust its child to a local passerby, before being repatriated with at least sixteen thousand other people. Confiscated as part of what the police call Operation Albanians, ferries of the Adriatica and Tirrenia lines accommodate thousands of people in their holds. They complement the military airplanes leaving for the short flight to Tirana. On one of those planes, many of the returnees sing in unison the 1984 hit by Italian pop star Eros Ramazzotti, "Una Terra Promessa" (Promised Land).

To this day, Enrico Dalfino, mayor between 1990 and 1991 and professor of law at the University of Bari, is one of Bari's most beloved mayors. Anna, his widow, affectionately keeps more than four thousand telegrams he received following those events, in which people from all over Italy thanked him and the city for their humanity in trying to receive the Albanian migrants.[13]

And yet despite some popular sympathy, the people in the stadium were not considered heroes to be welcomed with open arms. The pushback option was "palatable," to borrow from the relevant vocabulary of political

science. Albania was no longer communist. Solidarity was no longer institutionally sponsored as it had been with the first "brothers" of 1990.[14] The
widely broadcast image of Albanians was now that of violence-prone beg-
gars wearing rags, whom one needed to rescue, nourish, and clean.[15] A shift
in perceptions also occurred at the local level, elsewhere in Apulia. Face-to-
face interaction was possibly informed by the televised images of misery,
violence, and confinement in the port and the stadium. Pietro, a volunteer
with Misericordia (a lay Catholic brotherhood providing social and health
services) in the port of Otranto, was involved in the reception of Albanian
citizens from the first arrivals. He recalls that Otranto's local residents "at
the beginning" saw Albanian migrants as "brothers from the other side
[of the strait]."[16] But his understanding—perhaps colored by his visceral
anticommunism—is that these first arrivals were quite "*spregiudicati*" (cyn-
ical, amoral). They did not value individual labor and private enterprise,
thus creating resentment in those who were helping them but did not see
in their beneficiaries any willingness to "move on." Pietro also suggests that
a few insignificant thefts received undue media attention, which affected
the local perception of all Albanians. His words speak to the larger perception that Albanians were failing to make a positive return on the Italians'
gift of compassion and reception.[17]

Confinement in the Della Vittoria stadium helps legitimate the repatriation of the *Vlora*'s Albanians. Confinement in the stadium suggests to the
Italian public that immigration is exactly what President Cossiga, the interior minister, and the police intend it to be: first and foremost, immigration
is *a problem of public order* and containment. Quite significantly, then, the
stadium confinement constitutes an important early step in Italians' acqui-
sition of cultural knowledge and moralized evaluation not only of migrants'
"otherness" but also of the "immigration phenomenon" itself. These early
instances of confinement and pushback lay the precedent and the founda-
tions for more permanent sovereign structures. But they do so through the
systematic method of emergency. A methodical emergency that leads to the
need to confine is the institutional response to a maritime mobility that
seems to threaten public order.

With the essential support of hundreds of volunteers and of lay and
Catholic voluntary forces, during the 1990s Italian state authorities were
able to "assist" in Apulia "209,500 foreigners" including 67,000 Albanians,
3,000 Croats, 14,000 Somalis, 80,000 Yugoslavs and Bosnians, 15,000
Kurds, and 30,000 Kosovars.[18] Otranto's Misericordia alone, according to

one of its volunteers, in the two decades between 1991 and 2011 "received and fed" about 200,000 people, of whom 32,000 were minors.[19] But citizens and volunteers, as mentioned above, also acted without coordination, for example when bringing to the seaside "a box of cookies, a quart of milk, a jar of jam."[20] The relative lack of organization, institutionalization, and centralized confinement of migrants in the early 1990s points to a genuine spontaneity on the part of the locals, who were not too concerned with legal nuances and with the knowledge of "different" cultural preferences. Pietro mentions the "tortellini uprising" of March 1991 when he says a group of Albanian migrants in the Frassanito camping ground rebelled because of the pork they recognized in the tortellini stuffing, contrary to their dietary practice.[21] Many people who shared with me their experience of those years point out that "it is the poor who care for and give to other persons in need,"[22] underlying how the main agents of solidarity were common citizens, rather than local notables.

Working with migrants—including providing immediate assistance upon disembarkation—for many Catholic priests, parishioners, and lay individuals represented the beginning of an involvement later extended into other arenas of volunteer work. Some churches have since then served as shelters for migrants, and today they are used as meeting venues for diverse social actors who are keen on elaborating forms of solidarity with migrants and even resistance to immigration policies. Individual volunteers began working within parish or diocesan activities, and later used that expertise in working for local or state institutions of migration management. Still, some of the volunteers and priests involved in these reception efforts share with me a deep sense of frustration.

Franco, a middle-aged, mustached medical doctor to this day working in Apulia with newly arrived maritime migrants, regrets that the collective effort of the 1990s constituted a missed opportunity.[23] Incidentally, let me note that the phrase "missed opportunity" keeps reemerging as commentary to each umpteenth shipwreck and to each known episode of violence in holding facilities. In the doctor's words, the immigration-related hectic activities of the 1990s were a bit "like the Italian 1968 movement": the hope and expectation of deep social and political change was soon to be "shattered." For in his analysis, local volunteer and Catholic workers, expressing a humanitarian and generally receptive stance toward migrants, were not able to take advantage of the political leverage ensured by the state's dependency on their services. That loosely structured, nongovernmental involvement had been consistently solicited by the state administration, and for more than a decade it proved indispensable in the state's bureaucratic and humanitarian management of migration. But with very few exceptions, these nongovernmental forces were not able, or willing, to try and foster a shift in the state's "public order" approach to immigration. On the contrary, a humanitarian logic de facto enabled the institutionalization and centralization of migrant detention.

From Children's Colony to Penal Colony:
The Birth of Confinement

Several years later, during early spring 1997, social, political, and military upheaval characterize Albania, with thousands of people seeking safety abroad, including by crossing the Strait of Otranto.[24] Following the arrival in Apulia of about fifteen thousand Albanian citizens, in a situation of emergency, Law Decree 60 of March 20, 1997, authorizes police prefects to speedily expel foreigners they deem "undesirable." These 1997 events constitute a major turning point in the reception of migrants.

Working then with Otranto's Caritas, Don Giuseppe was involved in assisting many of those newly arrived fifteen thousand. He recalls that, as happened routinely, the police prefect of Lecce asked local voluntary organizations for logistical help. The Catholic Dioceses of Otranto and of nearby Lecce, in particular, were asked about any available sleeping quarters, needed to accommodate at least six hundred migrants. Don Giuseppe's Caritas made those six hundred places available—but spread across twelve different locations in the area. The prefect rejected that offer. As Don Giuseppe explains, "immigration was considered more as a problem of public order than as a political problem."[25] In other words, in line with their background in policing and with governmental expectations, state officials saw immigration as a challenge to public order and as a phenomenon to track and control. Migrants could not be dispersed in the territory because that would not be practical in terms of their bureaucratic manageability. Don Giuseppe is a strong opponent of migrants' confinement in holding facilities. In several conversations he emphasizes how he and his Caritas branch repeatedly proposed to state authorities hosting individual migrants in homes with local families, and migrant family groups in autonomous apartments that were available. He is convinced such a social and spatial approach would help migrants access the social, administrative, legal, and economic networks and resources necessary for everyday life and "integration." Don Giuseppe contrasts his entrenched conviction to the choices made by other persons and religious bodies. In particular, in response to the prefect's urgent request for accommodations in 1997, the Diocese of Lecce offered one of its facilities, the Regina Pacis. As a single site, it could accommodate up to five hundred people. The structure, donated to the diocese by a private citizen, used to be a *colonia estiva*, a seaside summer resort intended for young people, including underprivileged children.

I have the chance to see it myself in 2004. My first interview at the Regina Pacis is scheduled for September 22. It is a warm and sunny Wednesday. Early in the afternoon the city of Lecce, where I am residing for this leg of my fieldwork, is sleepy and quiet, with summer lingering. My burgundy Fiat Tipo is the only car on the road as I drive past the city's center toward San Foca, the small coastal village where the Regina Pacis is located. It is a half-hour drive. There is no traffic to worry about, so there is time to scan the pine trees bent by the constant sea breeze, and to get anxious. I am uneasy about my first visit to the center and my first interview with its director, Don Cesare. Both the center's fence and Don Cesare are already somewhat familiar because of their mass media exposure.

The clergy's conspicuous involvement with migration issues is not an exceptional case. The social role of Catholic priests and bishops in local communities; their moral and intellectual authority, charisma, and prestige; their experience with Italian emigrants abroad; and their charitable mobilization for immigrants, starting in the early 1990s, have contributed to making some clergy members public experts on migration. Don Cesare in particular, often hailed as "the migrants' priest," became an influential and knowledgeable voice on immigration management and human trafficking. He has given dozens of interviews to national and international media. Institutions at the EU level routinely have invited him as a consultant and a panelist. Institutional, official visits to the Regina Pacis holding center have been countless and conspicuous, including those of local politicians, members of the Italian parliament, ministers and prime ministers, EU and UN representatives and even Carlo Azeglio Ciampi, president of the republic (1999–2006). But I also know Don Cesare and the center from activists' denunciations. The pioneering Regina Pacis is the object of both celebration and vocal opposition. If I were to adopt activists' vocabulary, I soon would be entering and conducting an interview in a *lager*, a Nazi-like concentration camp.

The Regina Pacis is easily visible from San Foca's beach. Sand flies everywhere when it's windy, and I park in the dusty back of the center. I ask the carabinieri patrol how to get to the front entrance. Here I find more patrols and a checkpoint. I have an appointment with Don Cesare, I explain. The guard leaves his post to open the gate. I stand in the cement front yard. The gray of the cement and the silver of the aluminum fence starkly contrast with this sky. I have to show my ID card. I feel somewhat privileged. That Italian document, a token of my citizenship, makes me exempt from the possibility of confinement in such a facility. Once my identity is confirmed, the young soldier apologetically tells me, "it's routine." My presence and arrival time are annotated. Another soldier goes inside the center to announce my arrival to Don Cesare. Still in the cement yard, I notice a couple of women who are playing with their small children. Carabinieri chat and joke among themselves and with these women, here protected from their traffickers' outreach. Young workers are unloading a truck of shoes and food. Two Brazilian nuns also arrive and enter the center, guitar cases in hand. Most of the center's windows have bars. A few meters on the left lies a gorgeous public beach. Just a fisherman today; a few days earlier it would have been crowded with relaxing families and joyous tourists.

Ten minutes have gone by in the courtyard. Don Cesare—hectically busy as are all Italian priests you will encounter—greets me. He is a rather tall, middle-aged man, wearing dark clothes. Almost bald, he wears glasses and strikes me as a pragmatic and assertive figure. We walk to his office, the first room on the right in the long corridor. As you come from the sunny yard and your eyes have yet to adjust, the interior looks quite gloomy. The pastel ceramic tiles in the corridor remind me of my hometown's hospital.

The Regina Pacis is run by a foundation of the same name, under Don Cesare's leadership. The two-year convention signed in March 2003 with the prefect of Lecce—and therefore with the Italian state—stipulates that the foundation is to receive a daily reimbursement of forty-three euros per migrant. The center's management and staff comprise Don Cesare and several young colleagues. Among the latter, there are former *ospiti*, or "guests," as they are routinely called, from Iraq, Moldova, India, Albania, and Morocco, who can thus also help with translations. The center has been structured to host up to 180 migrants in twenty-seven rooms, and has additional spaces such as a kitchen, laundry, dining room, medical and dental rooms, rooms for the armed forces, a social hall, and a satellite television hall. Several professionals work or serve voluntarily in the center, including a social service assistant, a psychologist, a dentist, and a lawyer. But there is no independent oversight. No institutionalized mechanisms allow migrants to denounce potential ill treatment by the management, staff, fellow detainees, or armed forces.

Don Cesare shares his large office with close colleagues. They may easily listen to my conversation with him. A fax arrives from a minister's office. Then it's a phone call from the local police headquarters of Asti, at the opposite corner of the Italian peninsula. Asti police inform Don Cesare that two new migrants to be hosted will be arriving, escorted all the way from Asti. They might be "difficult cases": the police agent wishes Don Cesare "good luck with them." In the office I notice a small cabinet with dozens of keys, like those I was responsible for when I worked as a hotel night porter. Now it's the turn of a young man, a guest who knocks and enters the office. With imploring tone he asks Don Cesare when he may leave the facility. Before being transferred to the Regina Pacis he has spent two years in prison, he complains, and now he is undergoing "this," as if he hadn't been sufficiently categorized in prison. He "just can't bear it anymore." It is not uncommon for countries of origin to make repatriations difficult, for overloaded Italian bureaucracies to delay, and for holding facilities to see any empty bed as a missed state reimbursement. Looking toward this guest, Don Cesare replies he doesn't know—he hasn't looked at his case yet and right now he is busy with me.

I explain to him who I am and the research I am doing. For five long minutes, I reexperience the eerily familiar feeling of those oral examinations at my undergraduate alma mater, in Florence. I would always answer while looking the professor in the eye, occasionally without finding any clue as to whether my ongoing answer was ingenious or totally off the mark. In this case, Don Cesare responds by crafting quite a comprehensive statement. In the span of a few minutes, it includes references to a dichotomy between (his) humanitarianism and contentious politics; to Catholic social teachings on immigration;[26] to cultural change, socioeconomic integration, and social scientific work:

> For us, the human being is at the center of migrations. It is from this fact that we must try again to understand the phenomenon [of

migration]: where does it come from, what is its future. The migratory phenomenon is made up of human beings who carry a baggage
of culture, politics, and poverty. . . . If there is no such focus on
human beings, we will never be able to make laws, and to understand what's going on in the world. This is the inspiring principle
of our reception of migrants, even in the shade of controversy. But
controversy originates in politics, not in the appreciation of the
human being. If we really consider the human being we realize that
several things are not how politics make them appear. The [migrant]
human being carries a strength which we cannot but appreciate.
This strength is such that it can even change our culture, our history,
and our territory. This is how culture changes. What can we do
when a new *halal* [i.e., Muslim] butcher shop opens? But this is also
how we get to know the other's culture, in a mutually respectful
debate that results in the growth of a single society. We both are
part of this society, the other who arrived by boat yesterday morning, and me, arrived by birth. We must help our people—from the
common citizen to the great thinkers, and especially sociologists—to
understand that the human being is a value. . . . Then of course you
[the researcher] do your part of the job. You might analyze what I
do, but you culturally mediate it as well.[27]

Don Cesare strikes me with his nuanced understanding of the "mediat-
ing" facets of the social scientist. And he articulates a notion of culture as
inevitably subject to change; and of society as comprising both old and
new residents. Contrasted to the static understanding of culture and society
expressed by a number of secular politicians, Don Cesare's own normative
understanding appears more sociologically grounded. His emphasis on the
absolute value of each migrant and of each human being is a pillar of Catholic social teachings, and also a marker of his ambivalent relationship with
"politics." On the one hand, he would like to see better laws, and a more
complex institutional and cultural understanding of migration. On the
other, he is wary of what he deems ideology-driven controversies surrounding his work. In particular, he implicitly refers to the mounting contestation
of social movements—including anarchist and counter-globalization
ones—who blame him for what they see as the essential function of the
center: to implement administrative detention on behalf of the state. Others, like the procession of politicians approvingly visiting the center, see

only humanitarian motivation in what he does. Indeed the lawyer serving at the Regina Pacis proudly emphasizes that through her work and Don Cesare's own (discretionary) intervention in 2003 around 37 percent of the center's guests who had received an expulsion decree from the police successfully appealed it, or at least had the expulsion suspended or revoked for health or other reasons.[28] And she thinks it is a salient fact that the Regina Pacis also serves as a shelter for homeless or destitute asylum seekers and migrants, regardless of their documented or undocumented status and the lack of state reimbursement for them.

I ask Don Cesare about the institutionalization of the Regina Pacis. When in 1997 the prefect accepted the diocese's offer to provide lodging for five hundred migrants, Don Cesare, secretary to Lecce's Archbishop Cosmo Francesco Ruppi (1988–2009), became the first director of the center. In 2000 the newly established Regina Pacis Foundation, with Don Cesare and Archbishop Ruppi as its leaders, assumed control of the center, replacing the diocese. What follows deserves to be quoted at length: it is Don Cesare's account of the early days of the Regina Pacis as Italy's pioneering migrant holding facility:

> My service to migrants began with migrants, in the sense that it is they who came to our house. Especially in 1997, it was a reality that deeply affected our Salento region [southern Apulia]: many people arriving, no organized welcome and reception, no presence of the state. Even voluntary forces were scared by a phenomenon that featured extremely high numbers. Christian humanism doesn't fear numbers, because it makes available whatever it can, and tries to transform a difficult moment into an opportunity for doing good to others. In 1997 we had a migratory phenomenon welcomed with forms rich in charity. Maybe there was little organization, but certainly there was a shelter and a meal, and assistance and guarantees not offered by others, and certainly not by the state. It is evident that the transition from emergency to a situation of ordinary migration influx has brought migration facilities to grow as well. At the beginning we were an improvised camp of migrants; with time we have become a facility of welcome and reception with rules and several methodologies of specialized intervention. . . . Moreover, the Regina Pacis has carried the moral weight of being the first facility of reception in Italy. Therefore, of having the duty to dictate the

rule to other facilities, through forms of dedication to the human
being made up of small things, but still of value. It is obvious that
the interpretation of reception that the [immigration] legislation has
provided is completely different. Its understanding of migration is
completely different. Because following that kindness of reception,
we witnessed (from 1998) a legislation that has used a completely
different interpretive key. This key is related to preoccupations
about national security, invasion, Islamization, and to larger understandings that have changed the politics vis-à-vis migration.[29]

There are several themes emerging in these words, and an overall concern with the legitimation of the establishment, activities, and morality of
the Regina Pacis in regard to a larger legal and political framework. In
particular, Don Cesare verbalizes a consensus I have apprehended in speaking with volunteers, researching news archives, and participating in local
conferences. In summary: humanitarian and charitable activities preceding
the institutionalization of migration holding centers, in 1998, are seen as
disorganized and uncoordinated efforts to meet migrants' demands and
to compensate for the state's perceived inactivity. The 1998 "Turco-
Napolitano" Immigration Law (40/1998) institutionalized previously infor-
mal shelters and charitable activities. It centralized, regulated, and financed
ostensibly disorganized and isolated grassroots efforts. This "humanitarian" facet made the immigration law palatable to Catholic and other nongovernmental organizations. But it was a law mainly focused on policing
and migration regulation—in line with the obligations of the Schengen
Agreement, implemented in Italy since 1997.

The 1998 Immigration Law legally defined the Regina Pacis and similar
or forthcoming centers as *centri di permanenza temporanea e assistenza*
(centers for the temporary residence and assistance of migrants, or CPT).
The ostensible function of such facilities is detention and removal: to enable
the deportation of unauthorized migrants, providing shelter while their
identity and nationality are ascertained and means of transport are made
available. Holding of migrants is to be implemented by extending the "necessary assistance" and "full respect" for migrants' dignity (Law 40/1998,
Article 14). The law consolidated in detention centers the perceived improvisation of volunteer and case-by-case institutional responses. Arbitrariness,
discretion, and emergency were also to be confined behind bars, together

with the uncontainable demands of migrants, their social relationships, and their bodies.

It is not uncommon for immigration-related nongovernmental organizations to refuse to take part in such processes of migration governance, including administrative detention. This may happen for several reasons. For one, many such organizations refuse to compromise their nongovernmental qualities. As Davide Però explains in detail, the "subordination, cooptation, and conformism" experienced by NGOs participating in governance activities "draws attention to the high price and degree of compromise that such organisations have to pay (in terms of independence and freedom of action) in exchange for the resources, prestige, benefits and so forth deriving from being part of the governance establishment" (2005:13). Some organizations share views deemed incompatible with policy-oriented exigencies in the first place. This is the case of the Comboniani, a Catholic missionary order that in Lecce, not too far from the Regina Pacis, informally hosted a number of migrants. On November 15, 2003, the order organized a protest across Italy and in front of the Italian Parliament in Rome, distributing mock legal residence permits "in the name of God" and protesting against the immigration law and the police's long processing time for residence permits.[30]

About sixty thousand persons were hosted in the Regina Pacis between 1997 and the end of 2004, when its contract with the Italian state was terminated. No reasons were officially and publicly offered to explain the unwillingness of the Regina Pacis Foundation to renew the agreement. But several bishops, missionary orders such as the Comboniani, national Caritas, other Catholic and lay NGOs, and activists had expressed serious concerns over the church of Lecce's involvement, through its most visible figures, in the management of migration for the state. One might speculate that the pressure on Don Cesare, and indirectly on the Diocese of Lecce, was becoming politically unbearable. Informants of mine have alleged that institutional support for the Regina Pacis at the national government level was becoming more tepid. Nevertheless, in his latest public statements Don Cesare has once again argued for the continued need to cooperate with legislators, just as he had done when speaking with me: "It is evident that when you find yourself operating within a[n immigration] law that puts many limits on your activity, that tells you 'if you want to work in the reception of migrants, then you must respect certain rules,' then you must choose: either you act as a revolutionary kicking the law, or you act as a

revolutionary remaining close to the [migrant] human being, even accepting the pressure of the law."[31]

At the same time, Don Cesare has also publicly expressed his exhaustion
at working as a bureaucrat of exclusion, at the local church becoming a
servant of the state, and at "charity" being increasingly exploited by "politics." At a national conference on migration organized in Lecce by the
Italian Christian Worker Movement, Archbishop Ruppi—in his role as
leader with Don Cesare of the Regina Pacis Foundation—eventually con-
veys the point that political pressure, migrants' reception, and their detention are incompatible: "reception and legality are two sides of the same
problem, and are both necessary. Reception is a human, civic, and Christian
duty. Reception is such when it is free of physical and political bars. Chris-
tians are such when they welcome the other, when they remember that the
first immigrant is Christ."[32]

Finally, and perhaps more importantly, since 2001 Don Cesare has faced
prosecution for several instances of alleged abuses and embezzlement
related to his role in the Regina Pacis center and foundation. In 2005 he
was convicted along with local doctors, members of the staff, and carabinieri officers. As upheld in February 2010 by the Court of Appeals in Lecce,
the ruling found that in his capacity as director of the Regina Pacis center
he quietly assisted the brutal violence inflicted on a group of migrants of
North African origin, on the night of November 22, 2002, during the
month of Ramadan. Soon to be repatriated, the group had attempted an
escape from the Regina Pacis. Once apprehended, they were brought back
to the center and brutally beaten. At least one among the men, a young
Moroccan citizen, was not only kicked and punched but also treated as an
object of scorn for his Muslim religion. He dared to escape, causing unnecessary trouble to fatigued soldiers and personnel. A carabiniere used his
baton to force down his throat a piece of pork, retrieved from the kitchen.

For years, and even during judicial proceedings in 2005, Don Cesare
and the archbishop of Lecce received public expressions of support and
solidarity from ministers and politicians across the political spectrum,
major Catholic mass media, and mainstream media in Apulia. Most of the
people who had approvingly visited the center at its heyday stood behind
its founders and leaders. Those high-profile visits, actively publicized by the
local and national media and by the Regina Pacis Foundation itself, certainly contributed to the celebration of the center. Politicians, in turn,
through these visits promoted themselves as humane and responsible

leaders. Participating in the secular procession entering the Regina Pacis, conspicuously kissing the archbishop's pastoral ring, and shaking Don Cesare's hand provided moral and religious legitimation, possibly conducive to electoral success. More significantly, though, those visits have also circulated as icons showcasing the Italian state's institutionalization and exploitation of charity and solidarity as it manages national and EU borders. That secular procession has sanctified the state itself, by foregrounding its "charitable" detention practices.

The understanding of the Regina Pacis that was publicly showcased was that of humanitarian assistance, rather than of classical surveillance and policing. In his conversations with me, as well as in his media interventions, Don Cesare routinely underlined the charitable nature of the diocese's and foundation's investment in the Regina Pacis. He emphasized that "migrants' reception entails openness, charity and sacrifice," and that "it is not us who wanted gates and bars outside the center, but the Law."[33] Indeed, the well-publicized presence of the Regina Pacis helped to promote the idea that residents of Salento, the southern portion of Apulia, deserved the Nobel Peace Prize for a decade of maritime migrants' reception. *La Gazzetta del Mezzogiorno*, one of the most respected regional newspapers in southern Italy, first launched the idea in 1999. This was discussed in official venues of the European Parliament and in the Italian Senate, as the arrival of migrants to coastal Italy was increasingly under the spotlight. Although ultimately unsuccessful, the proposition stands as an indication of the dominant humanitarian understanding of the state effort to preserve public order in light of maritime migration. Lampedusa's residents and administrators[34] have been nominated for the 2014 Nobel Peace Prize.

Salvation Behind Bars

Don Cesare says the Catholic Church in Italy has built a net of solidarity and reception working as "*l'infermiera dello Stato*" (the state's nurse).[35] He deplores the absence of any serious state policy of migrants' "inclusion" and is critical of the institution of migration facilities such as the Regina Pacis itself, as they respond only to logics of control and public order. In this framework, he says, charity is exploited and its operators—such as himself—become bureaucrats of exclusion. Indeed, charitable institutions, often under church control, have historically been called to govern the "accidents, infirmities, and various anomalies" (Foucault 2003 [1997]:244) the modern state encounters. And in a world conceived as carved into nation-states, migration interrogates the naturalized overlap among state, territory, and sedentary citizenship, thus being the anomaly par excellence and routinely engendering emergency responses. Without the logistical and moral contribution of nongovernmental actors, which include dioceses, the Misericordia confraternity, parishes, the Red Cross, and a myriad of other organizations, "the state" would be unable to manage both its southeastern border region and the many arrivals related to the Mare Nostrum operation. These organizations, then, have been in effect working *for* and *as* the state by assisting, processing, feeding, sheltering, and detaining people on its behalf. In doing so, they have been working to cure, support, and nourish the state itself. The prolongation of migrants' lives through food and shelter might very well be due "to charity and not to right," to use Arendt's insightful words (1958 [1951]:296). But that charitable and humanitarian enterprise also serves policing ends.

While Immigration Law 40/1998 capped the maximum length of stay in CPTs to a maximum of 30 days, the more restrictive "Bossi-Fini" Immigration Law of 2002 (189/2002) reinforced the policing function of centers and brought confinement to a maximum of 60 days. Legal dispositions on security (Law 125/2008) formally renamed the old CPTs as "*centri di identificazione ed espulsione*" (centers for the identification and expulsion of migrants, or CIEs). Law 94/2009 brought confinement in CIEs to a maximum of 180 days, and Law 129/2011 to eighteen months, in select cases. CIEs detain several "categories" of people, who in theory should all be awaiting repatriation or the notification of an expulsion decree. Among these people, there might be migrants whose asylum claim has been denied, but who decide to appeal the adjudication; migrants who have been caught with expired residence permits or forged documents; migrants who have just been released from prison; people who are presumed not likely to leave Italy following an expulsion decree; and migrants, including those with proper residence permits or visas, who are considered threatening for public order.

In addition to ten CIEs (some temporarily closed or under renovation) as of 2014 there were five centers of short-term "*accoglienza*" (reception) formally intended for immediate assistance as authorities decide how to proceed with migrants, nine centers dedicated to the "assistance of asylum seekers," and four centers of "first aid and assistance" in areas of maritime arrivals in Apulia, Sicily, and Sardinia (see Chapters 4 and 5).[36] While there are important differences among these types of facilities, it should be noted that the same center can have more than one administrative function; and that the "categories" of people held vary also according to discretionary police dispositions, often related to factors such as geographical proximity to a police station, port, and airport or the urgent need for accommodations.

With few exceptions, regional and national newsmakers refer to such complicated and changing catalogue of facilities with the humanitarian euphemism of *centri di accoglienza* (centers of reception). Whether facilities are open or closed, migrants within these centers and in much public discourse are always defined as ospiti, never *trattenuti* (detainees). In Otranto, a small town of fifty-two hundred inhabitants, I often asked for directions to the local "center for the identification of migrants," as it used to be defined. People looked at me startled. Only after I rephrased my question, asking instead about the "center *for* immigrants," people could finally understand what I was referring too: "*Ah, il centro di accoglienza!*" ("You mean the reception center, then!"). Even the local police, in official documents I have seen, indicate such centers as centri di accoglienza. In the generic understanding of most local residents these are simply "centers *for* immigrants," then. There is little effort to use any more precise legal terminology. Such invariable insistence on hospitable "assistance" and "reception" is not emblematic of careless ignorance, but of a cultural knowledge of the moral aesthetics of confinement. In these aesthetics, centers are *for* immigrants for two reasons: they are where immigrants ought to be assisted, but also where they belong.

Cement courtyards, aluminum fences, automated gates, concrete walls, and omnipresent video surveillance are central to the aesthetic of migrant confinement. But holding facilities are to be examined also in their nexus—mnemonic and experiential, visual and mediatized—with the cold nights on the beach, the unruly scenes of the Bari stadium, the pots of food, the blankets, the clean clothes, the ostensible disorganization prior to the facilities' institutionalization.[37] Holding facilities expropriate the moral authority of the scattered instances of popular solidarity they confine and displace.

Such "humanitarian" function and legitimation is compatible with the moral economy of strictures and opportunities of voluntarism and of (Italian) neoliberalism.[38] It is also locatable within larger strategies of humanitarian immigration management and the global commodification of

salvation.[39] But as migrants receive food and shelter, they are also subjected
to additional layers of stigma. Reduced to objects of charity and humanitarian assistance, people in holding centers become incapable of reciprocating.
And as newly arrived foreigners, they are seen by some as not having earned
the right to receive food and shelter—especially at times of financial crisis,
cuts in public spending, and painful unemployment. Indeed if these centers
provide accoglienza, then they must have been established for the migrants'
own good. If guests escape, or rebel against their benefactors, they are just
ungrateful, and perhaps ought to be punished. Episodes of compassion
toward migrants "appear as privileged moments of collective redemption
eluding the common law of their repression" (Fassin 2005:375). As Ivan
Illich (1987:16) would put it, migrants' condition of physical detention and
social isolation, their "human miseries and burdens," are made irrelevant
to larger social and political experiences and priorities.

Images of civilians herded and locked in stadiums, like the ones in
Bari, perhaps bring to mind past experiences of totalitarianism, if not
massacres—like the aftermath of the September 11, 1973, coup d'état in
Chile. Holding centers might appear as more compatible with democratic
and humanitarian ideals, and are proliferating globally. In the case of the
Regina Pacis we have a criminal conviction that allows all of us—not just
me, the staff, and the migrants—to know the details: names, faces, lacera-
tions, fractures, the cut of meat used in the attempt to degrade a person
and his religion. The possibility for such "incidents" to happen needs to be
multiplied for each such facility, and for each migrant ever held in one.
Holding facilities exist primarily as institutionalized state structures in
order to identify, fingerprint, contain, deter, and selectively deport people.[40]
They not only displace practices of solidarity and hospitality but also seek
to encircle the gray legal area of bureaucracy and policing, as agents seek to
discern identities and ascertain deportability (see Chapters 4 and 5). In the
bureaucratic and material passage from the "sweet ship" to the docks, from
docks to stadium, from stadium to deporting plane, or from port to holding
facility, people and bodies are subjected to various kinds of thresholds.
They go through what one might phrase as "the experience of being-*within*
an *outside*" (Agamben 2009 [1993]:68; original emphasis). They are de facto
excluded from basic rights and democratic practice through spatial, administrative, and humanitarian inclusion behind bars.

But every detention center's wall has a street side to it. These walls are
increasingly covered in activists' murals, sprayed calls for action, political

manifestos, and the aesthetic of political antagonism—words of solidarity
with detained migrants, puns and provocations. In the early history of CPTs
and CIEs, such as in the Regina Pacis case, it was anarchist, communist,
and peace symbols that were sprayed outside the centers. Critical voices
were discounted from mainstream public discourse and attributed to the
alleged utopianism of leftist, anarchist, and Catholic groups, including the
Comboniani order mentioned above. For a long time, facing the contradictions emerging in such facilities has been procrastinated through further
forms of surveillance, confinement, and individualization—removing all
unnecessary furniture, putting bars on windows, creating a "Chinese box"
succession of locks and gates, isolating known troublemakers, using non-
flammable mattresses, bolting beds and cabinets to the floor, forbidding
the use of phones with cameras, restricting access by relatives and denying
any independent oversight, accepting abnormally low tenders (as organizations and multinational corporations bid on the administration of centers
on behalf of the state), confiscating anything sharp as it could be used for
self-mutilation or for aggression, liberally administering anxiolytics. But
"troublemakers" are made and remade in detention. And Prozac does not
solve anything, especially when "hospitality" follows the lowest bid to
secure a state contract, and is extended mechanistically and stingily. Prozac
does not create desire, when such hospitality is unwanted.

While the 1998 Immigration Law mandating CIEs is still in place,
important pieces of the detention apparatus are literally crumbling. Some
facilities are de facto closed or unusable; others are being renovated, following riots. A new one is (unofficially) in the making. Mayors and city councils in some of the cities where CIEs are located—including Bologna, Bari,
Milano, Turin, and Lamezia Terme—have adopted motions pressing the
Ministry of the Interior, which is responsible for CIEs, to reconvert them
into facilities for refugees. These initiatives have the most diverse motiva-
tions, from zoning and urban planning to concerns about public order and
human rights. The regional government of Apulia has joined a class action[41]
against the Ministry of the Interior for the degrading conditions of the
center in Bari. In discussing the case, Judge Francesco Caso of Bari's Civil
Tribunal has spoken of the CIE's conditions as "bordering on illegality,"
and asserted that migrants' conditions would have been "better" safeguarded and guaranteed, "at least on a formal level," had their cases been
under the responsibility of the criminal prison system.[42] In December 2012,
Judge Edoardo D'Ambrosio acquitted three migrants who had severely

damaged Crotone's CIE—the cheapest facility for the Ministry of the Interior to reimburse, given the extraordinarily low bid. According to the ruling, those migrants acted in "self-defense," they were "illegitimately" detained, and they "did not have any other instrument to defend their rights."[43]

Select healthcare NGOs have secured permission to enter CIEs, and have produced public reports. Medici per i Diritti Umani (MEDU, or Doctors for Human Rights), in addition to a focus on extreme forms of psychosocial vulnerability and on the degrading physical and sanitary conditions of most facilities, has made a point of insisting on the "inefficacy" of CIEs in the execution of their intended function. In 2013, some six thousand people were detained in CIEs, including, in decreasing order of presences, citizens of Tunisia, Morocco, Albania, Nigeria, Egypt, Romania, and Algeria. Of these, only half were actually repatriated, amounting to a negligible percentage of the undocumented migrants on Italian territory.[44] Riots, revolts, and vandalism have dramatically reduced the overall total capacity of CIEs. While some among the 2014 Mare Nostrum arrivals have been brought to CIEs, with the presumption they will be deported, the vast majority of arrivals had to be entrusted to a more dispersed network of churches' and cities' structures—gyms, schools, nongovernmental shelters, and parishes. The Italian Parliament is currently discussing an amendment—signed by Senators Luigi Manconi and Sergio Lo Giudice—expected to reinstate a ninety-day cap for detention (now at eighteen months). The "CIE system" might be on the verge of an "implosion," as MEDU puts it (2013): the perception of the costly, degrading, and ineffective qualities of detention and removal centers is growing.

While there is an emerging global critique of detention and removal facilities (in the United States, United Kingdom, Italy, Spain, Greece, and Israel, among other countries), it is also important to appreciate that a variety of social actors have different motives, and that salient critiques and effective strategies emerge when grounded in specific, locally existing legal, political, humanitarian, and migrant-initiated mechanisms, tensions, and contradictions. What is being pondered by Italian judges, journalists, lawyers, legislators, mayors, doctors, and others is whether detention and removal facilities are ambiguous thresholds—humanitarian-policing facilities with the potentiality to be reformed—or cages to be overturned. Migrants in detention, and activists outside, have long since come to their conclusions. A consensus might emerge, resulting in the legislative dismantlement of CIEs. Or as with other crucial junctures (such as the 1998 Immigration Law), "missed opportunities" might actively be pursued, and the status quo reinforced. Should CIEs actually be dismantled, where would their policing function be shifted—in the gray area of mixed-purpose holding facilities, on commercial ferries, perhaps beyond the external borders of the EU? Will the EU's ambitiously preemptive approach ever make detention and removal facilities on EU territory altogether unnecessary?

Half of the migrants in CIEs will be repatriated, escorted by the police on deportation ferries and flights. Many more will travel in the opposite direction, transiting through Greece, Albania, Turkey, Egypt, Libya, and Tunisia. These maritime travelers both hope for and dread the encounter with their Italian rescuers.

Chapter 2

Genealogies of Rescue and Pushbacks

Phantom Shipwrecks

It is not always the intended destination that shapes the journey of maritime migrants. It might be the contingencies of the journey that result in a certain point of arrival.[1] The experience of maritime migrants is often characterized by waiting.[2] Tunisian scholar Fawzi Mellah effectively renders their condition as he writes that they live "in a temporality of little immediate futures" (2001:42). Hidden and sometimes locked in countryside farms, people wait for the smugglers' decision to take them to the coast; for a boat; for more migrants to fill it beyond capacity; for good weather; for relatives to wire money and purchase their passage; for holidays when there might be fewer patrols; for patrols to rescue them. They also face the possibility of death at sea.

In these pages I examine two specific shipwrecks, of the *Yiohan* and the *Kater i Radës,* which occurred within just over a three-month period in 1996 and 1997. These events speak of the structural dynamics of sovereignty, mobility, and smuggling. They trace stories, networks of correlations, institutional silences, routes, and crimes that are current. Unlike with many other shipwrecks, the circumstances in these cases are known, and a judicial ruling has been made. Activists, survivors, and relatives have long fought in court. The *Yiohan* shipwreck—for years silenced in Mediterranean depths—stands as one of the most serious documented maritime disasters since World War II. The *Kater i Radës* shipwreck is locatable in relation to Italian pioneering blockades and pushback operations at sea. Italian-Albanian bilateral agreements foreshadow Italian-Libyan and Italian-Tunisian agreements. Efforts against maritime migration are pursued not only on the coast and at sea but also well beyond European territory. In particular, Muammar Gaddafi's Libya is recruited, through commercial and political treaties, as a partner in the effort to first "push back" and then "readmit" non-Libyan, sub-Saharan migrants at sea, to detain them, and to repatriate them through the Sahara. These policies of "externalization" crucially inform the new, post-Gaddafi Libya's relationships with the EU and in particular with neighbors Italy and Malta (see Chapter 5). Here I trace their genealogies, preceding Colonel Gaddafi's 2011 demise. At present, the EU is actively involved in strengthening unstable Libya's ability to control its borders and to manage foreign citizens on its territory, prompting questions about the geopolitical reach of European borders and the implications for democracy and human rights.

The Christmas Tragedy

The night of December 26, 1996, smugglers in the central Mediterranean expected less surveillance and fewer fishing boats, due to the Christmas festivities. The disaster happened at 3 A.M. A total of 283 would-be migrants, including Sikh Indians, Tamils from Sri Lanka, and Pakistani citizens died in international waters south of Sicily's southernmost promontory, Capo Passero. In Rome, passenger Syed Habib had been patiently waiting for the issue of his Italian residence permit, but he wanted to visit his sick mother, so he traveled back to Pakistan.[3] Without a permit, he could not return to Italy in an authorized manner, and had to use the services of smugglers. Even in small villages, it is easy to find somebody who knows about traveling to Europe. Brothers Anpalagan and Arulalagan Ganeshu, respectively seventeen and eighteen years old, intended to settle in London and study there.[4] They never reached their destinations. On the "mother ship," the *Yiohan*, they all met many would-be migrants from Pakistan, some of whom had left Karachi two months earlier.

Survivor and witness Shahab had paid $7,000, and owed another $7,000 upon arrival in Italy.[5] In Latakia, Syria, he had boarded the *Alex I*, and then somewhere in the Mediterranean the *Ena*, the *Friendship*, and finally the *Yiohan*. Shakoor Ahmad, another survivor, flew from Karachi to Dubai, Oman, and Cairo, and from there traveled by truck to the port of Alexandria, Egypt.[6] There he was told he'd work as a sailor to pay his passage to Italy. His contact, a woman, got all the necessary paperwork by corrupting local customs officers. He boarded the *Friendship*, a vessel with a Greek captain, a Russian crew, and Panama flag and registration. Additional groups were brought on the vessel by boats from Istanbul, Adana, and Antakya in Turkey and from India. After twelve days docked in Alexandria, waiting to take in as many passengers as possible, the *Friendship* eventually left port and transferred them to a Greek-staffed fishing boat, the *Sealine*. Later, there was another transfer to the *Yiohan*, which ended up carrying 464 people. The ship had a Honduran flag, Greek officers, Arab and Cretan sailors, Polish staff, and a Lebanese captain. Despite the scarcity of food, the "Arab cook," says Shakoor, was "the only humane crew member."[7]

Around 1:30 A.M. on December 26, 1996, waiting is over for most of the 464 people at high seas on the *Yiohan*: they are to be transferred to a much smaller wooden vessel, code-named *F-174*. Once a launch of the British Royal Navy, it has been recycled as a small fishing boat. It sails from Marsaxlokk, a fishing village in the southeastern part of Malta. The *F-174*, whose hold is occupied by freezers and boxes, has often brought food, alcoholic drinks, and water to the *Yiohan*. This time it has to take people in. More than 300 *Yiohan* passengers get on the *F-174*—at gunpoint, as some hesitate, realizing the hazards of so many people boarding a boat intended for eighty. Occupants standing on the deck obstruct the only possible exit for people in the hold. The captains of the small *F-174* and the larger *Yiohan*, respectively Zervoudakis Eftychios from Greece and Youssef El Hallal from Lebanon, deem the relatively inconspicuous *F-174* apt for taking people to Sicily undetected. The weight is too great, and not well distributed. The sea is stormy, and water starts to seep into the hold, probably due to a collision with the larger ship during the transfer operations. People on deck can hear screams and prayers as passengers below deck frantically use buckets to bail out water. Eftychios changes the *F-174*'s course and again veers toward the *Yiohan*, soon jumping in the water and abandoning the ship. The *Yiohan* also heads back toward the *F-174*. The two vessels crash, damaging the prow of the smaller ship and sending it to the bottom of the sea. Twenty-nine people survive, grabbing the ropes thrown by other passengers still on the *Yiohan*. The *Yiohan*, without calling an SOS, veers east, and after four days reaches the Greek Peloponnesus. There it disembarks the retrieved survivors and the passengers who had not been transferred to the *F-174*, a total of about 150 people. They are kept in farmhouses near Argos and Nafplio, under armed guard, but are finally let go. About fifty people reach the local police station to tell authorities about the wreck of the *F-174*.

Local prosecutor Jannis Pravataris believes their stories, and eventually prosecutes and wins the conviction of 11 people. On January 26, 1997, shipwreck survivors are repatriated, with the exception of 22 Sri Lankan Tamils, who intend to apply for asylum.[8]

The night of December 26, Maltese authorities had warned the Italian coast guard about the disappearance of a fishing boat, and allegedly of the possible shipwreck. On December 31, 1996, the Piraeus Rescue Coordination Center of the Hellenic coast guard transmitted news of the shipwreck to its Italian counterpart, based on survivors' testimonies. The Italian coast guard search-and-rescue operations began, with no findings. On January 5, 1997, Admiral Renato Ferraro, commander of the Italian coast guard, publicly assessed as "extremely vague" the accounts from Greece, and claimed that a more extensive search-and-rescue operation would be "impossible."[9]

Balwinder Singh, among the survivors in Greek custody, is convinced the whole world is talking about the tragedy he and his companions have experienced.[10] It is only eight days after the shipwreck, on January 4, 1997, that the major Italian news agency, ANSA, circulates the news. ANSA's statement uses the conditional tense, and mentions the skepticism of Greek and Italian institutions because no trace of the shipwreck has been spotted. On January 11, 1997, journalist Livio Quagliata's revealing article in *Il Manifesto*, the Italian leftist newspaper, offers a comprehensive survivors' account of the shipwreck. But Italian and Greek authorities opt for suspecting that the migrants have concocted or at least exaggerated the tragedy to manipulate public opinion and to avoid expulsion from Greece. In the absence of any corpse, and without indications on the exact position of the wreck, in institutional documents this becomes a "presumed" shipwreck. Most media speak of a *naufragio fantasma* (phantom shipwreck). The same tentativeness and indeterminacy emerges with every shipwreck that happens far from European coasts, in 2014 as in 1996. There are presumed shipwrecks and presumed dozens of victims on the way to Europe. Presumed—until bodies wash ashore on Tripoli's beach.

Later in January 1997, members of the Italian Parliament led by Tana de Zulueta bring the issue to the attention of their colleagues and the government. Migrants' relatives in Asia, and the migrant leaders of labor, ethnic, and kinship networks in Italy, ask for a more direct involvement of the Italian, Greek, Egyptian, and Maltese governments and police authorities. Nevertheless, the demonstration that phantom shipwrecks do not exist, but real ones do, is left to locally situated global activists such as Dino

Frisullo; to the investigations of relatives and conationals of the victims;[11] to the initiative of a handful of journalists;[12] and eventually to the efforts of prosecutors in Reggio Calabria, Siracusa, and Catania. And yet a real conversation involving lawmakers, administrators, coastal residents, and the national media does not ensue. Public opinion does not pose any obstacle to the forthcoming enforcement of stringent maritime border control.

The Naval Blockade: Expecting the Good Friday Tragedy

At the darkest hour of Good Friday people in towns of southern Italy take to the narrow streets in procession. Believers hold back their tears as they quietly follow the statues of the black-dressed Mother of Sorrow and of the dead Christ. The occasional lament of the trumpet pierces the night—everyone is to wake up in sorrow. At the end of the procession the priest blesses the crowd and the sea—a source of hope, wealth, and mourning for fishermen and their families. On the night of March 28, 1997, the thirty-four Albanian survivors of the "Tragedy of Good Friday" (as it is called in Italy) were taken by authorities to the Apulian port of Brindisi, on the Adriatic. They disembarked at 2:45 A.M. They were hastily put on a bus and taken away to a police station to be identified and interrogated. In Albania those survivors had left behind violent riots and widespread unrest.

In the early spring of 1997 the revolt against the state apparatus and its president, Sali Berisha (1992–97), is largely due to the collapse of pyramid financial schemes, the consequent widespread loss of savings, and the popular suspicion of politicians' corruption and even involvement in the schemes. Clashes involve petty criminals, gangs, organized crime, opposing party supporters, and security forces. Hundreds of thousands of rifles and guns are stolen from government depots. Soldiers are left with no access to weapons. On March 13 ports and airports are shut down. A state of emergency and curfew are of no use. Twenty-one people are killed on March 27 alone in the southern city of Vlorë. Italian citizens and other Westerners are evacuated by helicopters sent by their countries of origin. In a situation that many Albanian and international commentators define without hesitation as "civil war," attempts to leave the country at any cost intensify.

The Italian media, in the meantime, offer resonance to segments of the political spectrum voicing their frustration toward the navy, for its perceived inability to prevent Albanians' journey across the Strait of Otranto and arrival on the Apulian coast. Navy officers themselves are frustrated, as their job is tiresome and unrewarding. There is also a rivalry with the Italian finance guard, whose boats, helicopters, and planes have a longer and more established tradition in fulfilling policing functions. At this time there is an emerging consensus on the need to prevent arrivals from Albania. Newspapers and other media neutrally or approvingly report that the goal of the new institutional "hard line" is to "stop the Albanians," who are routinely described as "clandestine immigrants."[13] Phrases such as "invasion," "exodus," and "criminal invasion" are commonplace.[14]

On March 18, 1997, prominent Italian journalist Gad Lerner is in Otranto, on the Apulian coast, to provide live coverage of these events. His news and talk show, *Pinocchio*, airs on RAI1, Italy's most watched public television channel. About 130 unauthorized boats have already landed carrying "desperate people" from Albania. Some of the local entrepreneurs complain about the negative impact of Albanian arrivals on tourism, as summer is approaching and potential tourists are alarmed. Toward the end of the show, and over the following days, the headquarters of RAI1, of major newspapers, and even of left-oriented radio programs receive thousands of phone calls. At the national level there are vocal actors arguing for the need to "intercept" Albanian boats, and callers are angry with Lerner for his perceived partiality throughout the show, for siding with the Albanians and targeting the Italian navy.[15] On television, Lerner speaks to two high-ranking officers, Admiral Alfeo Battelli and General Rolando Mosca Moschini. Battelli is the regional head of the Italian navy, and Mosca Moschini is the national head of the finance guard. Lerner, premising that "any such decision would be a prerogative of the government," asks whether "in theory" the armed forces can do anything other than escorting to the port incoming Albanian vessels. What about "pushing them back"? His tone suggests a rhetorical provocation. General Mosca Moschini confirms that any option other than escorting these boats to Italian ports would be risky and difficult. There is the "risk of sinking them," restates Lerner, and this is confirmed by the general: "yes, there is no doubt about that."[16] A few days later, on March 27, 1997, self-professed devout Catholic member of Parliament Irene Pivetti—elected from the right-wing Northern League Party[17] and former president of the Italian Chamber of Deputies (1994–96)—suggests that the way to face the Albanians' "invasion" is to throw them back into the sea.[18]

On March 28, 1997, five Italian warships patrol the seventy kilometers (forty-five miles) of the Strait of Otranto. They are coordinated by the

Ionian and Strait of Otranto navy headquarters in Taranto under the leadership of Admiral Battelli and by the general navy headquarters in Rome. These warships, earlier patrolling the Adriatic during the Yugoslav conflicts, and routinely protecting Italian fishing boats in the Mediterranean, are now asked by the Rome headquarters' directives to do something entirely different: deter migrant arrivals and escort vessels back to Albanian ports. They are taking part in Operation White Flags, implementing a de facto naval blockade. For minister of foreign affairs Lamberto Dini, an eminent member of the center-left government led by Romano Prodi (1996–98), has written a letter to his Albanian counterpart on March 25, offering the Italian government's "assistance for the control and containment at sea of Albanian clandestine expatriations" by stopping Albanian vessels in Albanian and international waters, and "redirecting their course to Albanian ports."[19] It is an offer you can't refuse. Later that day, the Albanian government—unable to control not only the coast but also the country's southern territories—accepts it. By doing so, it secures Italian financial, police, and humanitarian assistance.[20] This exchange of letters serves thus as a bilateral agreement. It also stipulates that, starting on April 3, all Albanians managing to cross into Italy are to be summarily repatriated. The UN, especially in the figure of the high commissioner for refugees, severely criticizes the blockade as "illegal," as it is the result of a mere intergovernmental agreement.[21]

That Friday, March 28, about 120 people embark on a tiny guard ship in Vlorë, southern Albania, under the armed scrutiny of the local gang leaders who have arranged the trip. They leave around 3 P.M. crammed in the old Soviet-made *Kater i Radës*, a twenty-one-meter vessel built for a crew of ten. Around 4:30 P.M., in Albanian waters close to the island of Sazan facing the bay of Vlorë, the Italian navy frigate *Zeffiro* tries to dissuade the *Kater i Radës*. Its helicopter is hovering over the vessel; through loudspeakers, it directs the ship to turn back. Women on board hug and conspicuously hold up their children, only to provoke the *Zeffiro* captain's suspicion that behind the coats and bundles there are dangerous snipers in hiding. The *Zeffiro*, with a length of one hundred meters, tries various maneuvers in the proximity of the much smaller Albanian boat. Huge waves make safe navigation difficult, but Namik Xhaferi, at the helm of the *Kater i Radës*, does not change course. A second warship, the ninety-meter and 1,285-ton *Sibilla*, replaces the *Zeffiro* in the pursuit of the target. Its megaphones threaten immediate arrest upon arrival in Italy. It's almost 7

P.M., and it's dark, windy, and chilly. The people on the 56-ton *Kater i Radës*, under the powerful spotlight of the *Sibilla*, display a white flag, and again their children. Lights are off now. The navy warship is much faster; for a few moments it becomes invisible as it towers over the *Kater i Radës*. There is a collision, and the *Kater i Radës* capsizes in fifteen minutes. For the survivors, the distance they have to swim to reach the *Sibilla* seems prohibitive. They are brought to the port of Brindisi, and then hastily to a police station. It is the night of Good Friday.

The following days no member of the Italian government visits the survivors in Brindisi. Prime minister Prodi eventually travels to Vlorë on April 13, where he offers his condolences to a crowd of ten thousand people. He outlines the humanitarian and peacekeeping role of the forthcoming UN, Italian-led multinational security force of six thousand soon to be dispatched to the country through Operation Alba (Operation Dawn). He also promises the wreckage will be recovered. On the other hand, on Easter Sunday then opposition leader Silvio Berlusconi flies from his resort in Sardinia to Brindisi, to meet with survivors. He weeps on television. He hints at the government's moral responsibilities for its uncompromising effort to implement stringent border policies. He offers the survivors hospitality in one of his many residences, receiving in return the request that the wreckage and the bodies be recovered.

In that vessel, survivor Krenar Xhavara lost his wife, a six-month-old daughter, his brother, sister-in-law, and six nephews.[22] Krenar is also a witness, then, and the main narrator of the Italian-Albanian documentary *Jetoj* (Alive; Eshja and Soranzo 2004). Elvis, eleven years old, is the only child who survived. Hasim lost his brother and sister-in-law. Both residents of Italy, they had gone back to Fier, in southwest Albania, because of a death in the family. In the meantime, ports and airports had been shut down because of the riots. Afraid they would lose their Italian jobs and consequently their residence permits, Hasim's brother and sister bought their irregular passage on the *Kater i Radës*.[23] Ismete Demiri is one of only two female survivors. She intended to reach her husband in Brescia, northern Italy. She helped identify the man at the helm of the *Kater i Radës*.[24] The body of her twelve-year-old daughter was never found. Fifty-seven bodies were recovered. Relatives and Albanian authorities confirm the number of victims at eighty-one, including thirty-one under the age of sixteen. The bodies of twenty-four people were never found: *dispersi*, lost at sea.

Seven months after the collision, the wreck of the *Kater i Radës* was brought to the surface, by order of the Italian court. The ship was located thirty-five miles off the Italian coast, no more than ten or fifteen miles from Albania, in Albanian territorial waters. The boat, it became evident, displayed white flags. The people trapped in the wreckage intended to reach Italy without the preliminary authorization of the Italian government and police. Most carried some form of identification. On November 18, 1997, yet another Italian-Albanian bilateral agreement made possible the speedy repatriation of Albanian nationals who survived the maritime journey across the strait.

The first trial for the sinking of the *Kater i Radës* lasted from 1999 to 2005. Survivors and relatives could attend only some of the proceedings, as they faced Italian visa and economic difficulties. Leonardo Leone De Castris, the young and motivated prosecutor serving in Brindisi's court, lamented the lack of cooperation from navy headquarters, and in particular missing pieces of possible evidence, including radio communications and video footage and photographs that might have warranted the prosecution of navy admirals Alfeo Battelli and Umberto Guarino, in charge respectively of the Taranto and Rome headquarters. Nevertheless, De Castris did manage to obtain a conviction not only for Namik Xhaferi (four years in prison), at the helm of the *Kater i Radës*, but also for Fabrizio Laudadio (three years), the *Sibilla*'s captain. They were both held responsible for shipwreck and multiple manslaughter.

But in 2010 chief prosecutor Giuseppe Vignola of the Court of Appeals in Lecce argues in court that responsibility for the shipwreck should fall entirely on Xhaferi. Testimonies by Albanian survivors should be ignored as partial, possibly concocted, and self-interested, he suggests, while there is no reason to doubt the word of Italian officers when they maintain they have not implemented any form of harassment other than verbal dissuasion. Vignola maintains that navy vessels in the Strait of Otranto were always careful as they were intent on avoiding such "hemorrhage of *clandestini* who invaded Italy first and then the rest of Europe" (in Leogrande 2011:192–94). Despite Vignola's passionate efforts, in June 2011 the court upholds both convictions and stipulates reparations for survivors and family members.

The navy's argument that Xhaferi's suicidal maneuver and sudden change of direction were responsible is rejected. Both captains are convicted for individual mistakes. But their faults are technical. There is no involvement of the institutional actors envisioning the blockade and constituting the larger chain of command, including Italian and Albanian government ministers and Italian navy officers in Rome and Taranto. The prosecution is unable to demonstrate beyond reasonable doubt that navy headquarters gave the *Sibilla* specific orders on how precisely to "harass" and redirect the *Kater i Radës*. Speculations that the *Sibilla* was ordered to get as close to the other vessel "as to almost touch it" cannot be proved. Speculations that its crew was ordered or at any rate was trying to jam the *Kater i Radës*'s propeller with cables cannot be proved.

The question, never asked of the politicians who envisioned the blockade, remains: how do you force an unseaworthy and overcrowded civilian vessel to stop and change its course? This question applies in 2014 as it did in 1997, with Libyan, Tunisian, Turkish, and Egyptian patrols that are tasked precisely with this mission. This is not only a question about the ethical, legal, and political aspects of such political directives but also a fundamental question on their technical feasibility. In Otranto, professional fishermen told me that in their opinion the government's "naval blockade" was unrealistic, conceived by people who have never sailed and ignorant of basic rules of navigation. Indeed, the Italian navy and government have never acknowledged publicly that Operation White Flags was a blockade, the word used by most media. For "naval blockade" is a phrase and practice legally reserved for a state of war, and this was not a declared war.[25] I shall call this a crime of peace, then.

The War (Against Clandestine Immigration)

Friedrich Ratzel defines national boundaries as "the skin of the living state." Like the epidermis of animals and plants, boundaries "provide . . . defense and allow . . . exchange to occur" (qtd. in Prescott 1978:14). Ratzel was writing in 1897. He originated the concept of *Lebensraum* (living space) later appropriated by the Nazi regime.[26] Ratzel's metaphorical language may seem old-fashioned, especially as it deploys naturalistic metaphors to describe sociopolitical processes.[27] But early in the twenty-first century, European institutional discourses, practices, and technologies of border control do not fundamentally contradict the substance of his understanding. Among states, including those in the EU, there is widespread and institutionalized consensus to lift border controls for the flow of capital, nondestabilizing information, services, and (wealthy) people in demand.

But when it comes to poorer migrants and refugees, whether in North America or the EU, "the national state claims all its old splendor in asserting its sovereign right to control its borders" (Sassen 1996:59), managing the inflow of necessary labor.

Ratzel's description is productive and reflective of a naturalized interdependence between people, territory, and state. International migration does indeed have the potential "to challenge established spatial images," and to "highlight . . . the social nature of space as something created and reproduced through collective human agency" (Rouse 1991:9). And yet discourses on international migration also revitalize the spatial imaginaries that migration confounds in practice. As we see not only in the Mediterranean but also in desert settings, "flood," "flow," and even "hemorrhage" are often used to refer to human mobility that demands an immediate solution (Chavez 2001:74). Ratzel's metaphorical language has maintained its institutional and vernacular currency. Borders are made into consequential icons of surveillance, sovereignty, control, low-intensity conflict, and warfare.[28] In the coastal theater of operations in Italy, and even farther away beyond territorial waters, armed forces have been important players.

The Italian army has been often deployed with powers of police in Italian cities. It routinely guards Sicilian anti-Mafia tribunals. It has recently patrolled areas of Naples and Milan considered at risk of international terrorism or so-called immigrant riots. In southern Italy, in particular, it has traditionally been used in efforts to fight the conspicuous terrorism of the Mafia. But in 1995 the army was also deployed to control the maritime border. Between May and November of that year, Law Decree No. 152 authorized the Salento Mission of the Italian army. About 1,700 patrols were conspicuously dispatched to coastal Salento, the southern part of the Apulian peninsula, in order to "control the maritime frontier," fight organized crime especially involved in transnational tobacco smuggling, and thus "obtain a more pervasive control of public order and guarantee citizens' security." The army conducted, according to its own accounts, 767 vehicle searches, 2,604 procedures of identification, 10 arrests of "suspicious persons," and 3,029 arrests of *clandestini* (undocumented migrants). As the developer of the army website puts it, for soldiers participating in the Salento Mission "the threat to be faced is different: not strictly internal anymore, but rather coming from abroad."[29]

Since the early 1990s, the Italian finance guard military force has emerged as the predominant agency in Italy in preventing undocumented migration, mainly because of its traditionally large fleet, which includes naval vessels, airplanes, and helicopters.[30] Between 1989 and 2000, its budget almost tripled. Many of its boats and aircraft were equipped with military-style technologies such as thermal cameras and forward-looking infrared systems of night vision and surveillance.

The 1997 bilateral agreement between Italy and Albania allowed for Italian navy and finance guard vessels to be dispatched to Albania itself. Vessels were sent to patrol the northern, central, and southern coastal areas of Shëngjin, Vlorë, and Durrës and to the small island of Sazan facing Vlorë. As it is often the case, the agreement—signed at a time of social and political unrest and of massive emigration—outlasted the 1997 emergency. For almost twelve years (April 15, 1997, to February 25, 2009) the Twenty-eighth Navy Group operated in Albanian internal and territorial waters to prevent unauthorized emigration. It helped train Albanian officers, updated the local infrastructure of safety and surveillance, and restored the old port of Sazan (occupied by the Kingdom of Italy between 1920 and 1943) by installing a radar station that can ostensibly "ensure the discovery of fast targets that, involved in the trafficking of clandestine migrants, sail toward Italian coasts."[31] The finance guard also participated in the Italian effort of Albanian state building, including via the provision of technical equipment and military and intelligence expertise. Some thirty officers contributed to training their Albanian counterparts in the border patrol. Also, three military vessels supported Albanian police forces in curbing smuggling of people, weapons, and drugs. In August 2002 Albanian prime minister Fatos Nano ordered several boats, allegedly used for smuggling, to be publicly burned. More generally, authorized sailing of private motor boats became extremely difficult in Albania, and there was a specific moratorium (Law No. 10220) enforced between 2010 and 2013. As declared with exaggeration by the mission's chief, Colonel Cosimo Serra, the finance guard presence in Albania has "practically reduced to zero the trafficking of human beings between Albania and Apulia."[32]

In reality, to this day speedboats arriving from the southern Albanian coast and from the nearby Greek island of Corfu smuggle to Apulia tons of drugs, in particular heroin, cocaine, and marijuana, especially during the summer tourist season. And deterrence and militarization could not prevent the "Karaburun Tragedy," the Strait of Otranto's deadliest shipwreck after the *Kater i Radës*. Such an incident seems to substantiate what is routinely alleged by smugglers from Albania, Turkey, Libya, and Egypt: that

for smuggling mechanisms to work there are indispensable forms of connivance and corruption involving police and port authorities. The night of
January 9, 2004, several young people (mostly from Shkodër, in northern
Albania) departed from a village south of Vlorë toward Italy, at a cost of
1,500 euros each. A few hours later, a patrol boat of the Italian coast guard
retrieved twenty-one bodies not far from the island of Sazan and the Karaburun Peninsula, Albania's westernmost points just off Vlorë. People perished from hypothermia, following the stalling of their rubber speedboat's
engine and a fuel leak on board. Seven more people were missing. Eleven
were rescued, including the two boatmen, who were then arrested. The
head of Shkodër's antiterrorist police unit, father of one of the boatmen,
was also arrested, together with the vice-director of Vlorë's Port Authority,
uncle of the other boatman.[33]

Maritime emigration of Albanians to Italy through the strait has notably
subsided. The rising costs of smuggling operations in interceptions at sea,
arrests, confiscations, and repatriations helped to curb it. But it is primarily
the change in legal and economic relationships between Albania and Italy
that makes unauthorized maritime migration unnecessary for Albanian citizens. Factories and firms, including in the highly industrialized northeastern part of Italy, have notably decreased their demand for Albanian labor.
First, they are facing stagnation. Second, they can count on Romanian (EU)
workers who enjoy less restricted mobility.[34] Finally, Italian entrepreneurs
have outsourced some of their production, particularly to countries such as
Albania. There they pay each worker about 100 euros per month, one-tenth
of what the same worker would cost if working for the same firm in Italy.[35]
Most importantly, legal, authorized travel channels have been established.
On November 8, 2010, the EU[36] granted Albanian citizens possessing a
biometric passport the ability to travel to Schengen countries without a visa
(for sojourns shorter than three months).[37] To the citizens of Albania, as
well as of Bosnia and Herzegovina, Macedonia, Serbia, and Montenegro,
this was presented as a positive outcome of their countries' success in curbing organized crime, corruption, and illegal immigration, and more generally of improved security of documents and border control.[38]

But in the second half of the 1990s Albanians were only one of the
many groups trying to land in Apulia. Most notably, Kurdish citizens (often
politically active in pursuing independence and leftist antigovernment
agendas) were trying to leave Iraq, Iran, and Turkey via several routes taking them to Turkey, Greece, and Albania. From there, they headed to

Apulia and Calabria and then to northern European countries. In other words, while unauthorized exit from Albania was militarily prevented, the sources and reasons for transit emigration were not addressed—and they certainly could not be addressed in Italy, given the intractability of the Kurdish plight. Turkish and Kurdish organizations shifted their smuggling operations farther south and east, in Greece and Turkey. With the Italian coast, the Albanian coast, and the Strait of Otranto heavily patrolled, smugglers exposed migrants to longer and more perilous routes. Members of the Italian government asked Turkey to "stop the exodus and reinforce the control of its ports,"[39] which in practice would have entailed an even stronger and more severe repression of Turkey's Kurdish minority.

With the prospect of NATO military intervention in Kosovo-Serbia, the Strait of Otranto was subjected to further militarization. Fanav Formed, a NATO naval formation, joined in the patrolling effort of the Italian navy. NATO's humanitarian war in Kosovo-Serbia did indeed take place in 1999, ostensibly to protect Kosovo's ethnic Albanians.[40] In the meantime, Albanian passport holders who arrived in Apulia from Albania on speedboats were summarily repatriated. Among them, some were unaccompanied children. According to journalist Stefano Mencherini, in 2001 the Italian Consulate in Vlorë received 80,000 visa applications, granting only 12,700 of them.[41] A small, bipartisan group of senators suggested that Italian armed forces should shoot toward smugglers' boats upon their attempted return toward Albania, after passengers' disembarkation in Italy.[42]

The Italian government formulated a policy of temporary assistance and protection for Kosovar Albanians fleeing Kosovo, with refugee camps in both Albania and Italy. This policy was short-lived, lasting only until the conclusion of NATO's military campaign in June 1999. During summer 1999 a number of Kosovar residents, in particular Romany, were subjected to vandalism and revenge by extremist Kosovar Albanians, due to their alleged loyalty to the Serbian government. But NATO-led bombardment of Kosovo and of greater Serbia had officially ended. With the end of armed conflict, the logic went, it was not plausible that the Romany were being forced to leave. The sudden change in Italian policies meant that in Italy they were no longer considered refugees, but clandestini. And they were not just generic undocumented migrants but disparaged *Zingari* (Gypsies). The then governor of the Apulia region (1995–2000), Salvatore Distaso —an eminent professor of demography—publicly put it like this: "the mobility of the Romany people is extremely dangerous for the typology and the history of their people. . . . Gypsies, for the tribal traits they show, are a danger to our region [Apulia]: it is an undesired movement that could create tensions."[43] In response to this and other such concerns, the Ministry of the Interior allocated resources to install video cameras on street corners and beaches "at risk." In August 1999, as many as a hundred people, mostly Romany and including many women and children, died off the Montenegrin coast. They had fled neighboring Kosovo, and were trying to reach Italy on a fishing boat.[44]

In light of the militarization of maritime spaces and the criminalization of migration—embodied by unwanted Albanian and Romany citizens—the *Kater i Radës* disaster and the shipwreck off the coast of Montenegro are hardly accidents due to unseaworthiness, ruthlessness of smugglers, or stormy weather, to use some of the common explanatory phrases. They are the outcome of negligence, if not of purposefulness; of policies, of decision making, and of choices that have been made despite early warnings and alternatives that might have been considered. Such violent peace continues.

On July 24, 2000, two young finance guard soldiers died in the proximity of Otranto when their rubber speedboat collided with a vessel carrying Kurdish passengers. Six of the passengers also died in the collision. The comments of fellow soldiers and newspaper headlines made it finally clear that it was a "war" being fought. It was the "war against clandestine immigration," now finally talked about "because these are our dead."[45] The death of two among its own soldiers prompted the Italian government to ask for the assistance of the EU, "on whose behalf it was fighting that war" (Delle Donne 2004:153), and to envision new practices of dissuasion. The finance guard was concurrently fighting another "war," also off the Apulian coast—the war against maritime tobacco smugglers. A military operation, Operation Spring, was framed using bellicose language.[46] But there is an important difference between the "war" against tobacco smugglers and the fight against unauthorized migration. In the overarching rhetoric of wars conducted by Western liberal democracies, it is commodity smugglers (oil, arms, drugs, tobacco), pirates, terrorist cells, militias, infrastructure, and governments that are the intended targets. In the case of "human smuggling," the intended targets are the providers of unauthorized transport and their boats. But migrants on board risk becoming the collateral damage of such low-intensity conflict. It is at such a juncture, in the early 2000s, that new technologies and additional bilateral agreements were envisioned to support a more preemptive project of border enforcement and undocumented migration deterrence.

Then center-left minister of the interior, Enzo Bianco (1999–2001), publicly conveyed the emerging bipartisan consensus on the need to stop undocumented migrants in the ports of departure.[47] This Italian policy was pursued in Turkey, Albania, Tunisia, and eventually Libya, as discussed below, and was complemented by sustained investments in technology. Powerful Israeli-made radar was to be installed on the Apulian coast; and Italy acquired five Predator unmanned aerial vehicles from San Diego–based General Atomics. A specific new law, No. 178/2004, was passed to allow such unmanned flights in Italian airspace. By 2020, several European countries are expected to start collaborating in manufacturing EU-made drones, to be possibly used in the "surveillance of external borders or the fight against clandestine immigration in the Mediterranean."[48]

The commercial port of Bari was the first one to be equipped with Cargo Mobix 3800M 3.8Mev, a special police truck. The Mobix is able to scan commercial trucks with x-ray technology and to detect carbon dioxide and heartbeats, indicating the presence of unauthorized migrants. Vehicles cost approximately 3.5 million euros each. They can help save stowaways from suffocation, but also apprehend them and send them back to their ports of presumed departure. Important investments in technology also took place elsewhere in southern Europe. In the Strait of Gibraltar and southern Spain a complex surveillance system, the integrated external vigilance system, or SIVE, scans coastal areas and maritime space for migrants using high-resolution infrared cameras as well as radar systems in patrol boats and helicopters. The system, for which the Civil Guard in 1999 was allocated 200 million euros,[49] awoke "U.S. interest in SIVE for the war against terror."[50] Various Spanish NGOs, the Catholic Church, and local politicians opposed SIVE as a repressive and expensive measure. In response, the Spanish government emphasized its border responsibility to other European countries. It also stressed that SIVE had an important humanitarian component: it would help rescue migrants.[51]

As I speak about these technologies with a well-informed contact in Otranto,[52] he alleges that throughout the 1990s border patrol boats in the strait routinely used cables to jam speedboats' engines—as was alleged for the *Sibilla–Kater i Radës* deadly maneuvers. This would have posed a hazard for migrants. Hence, it would have received the applause of some politicians.

To this day, the words of minister of reforms Umberto Bossi (2001–4) remain particularly memorable. Replying to a journalist reminding him that migrant boats are often crowded with women and children, Bossi says solemnly: "Clandestine immigrants are to be kicked out. Only those with a job contract can enter the country. Others should be kicked out. There comes a moment when the use of force is necessary. The navy and finance guard must line up to defend our shores and use their cannons."[53] Roberto Calderoli, also minister of reforms (2004–6), declares on national television that border police forces should apply immigration law; instead of working for public order and security as they should, these forces instead carry on a work of "rescue and Red Cross"; thus, "migrants enter . . . and assail you, rob you, rape you, or perhaps assassinate you."[54] In the Italian political landscape, there is a tradition of disregarding such statements as empty expressions of populist folklore. They are, indeed, to be associated with the rhetorical hyperbole of the Northern League right-wing party, of which the two ministers are prominent leaders. What needs to be noted, though, is that during the second and third Berlusconi center-right governments (2001–6), several opposition, center-left leaders limit themselves to questioning the *efficaciousness* of strict border enforcement, not the political paradigm that substantiates it. To mention one example, Giannicola Sinisi, in charge of immigration issues with the center-left Margherita Party, during the summer of 2005 laments that "within 24 hours more than 800 people have disembarked [in Lampedusa], which shows the absolute inadequacy of the 'Bossi-Fini' immigration law. It is a continuous emergency. Where are the bilateral agreements with Mediterranean countries the government brags about so much? When tested by facts, they appear to be merely tools of propaganda."[55]

In the aftermath of the *Kater i Radës* shipwreck, the emerging institutional understanding was that maritime migration should be approached through deterrence, dissuasion, high-tech surveillance, and bilateral agreements allowing prevention, interception, and removals. Economic, legal, or political discussions were largely obliterated by the glitter of technology and the silences of diplomacy. But "border escalation"[56] engendered a vicious dynamic whereby stricter enforcement efforts in traditional, more approachable, safer, and shorter maritime routes elicited new and more perilous responses by smugglers and unauthorized migrants, in turn granting legitimacy to further attempts of border militarization and surveillance. In 2005 the Moroccan government agreed to increase surveillance of

migrants seeking to cross the Strait of Gibraltar, and in 2007 patrols by
Frontex started to operate as far south as Senegal.[57] These operations, and
possibly the deployment of SIVE, resulted in a drop in the numbers of
people attempting the crossing to the Spanish Canary Islands and to mainland Spain through the strait. But they also encouraged many to undertake
the long desert crossing to coastal Libya, and then to Italy.[58]

A Beautiful Postcolonial Friendship

Tekle, seventeen, is a student from Eritrea.[59] On September 11, 2005, his
story is presented to Italian readers by the widely circulated *La Repubblica*
newspaper. In other words: it is publicly known as of 2005. And it seems
reasonable that European authorities and intelligence services know a bit
more than newspapers. Like most of his friends, Tekle does not want to
choose between forced labor and indefinite conscription in his country's
military, which can turn everyone into an impoverished actor of governmental intelligence. He wants to flee the tensions with Ethiopia, the prospect of extrajudicial killings, disappearance, torture, arbitrary arrest and
detention, and restrictions on freedom of expression, conscience, and
movement.[60] Eritrea, a former Italian colony (1890–1947), is a one-party
state. Citizens are routinely abused by the apparatus led by President Isaias
Afewerki (1993–present).[61] Some schools have been closed to create an
incentive to pursue military training and military education. Droughts and
food scarcity afflict the population. An increasing number of international
extraction companies, among others, risk employing severely abused
"national service conscripts."[62] As many as four thousand citizens, including many minors, flee every month to Sudan.[63] An Eritrean refugee I met
in Italy suggests that his country's consular authorities, and citizens loyal
to the regime, actively keep track of antiregime members of the diaspora.[64]

Leaving Eritrea could cost Tekle his life, as would-be emigrants without
a selectively granted exit permit have to get through heavily militarized
national borders first, where "shoot to kill" is the norm.[65] And it could cost
his family in Eritrea imprisonment and heavy fines. Part of a group of four
hundred, Tekle manages to leave Eritrea, and to survive crossing the desert
on trucks through Sudan, Egypt, and Libya. Many more Eritreans, Ethiopians, and Somalis are smuggled across one thousand kilometers of desert
from Kufra, an oasis in the southeast of Libya, to the northern city of

Ajdabiya. From there, they travel to Benghazi, on Libya's northeastern coast. At every stage, they meet new requests for money. At every hour, they risk death and exhaustion in the desert, being sold to traffickers, and detention or deportation by Libyan authorities. They then travel by ship to Italy. Tekle sees fellow travelers drown in the sea facing Gela, Sicily. But he does make it to Italy. Eleven bodies are retrieved, while ten other persons are missing, either lost at sea or escaped before the rescuers' arrival.

Dissuasive measures put in place by Spain, Morocco, Mauritania, and the EU have considerably restricted the ability of migrants to cross the Strait of Gibraltar and to enter Spanish territory at the newly fortified African enclaves of Ceuta and Melilla.[66] In 1998 a verbal agreement was reached between the Italian Ministry of Foreign Affairs and the Tunisian ambassador in Rome, intended to bring Tunisian authorities to curb unauthorized transit migration, in exchange for more generous Italian entry quotas for Tunisian citizens. In December 2003 Tunisia and Italy signed an agreement that, in addition to allotting conspicuous financial aid and Italian investments in the North African country, enabled intelligence exchange and joint patrols over the 145 kilometers (90 miles) of the Strait of Sicily between Cape Bon and Trapani.[67] These factors, together with the corruption and connivance of officers in Gaddafi's Libya, contributed to migrants' prevalent use of the Libyan central Mediterranean maritime route to Europe, and in particular to Sicily and to Lampedusa, Italy's southernmost island.

Tekle is one of the 120,000 people who, between 2003 and 2008, traveled from coastal Libya to Italy.[68] This endeavor was and is enabled by pervasive smuggling networks. For example, Tuareg seminomadic and inherently transnational clans, often lacking basic citizenship documentation and severely affected by conflicts and disputes, have found their livelihood in goods and human smuggling across Chad, Niger, and southwestern Libya, complemented by Libyan and Nigerien officers.[69] Migrants using this route reach the hub of Agadez, in Niger—whose regional economy is increasingly shaped by the smuggling industry—and from there cross the desert to Sabha, in Libya, before reaching Tripoli on the coast. The other major route, in the southeast, leads from Sudan to the Libyan oasis of Kufra. Southern Libyan military bases and prisons are routinely used to detain African migrants and to organize their repatriation. It is worth noticing that Libya's vast land borders amount to nearly forty-four hundred kilometers. In northern Libya, smuggler facilitators include corrupt Libyan officers, competing militias, Egyptian intermediaries and boatmen, Tunisian

Figure 4. Fishing boat used by migrants, Lampedusa. A pair of eyes protects Mediterranean fishermen. Photo: Maurizio Albahari.

brokers who buy and sell old boats, and transnational traffickers of passengers who might also smuggle drugs. And there is no scarcity of passengers.

During the 1990s Libyan authorities, in the name of pan-African solidarity and to secure cheap laborers for the oil-rich country, encouraged immigration from Arab and African countries. They also recruited specialized workers, such as engineers, doctors, and nurses: Sabratha's hospital, in coastal northwestern Libya, was staffed by personnel from almost thirty countries.[70] Prior to the 2011 war (Chapter 5) Libya was inhabited by 5.5 million citizens and by at least 1 million foreigners. Among the latter were Egyptian bakers, Tunisian waiters, Ghanaian hairdressers, Nigerien sanitation workers, Chadian tailors, international students, and a variety of other workers and (unrecognized) refugees from Ethiopia, Eritrea, Somalia, Iraq, the Philippines, Bangladesh, Nigeria, and Sri Lanka, among other countries. Their presence has often been contested. In a most dramatic example, in September 2000 simmering social tensions, episodes of petty crime, rumors of cannibalism, and plain racism erupted in brutal violence, and 560 foreigners, mostly Nigerians, Ghanaians, Chadians, and Sudanese, were killed in Zawiyah on the northwestern coast, not far from Tripoli. As a governmental response, between 1998 and 2003 at least 14,000 people, including women and children needing refugee protection, were deported to the desert border areas.[71] And hundreds of migrants die in the desert between Libya, Niger, and Algeria, usually as they travel northward,[72] but also in the lengthy process of Libyan repatriation to sub-Saharan countries.[73] No one who has made it to the inhabited, northern part of Libya dreams of "going back" through the desert, especially with the burden of a debt to pay. They can seek employment in Libya, or venture farther north.

For Tekle, the seventeen-year-old Eritrean who has survived the perils of such a journey, "the fear arrives now," in Lampedusa. It is the fear of deportation to Libya: "Italian policemen are very nice, they rescued us, they fed us, and are helping us, but we know they will send us back. We don't want this," he pleads. The possibility of deportation he dreads is made possible by a lengthy process of rapprochement between Italy and its southern neighbor and former colony, Libya.

Between 1969 and 2011 Libya was governed by an authoritarian regime under the leadership of Colonel Muammar Gaddafi. After years of international sanctions and isolation, following in particular the Lockerbie bombing of PanAm Flight 103 in 1988, in 2003 Libya's government admitted responsibility for the actions of some of its officials and paid compensations. It also renounced its weapons of mass destruction programs. The way was paved for overt international trade, including in weapons; for further economic cooperation; and for Colonel Gaddafi to receive international honors and recognition.

Italian prime minister Silvio Berlusconi visits Libya in February 2004, soon followed by British prime minister Tony Blair. In June 2004, in turn, Gaddafi is invited to the EU headquarter in Brussels, where he is welcomed by the EU Commission and in particular by its president, Romano Prodi. On October 7, 2004, Gaddafi and Berlusconi meet in Mellitah, on the northwestern Libyan coast, and publicly cement the "friendship and cooperation" between their respective countries. Indeed, Italy and Libya already had a long story behind them: the Cyrenaica, Tripolitania, and eventually Fezzan regions had been Italian colonies between 1912 and 1947. Italian colonialism had been particularly brutal in crushing any resistance. Especially during the early conquest and later under the Fascist regime, civilians faced the lethal brutality of concentration camps; of massive expropriations; of forced migration and death marches across the desert; of the massive destruction of sheep, horses, and camels; of summary executions and assassinations. Soon after the 1969 military coup, carried on with his Free Officers Movement, Gaddafi ordered the expulsion from Libya of all remaining Italian nationals. Sixteen thousand to twenty thousand Libyan-Italians were thus ordered to leave Libya on October 7, 1970, and that date was celebrated as an anniversary, the "day of revenge." Since then, the complicated relationship between Libya and Italy was characterized by Gaddafi's requests for postcolonial reparations, instrumental to a sense of closure.

Following the 2004 bilateral meeting with Berlusconi, the "day of revenge" (October 7) is to be newly celebrated as a "day of friendship" with Italy—even if Gaddafi is known to be an astute negotiator and a mercurial friend. The occasion for the bilateral meeting, and for the newly cemented friendship, is the inauguration of Greenstream, the longest underwater pipeline ever laid in the Mediterranean, bringing gas from Mellitah on the Libyan coast to Gela, in Sicily. Gaddafi also thanks Berlusconi for his role in lifting the arms embargo on his country.[74]

The Council of the EU, bringing together member states' foreign ministers,[75] does lift the EU arms embargo on Libya on October 11, 2004. In a news release, the council expresses its concern regarding the "human rights situation" in the country, in particular regarding "serious impediments to the right of free speech and association, credible reports of torture of suspects and miscarriages of justice and inhuman conditions of detention." Nevertheless, the council invites Libya to intervene urgently and effectively in the issue of transit and maritime migration: "In reviewing the elements relevant to the development of relations with Libya, the Council recalled its conclusions of November 2002 that cooperation with Libya on migration is essential and urgent. It reiterated its concern about the level of illegal traffic across the Mediterranean from, or via, Libya. The loss of life at sea, maintenance of public order at the ports of entry and the burden of illegal immigration from, or via, Libya now require effective action by Libya. In this context, the Council also underlined that Libya should respect its international obligations."[76]

In November and December 2004, a European Commission delegation visits Libya and some of its migrant holding facilities. In the official report delegates write that "many of the illegal immigrants [we] met in the centres seem to have been arrested on a random basis. The decision to return illegal immigrants to their country of origin seems to be taken for groups of nationalities rather than after having examined individual cases in detail."

The conditions of the holding facilities they find vary "from relatively acceptable to extremely poor."[77] In addition, Libya, while a signatory to the 1969 Refugee Convention of the Organization of African Unity, is not party to the 1951 "Geneva" Convention Relating to the Status of Refugees. In the absence of a national asylum system, registration, documentation, and determination of refugee status are activities carried out by the Office of the United Nations High Commissioner for Refugees (UNHCR), with limited funds. Even being registered with the UNHCR does not grant particular benefits, other than the possibility of assisted repatriation and, more remotely, resettlement. Most importantly, until recently relationships with the Libyan government and the police have been very difficult, resulting in the UNHCR's inability to access detention facilities and extend its assistance to particularly vulnerable persons, including Eritrean and Somali nationals.

The Italian government in 2004 provided a "substantial economic contribution" for charter flights taking about 5,500 unauthorized migrants from Libya to their presumed countries of origin, including Pakistan, Egypt, Ghana, Nigeria, and Bangladesh,[78] but also Sudan and Eritrea,[79] and therefore probably in need of humanitarian protection as refugees. Between 2004 and 2005, deportations were also carried out using desert routes, resulting in 106 migrant deaths in four months.[80] In Italy, between October 2004 and August 2005 armed forces implemented the collective, summary deportation to Libya of migrants, mostly non-Libyans, who had arrived at Lampedusa. For example, according to Amnesty International (2005), "on 17 March [2005], the Italian authorities forcibly returned 180 people to Libya, where they may be in grave danger. Non-Libyan nationals risk detention on charges including illegal entry into and exit from Libya."[81] At this time, migrants in Tripoli were terrified by the prospect of police raids, detention, and deportation.

Gaddafi's Libya, in short, had long been under international scrutiny for its human rights record and the lack of refugee protection. This did not prevent intergovernmental and EU cooperation in matters of migration. Many of the people collectively deported to Libya would face extended detention and harassment in inhumane, degrading, unsanitary, exploitative, and violent settings, or summary deportation to their presumed country of origin. In either case, no jurisdiction was protecting their dignity and safety.

The Italian government helped finance in Garyan, not far from Tripoli, a "Center of detention for irregular foreigners to be repatriated, with a capacity of 1,000 places."[82] This center, ostensibly built "in line with European criteria," would be complemented by two new camps to be financed in the south of the country, in Sabha and Kufra, respectively in the southwest and on the southeastern border with Egypt and Sudan.[83] Moreover, the removal of weapons and military equipment sanctions in 2004 allowed Libyan officers to be trained by Italian agents and surveillance and police equipment to be sent to Libya, including vehicles, cameras, and nighttime viewers. Together with five hundred lifebuoys and five hundred life jackets, "1,000 sacks for corpses transport" were also donated by Italy.[84] Italian and EU authorities have long expected migrant deaths.

Deportations to Libya, in 2005 implemented by Italy through special flights, were strongly condemned by the UNHCR and by the EU Parliament—the only EU institution directly elected by EU citizens. The EU Parliament's "Resolution on Lampedusa" of April 2005 clearly and uncompromisingly highlights that—among several violations of basic human rights—collective deportation constitutes a breach of the 1951 and 1967 Convention and Protocol Relating to the Status of Refugees (article 33.1), which requires cases to be genuinely examined individually and prohibits the expulsion or return of refugees. More generally, the resolution is concerned with the semisecret bilateral agreement between Libya and Italy, whose effect is "to give the Libyan authorities the task of supervising migration," also committing them to readmission of "people returned by Italy." The resolution expresses concern over the treatment and deplorable living conditions of people held in camps in Libya, as well as over the massive repatriations of third-country nationals from Libya to their countries of origin.[85]

Despite the mounting concern regarding immigration agreements with Libya, and the widespread perception that the Libyan regime managed emigration from its coasts to gain leverage in international relations, in August 2005 the North African country and the International Organization for Migration (IOM, the preeminent intergovernmental organization) sign an agreement that, in the wording of the Libyan representative, would result in "curbing irregular migration and promoting orderly and humane migration management."[86] In 2006, giant Italian conglomerate Finmeccanica (the Italian government is its controlling shareholder) sells to Libya ten of its AgustaWestland A109E-Power helicopters, with the stated purpose of controlling coasts and borders. Following the lift of the arms embargo in 2004, Libya needs to renovate its arsenals. Between 2005 and 2009, Italy leads in arms exports to Libya, including bombs, rockets, missiles, military planes, and electronic equipment. It is followed by France and the United Kingdom.[87] In the meantime, between 2006 and 2007, the Libyan government claims to have arrested 95,370 undocumented migrants.

In October 2007, ENI (the multinational gas and oil giant, of which the Italian government owns 30 percent) secures a renewal of its fossil-fuel-extracting concessions in Libya for the following twenty-five years, with an estimated 20 billion euros to be invested in the 2007–17 decade.[88] Later in 2007, in November, the Italian center-left government, again led by Romano Prodi (2006–8), reaches a preliminary agreement with Libya, which also involves postcolonial reparations. Like others before him, foreign minister Massimo D'Alema promises the construction of a new highway in coastal Libya, all the way from Tunisia to Egypt, at an estimated cost of 3 billion euros. The highway would replace the one made during Fascist colonialism, in 1937. As a major infrastructure, it would demand the labor of immigrant workers.

In December 2007, the two governments sign a "technical agreement." Because it is a "technical" agreement, its approval is simplified and only subjected to the scrutiny of the executive, without parliamentary discussion and public debate. The bilateral agreement stipulates the delivery to the North African country of six fast patrol boats with mixed Italian-Libyan crews, to more effectively patrol the Channel of Sicily in Libyan and international waters.[89] Giuliano Amato, Italian minister of the interior and key facilitator of the agreement together with his counterpart Abdurrahman Shalgam, asserts that the agreement is intended to "reinforce the fight against criminal organizations engaged in trafficking and in the exploitation of clandestine migration."[90]

In August 2008, Italian prime minister Silvio Berlusconi (2008–11, leading for the fourth time a center-right coalition) and "Leader of the Revolution" Muammar Gaddafi sign in Benghazi a Treaty of Friendship, Partnership, and Cooperation, ratified by the Italian Parliament in February 2009 with only a few votes against. With the treaty, the two countries intend to "permanently close the painful chapter of the [colonial] past" and to highlight their "awareness of the deep relationships of friendship of their people and of the common historical and cultural heritage."[91] As they have been doing for years, once again Libyan authorities promise they will extensively cooperate in the fight against unauthorized migration. Article 19 deals with the "fight against terrorism, organized crime, drug trafficking, and immigration"—all in one article. In addition, the treaty deals with issues such as education exchange programs, infrastructural development, political and military cooperation, and most crucially economic partnership. ENI, the Italian energy company, has once again secured its continued access to Libyan natural resources. And as a form of reparation, Italy commits to invest $5 billion over twenty years. Italian company Selex Integrated Systems is awarded a 300 million euro contract to build and implement radar and electronic systems of control of Libya's land borders with Chad, Sudan, and Niger, with the costs shared by Italy and by the EU.[92] Selex is a subsidiary of Italian conglomerate Finmeccanica. The Italian government, as the conglomerate's primary shareholder, ensures cooperation and friendship with Libya, secures lucrative contracts at times of economic stagnation, and transfers the tasks of border enforcement and migrant detention and removal to reluctant Libya.

The Creation of Adam in Tripoli

On May 7, 2009, minister of the interior Roberto Maroni (2008–11), of the Northern League, calls a news conference at the ministry's Viminale Palace in Rome. He has a story to share, about the important operation that has taken place only hours earlier.[93] He announces a turning point in the campaign against clandestine immigration, especially regarding arrivals from Libya at the "Italian, Maltese, and European coasts." The night of May 5–6, he says pointing to a map, three migrant boats, with a total of 227 people on board, "asked for help" and were intercepted as they were headed from Libya to Lampedusa, in the search-and-rescue area (SAR) of Maltese jurisdiction. They were "taken" by Italian vessels and "brought back" to the Libyan port of Tripoli, in agreement with Libyan authorities.[94] Hesitation, awkwardness, and triumphalism emerge in the minister's tone. He emphasizes that this Mediterranean operation, for the first time, affirms the principle of respingimento toward migrants' country of departure, rather than the country of origin. He insists it has never happened before that a country agrees to "take back" third-country nationals, noncitizens. Prior to this turning point, he explains, the rule was that once migrants arrived in Italy or Malta local authorities had to identify the countries of origin for each person, and then repatriate them accordingly. Indeed, in the minister's

account there is no mention of where the pushed-back immigrants originally came from, or whether they might have been entitled to apply for
asylum in Italy. Minister Maroni did not mention any of this because he
did not need to know. He "knew" these to be non-Libyans, and the only
way to (mistakenly) presume this without interviews is by skin color. But
in light of the groundbreaking respingimento practice, these became redundant details. The Northern League had long cherished respingimenti as a
slogan. It still does. Maroni, in charge of "law and order" within the center-
right coalition, finally delivers what had been promised at rallies during the
electoral campaign, a year earlier.

Enrico Dagnino, an Italian photojournalist working for the French
weekly *Paris Match*, is on board the patrol boat *Bovienzo* of the Italian
finance guard, when the pioneering respingimento is carried out. His photos, later awarded the prestigious 2009 Louis Hachette Prize, are circulated
by Italian and European media. Together with a related journalistic piece,
they document events as follows. Maritime travelers, tired and scared, are
transferred from their boats to the *Bovienzo*, by officers with surgical masks
and batons. Men, pregnant women, and three children have survived the
perils of the desert, including torture, and thirst, hunger, and gasoline
burns after five days at sea. They are reassured, and told they are headed to
Italy. They are visibly grateful to their Italian rescuers. The trip to
Lampedusa seems to be taking longer than expected though. Those are the
lights of Tripoli, and of its port. Some passengers on board the *Bovienzo* try
to physically resist being handed over to Libyan authorities. Many had
already attempted the journey. Two groups in particular, of eleven Eritreans
and thirteen Somalis, had been rescued almost a year earlier, by a Spanish
commercial boat. Returned to Tripoli, they had been arrested.[95] An Iveco
Trakker, a truck made in Italy and equipped with containers with only a
few slits for air, is now waiting for them on the dock in Tripoli. Some men
become completely naked as they try to resist. Others have to be physically
dragged. One photo shows a young black man wearing a cap with a small
Cuban flag, and a leather jacket over a green shirt. He is down on his knees.
Tears dot his face. He grabs with both hands the left hand of a finance
guard officer, recognizable by his gray uniform. But the imploring man
cannot touch the Italian officer. Their hands are separated by the baby blue
latex gloves worn by the latter.

This image does not need to be reproduced here. It does not need to be
translated, and words alone could not do it justice. It is not degrading for

the migrant. It does not bring to the public the usual indistinct "mass," but the face, expression, and strong will of a plausible person. It summons the unjust nature of the encounter it documents. That encounter is not an event, but a situation of structural injustice whose conditions of possibility these pages have described. What brings that man to implore is not humility, physical weakness, or emotional exhaustion, but the existential awareness of the deep injustice to which he is being subjected, with others. The experience of the migrant and the career of the soldier—executing policies envisioned far from the sea—intersect in an encounter that marks them for life. The rescue, the hierarchical encounter with Italian and Libyan authorities, the naked bodies, the gloves, the baton, the faces, and the bystanders are a rendition of what border enforcement, pushback operations, and overarching immigration policies look like—materially, not symbolically—in a liberal democracy.

The photograph looks uncannily familiar, though, in a visual and symbolic way also. The tension of the two male figures in a hierarchical relation reminds me of the tension in Michelangelo's *The Creation of Adam*, part of the Sistine Chapel frescoes in the Vatican. In what is one of the most widely reproduced artworks in the world, God's right arm is outstretched to give life to Adam. There is movement captured in the painting, as their fingers and hands are not yet touching. "We" are Adam, in Tripoli. Our gloves separate us—those north of the Mediterranean, in this situation—from that outstretched arm. Latex gloves are among the "individual protection devices"[96] that build our immunity against the touch of structural injustice and of others' yearning to live and to prosper with us. They sterilize life, death, human rights, democracy, sovereignty, and entrenched asymmetries of power into statistics of rescue, apprehensions, and deportations; into quandaries of "burden sharing" and "bogus asylum seekers"; into the naturalized necessities of liberal democratic sovereignty; into vague humanitarianism. They transform every person they manage, assist, and deport into yet another clandestine occupant of our conscience.

Italian pushback operations were carried out throughout the summer months and until November 2009.[97] Various factors account for the de facto termination of such policy. First of all, Gaddafi's government and police did eventually tackle smuggling and unauthorized emigration through the country. Massive raids apprehended migrants, including refugees, to be detained and eventually deported. Some migrants left the increasingly unwelcoming country voluntarily. Arrivals in Italy during the second half of 2009 dropped. Italian sailors became increasingly disgruntled. Courts in Sicily began investigating the pushback operations and the Italian chain of command. Finally, various organizations, including UNHCR, voiced their strong objections to such practices, prompting unofficial diplomatic pressure on Italy at the EU level.[98]

In February 2012, the European Court of Human Rights (not an EU court; see Chapter 3) in the case *Hirsi Jamaa and Others v. Italy* condemns the Italian pushback practice as it has resulted in Eritrean and Somali nationals being collectively returned to Libya without having been given an opportunity to lodge asylum claims in Italy—as boarding an Italian vessel should have entailed, according to maritime laws. While the court does not find the pushback to Libya inhumane or degrading per se, it does find that people were put at risk of inhumane and degrading treatment, both in Libya and in the *potential* case of repatriation, that is, even if repatriation to Somalia and Eritrea did not happen.[99]

Between 2009 and 2010 the Italian finance guard delivers six of its armed vessels to the Libyan coast guard, as stipulated by the 2007 "technical agreements." In July 2009, one of those very vessels is used to intercept and confiscate two fishing boats of Sicilian fishermen, allegedly in Libyan territorial waters. In September 2010, again a former finance guard vessel intercepts another fishing boat, *Ariete*, from Mazara del Vallo, Sicily.[100] Shots are fired at the *Ariete*. There is damage to the boat but there are no casualties. On the Italian morning television show *Mattino Cinque*, Maroni confirms that the operating crew on these Italian-made and Italian-donated vessels is indeed Libyan, but also that Italian finance guard officers are routinely present on board to provide "technical assistance." In that specific incident, he asserts, Italian officers were below deck. The explanation for the shooting incident, he suggests, might simply be that the Libyan patrol boat thought the *Ariete* was carrying "clandestine immigrants."[101]

The Emigration of Sovereignty and Rights

Frontex was established in 2004 as the European Agency for the Management of Operational Cooperation at the External Borders of the Member States of the European Union. Nevertheless, decision making regarding policing, judicial cooperation, asylum, and crime prevention is still located "at the intersection of intergovernmental and supranational institutions"

(Walters 2002:568). Under current EU policy, migration remains largely a question of national sovereignty. The EU's Global Approach to Migration and Mobility (established in 2005) encourages, but does not require, a truly European cooperation. It has resulted in several "mobility partnerships" between select EU countries and countries that facilitate the readmission of unauthorized migrants. Frontex does receive EU funds, but it is understood as enhancing states' "management of operational cooperation." In particular, its Mediterranean operational activities depend largely on individual countries[102] that operationalize specific missions with airplanes, helicopters, and patrol vessels. This is true also for the Triton Mission. Frontex is in the process of negotiating cooperation in emigration and readmission matters with Turkey, Libya, Morocco, Senegal, Mauritania, Egypt, Brazil, Tunisia, and Azerbaijan. It has formalized "working arrangements" with Albania, Canada, Cape Verde, Croatia, Macedonia, Serbia, Bosnia and Herzegovina, Georgia, Moldova, Montenegro, the Russian Federation, Ukraine, Nigeria, Armenia, the United States, and Belarus. Belarus, Frontex's partner in managing migration at one of the EU's external borders, has since 2006 been subjected to EU and U.S. sanctions for the alleged violation of human rights under the presidency of Alexander Lukashenko, in power since 1994.

Italian agreements with Libya, Albania, Egypt, and Tunisia (see also Chapter 5) suggest once again that crafting and implementing the governance of the external borders of the EU is partly a prerogative of individual member states. But member states, Frontex, and various EU institutions are progressively and cumulatively also externalizing immigration control.

Since the mid-1980s, carrier sanctions have also become particularly relevant: private transport companies taking to the EU persons who do not hold the necessary visas or travel documents face fines and repatriation costs. A limited number of EU countries do discretionally waive these fines (up to 500,000 euros) once and if the traveler is recognized as in need of protection. But transport companies prefer not to risk making the wrong decision, and simply refuse the sale of tickets to persons without visas, including potential refugees. As the European Council on Refugees and Exiles (a consortium of eighty-two NGOs) puts it, carrier sanctions "confer on [such] private actors responsibilities which by nature pertain to public authorities. They privatise functions in the field of migration control to non-state agents that cannot be held accountable for ensuring the rights of refugees under international law."[103] As we have seen, Italy and EU member states and institutions also intervene abroad by providing military and humanitarian equipment, technical assistance, and police training; establishing or financing migration detention facilities; and formulating bilateral and readmission agreements, called by a Libyan acquaintance of mine "money plus diplomacy" for the conditionality of development and technological aid. The proliferation of such bilateral agreements often amounts to a fragmented and improvised policy,[104] but it does betray an overarching aspiration. This is that would-be migrants, often including "mixed flows" with potential asylum seekers and persons needing protection, do not reach the territory of EU countries in the first place.

In 2003, the EU Commission had already proposed the establishment of "protected entry procedures" allowing persons who wish to claim asylum in an EU country to approach the relevant embassy, rather than "having to risk the dangerous journey to the country itself," as a study commissioned by the EU Parliament puts it.[105] In case of approval, the person could travel to that country. This is similar to what happened in Albania in the summer of 1990. In reality, European and other embassies and consulates worldwide have considerably stepped up security. In turn, this provision if ever implemented could also lend itself to the externalization of asylum processing, in the sense of potentially not allowing applications to be lodged in the EU itself or outside one's own country.

Readmission agreements oblige signatory countries—gatekeepers, buffer states, and "safe third countries"—to (speedily) "take back" not only their citizens but also third-country and stateless nationals. The cases of Italy (especially with Tunisia and Egypt) and Greece (with Turkey) are paradigmatic of agreements that do not incorporate "proper human right guarantees" for persons returned (Crépeau 2013:16). Shifting the responsibility of migrant control also means that "the recourse of those migrants to human rights mechanisms within the European Union becomes legally restricted or practically impossible" (14). As I illustrate in Chapter 4, migrants' detention in particular—both in the EU and in countries of transit and readmission, and often in the absence of deportation proceedings—is often characterized by the failure to guarantee proper legal representation and access to consular and translation services, the inability to detect vulnerable individuals, the lack of access to NGOs and to asylum procedures, and the lack of external and independent monitoring. UN special rapporteur on the human rights of migrants and legal scholar François Crépeau suggests that, when it comes to migration, approaches that fail "to fully integrate human rights and legal guarantees can be termed repressive, and undermine the capacity of the European Union to act as a model for the protection of human rights worldwide" (19).

Additionally, the surge in bilateral, "technical," and intergovernmental agreements fosters a depoliticization and technicalization of governance. Parliaments, at best, are relegated to ratifying provisions. This surge in technodemocracy also allows governors and migration control officials to avoid much of the judicial scrutiny they ordinarily face nationally,[106] limit migrants' access to the judicial system, take extremely consequential decisions that remain opaque to the vast majority of citizens and media, and ultimately shift the responsibility of external border enforcement to non-EU countries farther to the EU's east and south.

The southern borders of Italy and of the EU, then, do not coincide with territorial and international waters. They are delocalized and extended much farther, into the home countries of potential emigrants and into the transit countries they intend to reach. Such a preemptive approach to migration, including the delocalization of migrant processing and deportation, is not merely an administrative outsourcing enterprise: it results in the potential delocalization of human rights, of ill treatment, and of death.

PART II

MIDDLE WORLDS

Chapter 3

Sovereignty as Salvation: Moral States

"Moses Was the First Smuggler in History": Buying and Selling Salvation

Enver, in his mid-thirties, is employed as a construction worker in Bari, Apulia. He grew up in a small village near Vlorë, across the Adriatic: "I had finished my studies; what should I have done stuck in Vlorë? My life, sitting all day in a café doing nothing, was not worth living, so I crossed, even if I knew people who had died in the attempt. At least I made a choice."[1] It is becoming increasingly clear that restrictive immigration and asylum policies are merely "*one* (and not even the most important) factor" influencing the geographic distribution of asylum claims[2] and of migrant arrivals. Enver's words point to the inadequacy of "prevention-through-deterrence" assumptions.[3] It has also become apparent that militarized border enforcement is extremely relevant to the routes privileged by smugglers and boatmen. While passengers are keen on reaching the coast, boatmen are anxious to avoid arrest. In other words, they want to avoid interception by the coast guard or armed forces. As is true for African-European routes, the militarization of the Strait of Otranto also resulted in a maritime reroute, with Syrian-, Turkish-, and Greek-based organizations opting for the crossing to Italy farther south in the Ionian Sea. Longer routes, the deployment of fleets comprising large ships (common in smuggling out of Egypt and Turkey, more than Libya), riskier maneuvers, and evidently higher fees are the smugglers' response to further patrols and policing. All of this, in turn, increasingly requires coordination of migrants' air travel, residence in hostels or farmhouses, the corruption of officers, and maritime transportation. Multibillions in profits are recycled and reinvested. The militarization of straits has been effective as a deterrent only insofar as it has deterred people traveling shorter and safer distances on smaller boats, with or without the services of small-scale smugglers. Conversely, it has contributed to the profiteering success of larger organized criminal enterprises, better equipped to provide transport in light of the more demanding circumstances.

Carretta del mare: an overcrowded, old, rickety boat. It has been the media's word of choice for migrant boats since the *Kater i Radës* disaster in 1997. The way that particular shipwreck was described is illustrative of the political grammar of shipwrecks' representation and explanation. A *carretta del mare* by definition puts people on board at risk. Passengers are desperate, irrational, perhaps even responsible for their own death, because they knew they were risking their lives in the first place. In addition, the *Kater i Radës* was trying to force a blockade, or at any rate cross a maritime border in an unauthorized way. Passengers are thus in a situation of illegality, and a sovereign entity has the right and duty to intervene when its borders are breached. Soon after the shipwreck, the navy chief of staff, Admiral Angelo Mariani, told the Italian public that Namik Xhaferi, at the helm of the *Kater i Radës*, had behaved irresponsibly and unpredictably, thus causing the impact with the Italian warship. As happens routinely, mechanisms and relationships of causality are simplified, and responsibility shifted entirely to smuggler boat drivers. And when it is not smugglers' fault, immediate agents of death and causes of death are conveniently conflated: people die, it is said, because of oxygen deprivation, water inhalation, dehydration, exposure. The rickety boats. The desperate people. The unforgiving elements. The unscrupulous smugglers. Unstable countries. They provide an undemanding explanation.

Scafisti: boat drivers. Local and national media reporting the arrival of migrant boats to Lampedusa, Sicily, and coastal Apulia and Calabria never fail to address the question of *scafisti*. They are always newsworthy, both when they are identified and arrested and when they manage to leave the scene. They make it to the news whether they are minors or adults; whether they are from Tunisia and Egypt or from Apulia, as in recent (2014) arrivals to the region. They are always "*killers*" and *negrieri* (slave traffickers). They might very well be reckless criminals. Upon departure, some force people onto their overcrowded boat at gunpoint, and then again out of the boat, but still too far from the shore. Alternatively, in the proximity of the coast they might throw overboard compasses and satellite phones as incriminating evidence. At other times, though, boat drivers might be smuggled migrants themselves, either forced to take the helm or convinced to do so in exchange for a discounted or free passage. Many *are* knowledgeable about the sea. Consider that small-scale fishermen in West Africa are seeing rapidly declining fish stocks, which incidentally might be due to overfishing by EU-subsidized and Asian vessels, and decide to emigrate, including driving a boat.[4] Or that with certain currents fishermen in northwestern Algeria might find 40 percent of their catch to comprise plastic trash that floats in the Mediterranean.[5] Scafisti are most often menial laborers executing the last and most hazardous part of trips organized by larger, often transnational, cartels. They sometimes drive passengers collected from larger ships. They are likely not to know the higher levels of the organization for which they work. At other times, there is no pyramidal organization, but a chain of "area managers" who "outsource" to smugglers the actual journey (Di Nicola and Musumeci 2014:91). Especially in this case, smugglers and scafisti have an interest in minimizing the risks of the maritime journey, to preserve their reputation with potential clients.

Passengers have to stay below deck, "even if they vomit." The center of gravity on the boat has to stay low. One has to be "tough" with them, because if they come up there is a risk of sinking. Thus speaks Aleksandr, a Russian sailor, entrusted by a Turkish organization with the lives of migrants he is taking from Greece to Apulia. He continues: "I know I'm the best. Passengers pray during their crossing. I am their only hope. I could have given the helm to one of them, take the dinghy and go back. Leave them to their fate. But I don't feel like having them risk so much. It would be a crime. Is smuggling a crime too? I think Moses was the first scafista in history! And I'm like him, like Moses!"[6] When arrested in India, Pavlo, one of the *Yiohan*'s crew during the 1990s, declared that the Indian government should in fact be grateful to him, for in his smuggling career he helped at least fifty thousand Indian citizens get to Europe.[7] Youssef El Hallal, the *Yiohan*'s captain, claimed to have saved thousands of men from war.[8] In a newspaper interview, El Hallal also alleged larger responsibilities for the Christmas 1996 collision between the *Yiohan* and the *F-174* and the sinking of the latter: "I don't want to be the only one to pay for an activity that involves hundreds of powerful individuals: shipowners, diplomats, police heads of all the countries of the Mediterranean. That shipwreck was a tragic accident during a business recognized and tolerated by governments."[9]

The merits of El Hallal's allegations about the role of diplomats and police officials are beyond the scope of this work. And yet let us note that

legality (or its pretense) is routinely sold and bought. Real visas and pass-
ports, as well as forged documents, also come with comfortable flights.
Already in the security-conscious, post–September 11, 2001, era, Dajti, an
Albanian citizen now resident in the United States with his wife and teenage
child, managed to buy Italian passports for him and his family in Albania.
He paid $35,000 for the passports, the American visas, and the flight to the
United States.[10] Dajti and his family were given real Italian passports, with
Italian names and supporting documents from the Italian municipality of
pretended birth. I know Dajti is not the only person who benefited from
such schemes in Albania and in Italy. Such a well-organized enterprise
implies the active involvement of transnational organized crime, and negligence or corruption within relevant institutions.

To those who could not afford such luxurious packages, during the
1990s Albanian scafisti offered pioneering unauthorized transport. Like
Aleksandr, Pavlo, and El Hallal, they also used moral undertones in their
accounts of the smuggling enterprise, emphasizing their role in "saving"
not only the people they transported but also the Albanian economy. Sali,
a native of the southern city of Vlorë, says that in the heyday of Albanian
smuggling to Apulia in the mid-1990s, "one boat could give something to
eat to a hundred people."[11] Smugglers were convinced, with some factual
accuracy, that Vlorë survived because of their work, including the remit-
tances sent by the many citizens they helped to cross. In 1996 one could
count in Vlorë's port approximately 70 rubber speedboats; in 2000, about
250. Some of these carried from twenty to forty persons each night, charg-
ing $600–650. Non-Albanians including Kurdish, Bangladeshi, Chinese,
Pakistani, and Filipino citizens paid an additional $200–250. Smugglers
claimed to have a moral duty to serve Albanians first, although in fact they
preferred Chinese and Filipino clients who were able to pay more and were
physically smaller—thus allowing more passengers. They usually carried at
least one passenger who could not afford to pay, such as a woman, a child,
or an invalid. Some ten people attended to each vessel preparing the trip.
There was a shuttle driver taking clients to Vlorë from other villages and
towns, and delivering the fuel for the boat.[12] There were two people always
guarding the boat, and a cashier in charge of collecting payments who also
took care of the clients before departure. When departures were delayed
because of the weather, because of heightened policing, or because the full
passenger load had not been reached, the cashier would secure food and an
accommodation. There was a person, with a regular residence permit in

Italy, who joined the clients on the boat for the ride—averaging two hours—across the strait to Otranto. Knowing Italy and Italian, upon arrival he would help the clients to a railway station. The following night, he would take a regular ferry and go back to Albania. There were the boat owners, a group or an individual; and two or three scafisti, who would brag about their skills and the many trips already completed. Payment was often collected from the migrants' relatives back in Vlorë, but only if the traveler had not been repatriated. Alternatively, there was the guarantee that passengers who did not make it to Italy, or were repatriated after a few days, would either receive the payment back or be transported again for free.

Coastal residents in Apulia, whether Italian or Albanian citizens, participated in the smuggling enterprise from the shores, signaling with lights the possible presence of police forces and the precise point of disembarking. They provided fresh clean clothes to the migrants, and occasionally worked as overcharging taxi drivers, driving migrants to the Lecce, Brindisi, or Bari railway stations, when not directly to northern Italy. Organized criminal cartels in southern Apulia were not interested in the business of human smuggling directly, but they tolerated it. Affiliates of the Sacra Corona Unita, as they call themselves, were much more involved with tobacco smuggling from Albania and Montenegro. Sacra Corona Unita is a younger organization in comparison to the Mafia, Camorra, and 'Ndrangheta. It was established in the early 1980s when a group of Apulian inmates decided to create their own autonomous criminal enterprise. The name they chose for themselves is worth noticing: "united sacred crown," where "sacred crown" stands for the Catholic rosary, in which every bead—the individual member—is linked to others. Insiders also use prayer cards in their rituals of allegiance and affiliation. Domains of prophecy, sacredness, and salvation are appropriated by persons seeking to legitimize themselves, such as smugglers, and by (criminal) organizations that need to foster internal solidarity and loyalty. Competitors include other organized crime formations, the church, and state actors.

Scafisti, in the self-interested representation by Italian and EU authorities, are ascribed an explanatory power: they explain migrant arrivals. In other words, if all smugglers could be arrested, and smuggling eliminated, (maritime) migration would cease to exist. And they serve as an easily identifiable culprit for the frequent shipwrecks. As both successful immigration and deadly attempts are explained by smuggling, questions about international relations, labor, access to asylum, immigration laws, and family reunification risk not being posed, let alone answered. And as Italian and often European public discourse routinely equates scafisti and smugglers to traffickers of coerced and desperate people, sovereign provisions of salvation are legitimated.

The Law of the Sea

The Christmas 1996 "phantom" shipwreck of the *F-174* off the southern Sicilian coast was forgotten and relegated to an official blend of presumption and concoction for four years. It was a journalistic investigation that made the *F-174*, sunk with its 283 people, to resurface in the Italian public awareness and political agenda. While the word of migrants had been taken with skepticism, pictures of the wreckage had the aura of incontestability. The search for the wreckage and the costly submarine pictures, in June 2001, were not commissioned by Italian or Maltese authorities, but by *La Repubblica* national newspaper, based on a local fisherman's report.[13] But why did it take four years for evidence of the shipwreck to emerge?

On January 2, 1997, Portopalo's fishermen were back at sea, following a few days of rest. Together with their usual catch they hauled shoes, shirts, and pants. For months they found in their nets direct evidence of a major shipwreck. One recalled: "We found dozens of them. They ended up in the nets, and we took them up on board with the fish. At the beginning it was whole corpses, then parts; finally white, clean bones."[14] Most fishermen became used to this. Those who initially vomited at the scene did not get upset any longer. Corpses were routinely tossed back into the sea, and the authorities never alerted.

But in January 2001, local fisherman Salvo Lupo realizes that his fishing nets are getting snagged on something. They are considerably torn, and contain a pair of jeans. Coins fall from the pockets, together with a plastic ID. He notes his own boat's position. It has to be the position of a wreck on the seabed, so he alerts local authorities. The latter do not deem the information relevant, so he decides to contact journalist Gian Maria Bellu of *La Repubblica*. Why, then, were these corpses routinely tossed back into the sea, and the authorities never alerted before Salvo Lupo took the initiative?

A few months prior to the *F-174* shipwreck, a fisherman had found another corpse, taken it on board, and brought it to the port and to the attention of local coast guard and police officers. Police questioning and a lengthy bureaucracy blocked use of the fishing boat and prevented its owner from sailing for weeks, causing the loss of workdays and consequent financial loss for a family whose only source of income was fishing. Another fisherman from Portopalo states it quite unequivocally: "When, toward the end of 1996, we noticed all those corpses, there was no need to reach any explicit agreement between us fishermen. We all knew that if we reported our findings, the whole fleet would be forced to stop. We just couldn't afford it."[15]

The fishermen's indifference, in this case, relates to corpses. But it also speaks to the behavior of potential good Samaritans, which is always to be located within social, legal, and political mechanisms.[16] In other words, legal norms and sanctions, institutional incentives and hurdles shape the intervention of fishermen and coastal populations, whether they consider hauling body parts or rescuing somebody in distress at sea.

The night of August 7, 2007, seven fishermen from the town of Teboulba, on the Tunisian coast opposite Lampedusa, are sailing on the *Mohamed El Hedi* and *Morthada*. Waters are choppy. They note a deflating dinghy in distress. Passengers include children and a pregnant woman. The fishermen broadcast an SOS, and then do what every sailor and shipmaster is expected to do at sea: help fellow seafarers. Rescuing people in distress at sea is the universal and unwritten "law of the sea." They take on board people sailing from Libya but originally from Sudan, Eritrea, Ethiopia, Morocco, Togo, and Ivory Coast.[17] The captains of the *Mohamed El Hedi* and *Morthada* intend to continue sailing toward Lampedusa, the closest safe port. Italian patrols soon reach them. A doctor summarily assesses that nobody on board requires immediate medical attention. The *Mohamed El Hedi* and *Morthada* are therefore ordered to take the migrants "back" to Tunisia, even if the vessels are sailing thirty miles off the coast of Lampedusa and ninety miles from Teboulba, Tunisia. Coast guard vessels try in vain to dissuade them from keeping their route toward the Italian island, including by sailing at close proximity to the fishing boats.[18] Upon arrival at Lampedusa, two children, their mother, and a nine-months-pregnant woman are flown to urgent care in Palermo, Sicily.[19] The Tunisian fishermen are arrested.

The Tunisian captains followed the unwritten law of the sea. But the duty to rescue any fellow seafarer in distress is also the written, codified law of the sea, both nationally and internationally. First, a fundamental notion of Italian law is *omissione di soccorso* (failure to rescue). As clearly phrased by Rudzinski (1966:91–93), "in contrast to Anglo-Saxon law, which discourages interference in another person's affairs even for the purpose of saving him from imminent danger of death," several European countries have "specific provisions in their criminal codes stipulating a duty to rescue." In one example: in the United States, charges of abandoning the place of an accident in which one is involved stem from "the positive act of fleeing, not for an omission"; in Italy they stem from *omissione di soccorso*, according to Penal Code Article 593. At the international level, the unwritten law of the sea is essentially accepted and codified as binding, and it crucially includes the 1974 International Convention for the Safety of Life at Sea and the 1982 UN Convention on the Law of the Sea, which oblige all shipmasters to swiftly provide assistance to persons in distress if they are made aware of the need and are in a position to provide help. Additionally, the International Convention on Maritime Search and Rescue (SAR), often referred to as the "Hamburg 1979 Convention," establishes that states have an obligation to ensure effective communication and coordination of rescue operations in designated areas for which they are responsible, called "SAR areas." Quite importantly, international maritime law leaves it to shipmasters to assess where the closest "place of safety" to take rescued persons is.

Indeed, the seven Tunisian fishermen were acquitted: the court of Agrigento, Sicily, did not find them guilty of aiding and abetting illegal immigration.[20] But this cost them and their Tunisian employer a month of detention, the dishonor of being represented in the media as human traffickers, the confiscation and disrepair of the boats, the Tunisian authorities' confiscation of their fishing permits, enormous financial loss, and considerable psychological stress. And yet the two captains, Abdelbaset Zenzeri and Lotfi Nouira, would do it again, they say.[21] Indeed, there is no worse offense for fishermen everywhere—in Sfax, Teboulba, and Monastir (Tunisia) as in Lampedusa and Otranto—than for it to be hinted or implied that they have failed to rescue or assist people in distress at sea.

Even if there are no known cases of Italian fishermen who have actually been found guilty of aiding and abetting illegal immigration after rescuing migrants, there have been cases of fishing boats that have been inspected and impounded and workdays that have been missed. The experience of the seven Tunisian colleagues, widely known from Tunisia to Sicily, serves as a warning of possible legal trouble. Moreover, rescue operations at sea are inherently hazardous, given the possibility of collisions and capsizing;

and they carry the risk of income loss and of one's home being searched by the police. Let us also consider the difficult economic context of the fishing industry. In Lampedusa, in particular, gasoline is 50 percent more expensive than in Sicily proper. Fishermen routinely complain about the paucity of fish.[22] These multifaceted concerns might help explain how several migrant accounts speak of boats in distress and of nearby fishing boats failing to assist them. They might also explain why fishermen toss back human remains without alerting the authorities. The fishermen's indifference is warranted by mundane and legal concerns, and it enables sovereign claims to the monopoly of salvation.

Documenting Death: Open-Source Intelligence

The *Kater i Radës* and *F-174* shipwrecks indicate that national and international institutions, humanitarian actors, and concerned citizenry have long been cognizant of the growing death toll at sea. In 2002 Italian minister of the interior Antonio Pisanu (2002–6) was already publicly declaring: "It is reasonable to speculate that many [migrants] remain missing at sea, without leaving any sign of their shipwreck in international waters. . . . For each rickety boat that makes it to our coasts, how many have drowned?"[23] In 2004, he stated that "in the last few years" to his knowledge 1,167 "clandestine immigrants" had drowned in Italian territorial and "nearby" waters.[24]

The vast majority die by drowning and suffocation in the Mediterranean. Others die in rivers, such as the Meriç/Evros between Turkey and Greece; of asphyxia in trucks or cargo containers; of hypothermia in boats or on planes; in minefields, including at the Greek border with Turkey.[25] These are the immediate causes of death for people trying to reach the EU without authorization. The International Centre for Migration Policy Development, a European policy-oriented research center with UN observer status, estimated that in the decade 1993–2003, at least 10,000 persons died in the Mediterranean trying to reach Europe.[26] In 2010, UNITED for Intercultural Action, a network of 560 European NGOs, listed and documented (since 1993) a total of 13,824 "refugee [i.e., migrant] deaths through Fortress Europe."[27] *Fortress Europe* is also the name of a blog edited by journalist Gabriele Del Grande, who from 1988 to October 11, 2013, collected every piece of information related to migrant deaths from Euro-Mediterranean news sources. He compiled a list of 19,372 documented deaths in that time span. The year of the Arab Uprisings and of the war in Libya, 2011, was "the deadliest year on record," with 2,352 deaths.[28] According to the UNHCR, 2014 became yet another "deadliest year on record," with 2,500 people who had died or gone missing in the Mediterranean between January and the end of August.[29] The organization produces its figures by compiling accounts of survivors, family members, and media reports. According to the IOM, in the first ten months of 2014, at least 3,072 people died or went missing in the Mediterranean.[30] At the end of January 2014, IOM's Rome-based office also reported that "over 20,000 people have died in the past twenty years trying to reach the Italian coast."[31]

A consortium of twelve journalists from six countries has recently taken up the challenge of cross-checking and systematically assembling such data. Beginning their activities in August 2013, this "Migrants' Files" team drew on data collected by UNITED for Intercultural Action, on data in Del Grande's database, and on the automated surveillance of news media carried out by PULS at the University of Helsinki.[32] The Migrants' Files approach is essentially one of "open-source intelligence," where real-time global news on asylum seekers, migration, smuggling, and trafficking in and around Europe are monitored and analyzed. The team also collects data from other publicly available sources, including governmental publications, white papers, and conference reports. These efforts require extensive data cleaning and fact-checking. And while some of this can be accomplished by algorithms, sixteen students from the Laboratory of Data Journalism at the University of Bologna, Italy, notably contribute to the enterprise. They pay attention to name, age, gender, and nationality of casualties. Every incident is recorded with its date, latitude, longitude, number of dead and missing, and the immediate cause. When duplicates are detected, they are manually removed, one at a time. The students review and double-check other sources of intelligence, and possibly testimonies, before registering an incident in the database. "Accuracy is laborious," say these journalists.[33] Nevertheless, some events and individual deaths cannot be documented, and the "true numbers of dead are doubtless higher than recorded." The journalists' consortium has created what they believe to be "the most comprehensive survey of European migration fatalities available today." An interactive Euro-Mediterranean map, including all the available information on each deadly event, is available online.[34] A Creative Commons license allows anyone to borrow and use the online data set. Between 2000 and the end of

August 2014, Migrants' Files document at least 25,000 deaths of people headed to Europe, including missing persons.

Rescuing Lives, Deporting Persons: Safe Ports and Human Rights

Italian, Maltese, Greek, and Spanish citizens and policymakers, among others, have been watching the Mediterranean chronicle of death from their living room, if not from the veranda of their coastal homes. For two decades we—citizens, consumers, policymakers, rescue workers, fishermen, navy sailors and armed forces personnel—have reconciled ourselves with the seemingly distant evidence of migrant deaths.[35] How?

I have already indicated that legal and mundane concerns might prevent bystanders from more direct involvement. I have also indicated that the political grammar of unseaworthy carrette del mare and of unscrupulous scafisti, together with the very real reiteration of migrant death, might nourish a naturalized sense of inevitability to the loss of life at sea. In the rest of this chapter I intend to ask two larger and interrelated questions: whither human rights, then, for migrants? And is there a sovereign and liberal-democratic rationalization for these deaths, especially at a juncture such as this otherwise characterized by pervasive moralizing?

On Saturday November 21, 2009, the Italian news agency ANSA circulates the story of a rubber dinghy in distress on the high seas, in international waters within the Maltese SAR area of responsibility. Its occupants, about eighty people, have managed to launch their distress call via a satellite phone. They have contacted people in Italy and Malta. They have declared their Eritrean and Somali nationality. Accordingly, most probably they would meet "the conditions to apply for asylum," in the wording of the news item.[36] Reporting on the same story, on November 22, 2009, *Times of Malta* writes that "Libyan rescue services have rescued around 80 illegal immigrants who were in distress on the high seas, just 60 miles from Lampedusa." Let us examine this from another vantage point. A Libyan patrol reaches the boat in distress, some 120 miles north of the Libyan coast and 60 miles south of Lampedusa. Italian rescue authorities in Sicily, maintaining contact with the Armed Forces of Malta's Rescue Coordination Centre, coordinate the Libyan operation. Eritrean and Somali migrants are brought back to Tripoli and arrested.[37]

Was this an operation of rescue, then, or a pushback operation? *It was both*. It stands as paradigmatic of sovereignty's humanitarian-policing nexus, showing it in its materiality, rather than merely as a legitimizing discourse. Lives were rescued, but persons were deported.

This could have worked otherwise. First, maritime law, as well as custom, stipulates that people rescued at sea must be taken to the nearest safe port, which in this case would have been Lampedusa. Second, a "safe port," when related to migrants and in particular refugees, entails additional qualifications, which arguably cannot be met in Libya. Clarifying what makes a port "safe" illuminates what is at stake in competing definitions of human rights. And clarifying what is at stake in competing definitions of human rights illuminates sovereign legitimations.

As the UNHCR understands it, a safe port implies that asylum applications can be lodged. It is a place where the dignity and human rights of those rescued are safeguarded, without regard to citizenship and legal status. This entails immediate personal safety, including protection from torture and cruel and degrading treatment and punishment, but also the possibility of seeking international protection and the guarantee of non-refoulement. The principle of nonrefoulement, enshrined in the 1951 and 1967 Convention and Protocol Relating to the Status of Refugees (Article 33.1), prevails over any bilateral or multilateral extradition agreement. It is customarily understood as prohibiting states from returning a refugee or asylum seeker to territories where there is a risk that his or her "life or freedom would be threatened on account of race, religion, nationality, membership of a particular social group, or political opinion."

In a liberal democracy, then, any attempt to deter or push back refugees to a port that is not "safe" is either illogical or dishonest. It would be logical only if policymakers or border guards were guided by the a priori belief in the "bogus," nongenuine nature of refugees' vulnerable condition. It would be honest (not necessarily right) only if policymakers and border guards had a very limited understanding of human rights. And it is this second possibility that I need to explore here, for simplistic understandings of human rights are extremely consequential, and detrimental to their actual implementation.

Soysal, in a pioneering way, argues that "national citizenship is losing ground to a more universal model of membership, anchored in deterritorialized notions of persons' rights" (1994:3). This author acknowledges that "the exercise of universalistic rights is tied to specific states and their institutions" (157), but she also argues that what were previously defined as national rights become entitlements legitimized "on the basis of personhood." Postnational citizenship, Soysal writes, "confers upon every person the right and duty of participation in the authority structures and public life of a polity, regardless of their historical and cultural ties to that community" (3). Conversely, let us note that even for EU citizens there is no legal and political membership in the EU detached from *national* membership: "European citizenship is not decoupled from but premised on a person's nationality. Only the nationals of [EU] member states are Euro-citizens" (Joppke 1998:30).[38] Moreover, it appears to be the case that the "territorial state" has a "basic and distinctive interest in being able to control the flows of persons across its borders—in being able to compel, induce, discourage, and forbid the entry or exit of *particular categories* of persons" (Brubaker 1992:25; my emphasis). And let us note that the modern state "does not have the right, although it does have the capacity, to compel the exit or prevent the entry of *its own citizens*" (Brubaker 1992:180; my emphasis). Dembour writes that "although the ideology of human rights does away with the concept of the state to concentrate on the equal value of all human beings, its practice relies on the way in which individuals are classified *in relation to a state*" (1996:29; original emphasis).

Thinking of refugees, and expanding the discussion beyond state-centered and identitarian membership and belonging, we still have to acknowledge that "having another place to go to, to appeal when you lose in one venue" presupposes "a belonging whose fragility those very same rights are supposed to protect us against," as Honig puts it (2009:117). Honig explains: "In the international arena no less than in the national, rights still presuppose *belonging*, now not only to states but . . . also *to a legal, bureaucratic and administrative order* or to the EU" (117; my emphasis). New forms of protection such as those afforded through the European Court of Human Rights (see *Hirsi Jamaa and Others v. Italy*, Chapter 2) do indeed aspire to protect everyone *within the jurisdiction* of the forty-seven states of the Council of Europe, crucially including those less able to see their human rights implemented, such as unauthorized migrants and refugees. Still, the general norm is that the European Court proceeds with a case only after domestic remedies have been exhausted, in other words only after an individual has employed, without success, all remedies available under domestic law.

It must be acknowledged that any simplistic dichotomy between citizens and noncitizens fails to highlight the difference in legal rights and protections enjoyed by different kinds of noncitizens, modulated by residency, race, gender, and class (Carens 2013:96).[39] And we may legitimately desire that the legal rights people enjoy "have little or nothing to do with their possession of citizenship in their country of origin" and "everything to do with the norms and practices of *the legal system in which they find themselves*" (93; my emphasis). But whether this is an accomplished fact or an admirable quest remains to be researched (and fought for) empirically in specific situations, and for different categories of people.

In summary: based on my ethnographic experience and on legal-political considerations, I do not see evidence that discounts Arendt's call for the right to have rights (1958 [1951]).[40] This is as relevant today as it was after World War II, even if we need to acknowledge that noncitizens are not a homogenous group; that states are not the only actors capable of implementing the right to have rights or willing to do so; that post–World War II institutions might offer legal and bureaucratic venues where the right to have rights can be recognized and implemented in the first place; and that states and other interested parties, from nongovernmental organizations to EU institutions, might manipulate the "Human Rights regime" (Hopgood 2013) to their own advantage, in neo-Westphalian fashion.

And so the question remains: who, in actuality, protects the human rights—to life, to physical integrity, to relational dignity—of those who fall through the expansive cracks between legal systems, spheres of jurisdiction, and sociopolitical and bureaucratic membership? Having built situational gates around those cracks, instead of safe and protected exit routes, sovereign actors also claim their role as saviors for those who, against all odds, manage to climb out. They do so by deploying a conveniently narrow understanding of what human rights, and a safe port, mean and entail.

Impossible Sovereignty: Governing with the Saved

The Italian police headquarters of the Centro Nazionale di Coordinamento per l'Immigrazione (National Immigration Coordination Center) was inaugurated on February 17, 2012. It is from this facility in Rome that all Italian

armed and police forces are coordinated in their operations against unauthorized migration. The facility is one of the first of its kind in the EU. It is
part of the larger Eurosur (Chapter 5) network of intelligence, statistical
elaboration, and situational awareness at the EU's external borders. Members of the government, the national chief of police, the head of Europol
(the EU criminal intelligence agency), and IOM's leading coordinator for
the Mediterranean were also present, marking the significance of the new
facility. Italian minister of the interior Annamaria Cancellieri (2011–13)
solemnly declared that "to fight the phenomenon of clandestine immigration is a civilizational duty, against the merchants of human life, people
who smuggle hope and get rich in a despicable way."[41] Frontex's director
was also there.

Finnish Colonel Ilkka Laitinen has been Frontex's executive director for
a decade, since the inception of the organization in 2004. In recent years,
Frontex has produced a variety of news kits, online materials, interviews,
and reports that, responding to humanitarian concerns, seek to convey its
practices as transparent and as respectful of human rights. In one of such
public statements, Colonel Laitinen admits being particularly proud of the
successes of Operation Hera. Hera is a multiyear operation essentially
aimed at preventing migrant arrivals to the Canary Islands, the Spanish
archipelago in the Atlantic off the northwest coast of Africa. Hera comprises
several components, from patrolling off the African coast to interviews with
immigrants upon arrival at the islands.[42] In the wording of Frontex's official
website, during 2012 the operation's aim was to improve "cooperation with
Senegalese and Mauritanian authorities in order to combat illegal immigration from North Africa to the Canary Islands."[43] In 2008, with a budget of
more than 10 million euros, the objectives were: "To carry out an exhaustive aero-maritime surveillance in the waters close to Mauritania and Senegal in order to reinforce the early detection of immigrants by sea. To involve
more closely the SAR Canary Islands Area Coordinator in the Joint Operation for those aspects concerning the information gathering, identification
of the migrant traffickers and any other relevant aspects [in] regard [to]
the objectives of this Joint Operation. To identify facilitators that transport
migrants from Africa to Europe. To detect as early as possible any new
trends being used by trafficking organizations."[44] In Colonel Laitinen's
account, "Operation Hera stands out. By implementing preventive measures off the West African coast, Hera has almost completely stemmed the
flow of irregular migration to the Canary Islands via this particularly

hazardous route. As a result, hundreds if not thousands of lives have been saved."[45] The statement provides a glimpse of the preemptive logic emerging in EU and member states' approaches to migration. And it stands out as paradigmatic of the conflation, in rhetoric and to a degree in the very practice of border enforcement as currently implemented, of salvation through a flexible, offshore, outsourced sovereignty.

Lieutenant Antonio Morana is Lampedusa's coast guard commander.[46] He is a relatively young officer, wearing the typical white uniform. He greets me expressing admiration for the basketball teams from Notre Dame, where I teach. As you enter the coast guard building, the Latin motto is prominently displayed, frescoed on the left side of the hall: *In Asperitate Maris Pro Humanitate* (in the adversity of the sea, for humanity). The captain's office overlooks the small port and the coast guard's four search-and-rescue boats and three patrol vessels. The first thing he emphasizes is that the coast guard has nothing to do with migrant interception at sea. He ascribes these tasks to the finance guard "and others." Finance guard vessels do routinely rescue migrants, but as part of their patrolling activities close to the coast. Morana says that the mission of the coast guard, in the domain of maritime migration and navigation more broadly, is quite simply to save people. "People are people," without any other qualification needed, he says. They are to be saved at the cost of one's life and with no preliminary consideration for their legal status. Marking further distance from the armed forces (coast guard vessels normally do not carry weapons on board), he asserts that only the coast guard has the technical capability of sailing in extreme weather conditions. And he emphasizes that "what originated as a job becomes a mission: you set sail to save others' lives; it's about emotions, values, human proximity, and a sense of usefulness in helping and saving lives."

The caring, "missionary" concern expressed by Colonel Laitinen and Lieutenant Morana is to be understood differently. Laitinen is deploying humanitarianism and salvation to legitimize the bilateral agreements and offshore border enforcement implemented by Frontex. Morana is characterizing the activities of the coast guard as humanitarian precisely to mark a difference in relation to the colleagues and "competitors" of the finance guard and Frontex. We have to note, though, that both Frontex's and the coast guard's activities, together with Mare Nostrum and Eurosur, are translated and annexed into larger governmental discourses of salvation through sovereignty. Such discourses claim the salvation of migrants' physical and moral wellness, for example by providing food and shelter in holding centers; by preventing trafficking and drowning through the preemption of emigration; and by preventing a life of vagrancy and prostitution through detention and repatriation. The costly national and EU project of human mobility regulation is legitimized not only as protection from external threats but also as a humanitarian endeavor. The borders of liberal democracy function also as thresholds of salvation, and geopolitical sovereignty as moral sovereignty.

The border is increasingly understood as a spectacle. Something, we are etymologically reminded, akin to a show which we look at. It is a theater of operations, in the military and literal sense.[47] But rather than as passive spectators we participate in it as an interactive public and with daily social relationships.[48] As Donnan and Wilson put it, "all organizations of power utilize rituals to bind people together, to the hierarchy, and to others in the past and the future" (1999:66). The border as a theater, as a ritual, as a symbol, and as the primary locus of the spectacle enacted by national and supranational authorities is a main constituent of an aesthetic of sovereignty and immigration regulation that is extremely complicated. What I want to note here is that what happens at the border should be understood both in its military and humanitarian facets, as a *single* spectacle. In the Mediterranean, and in mainland Italy, for more than two decades it has included batons and stretchers, guns and surgical masks, military trucks and ambulances, gates and hospitality, fences and food, armed forces' uniforms and health workers' uniforms, the coast guard and the finance guard, salaried bureaucrats and unpaid volunteers, smugglers and victims, refugees and trespassers.

There is one spectacle, then, but it is understood differently by different publics. Think perhaps of light that passes through a kaleidoscope, refracted and reflected differently based on angle, movement, weather conditions, illumination, time of day, and the perception of the viewer. The sovereign spectacle of surveillance, policing, and deterrence is also the sovereign spectacle of rescue and secular salvation. This sovereign military-humanitarian enterprise speaks differently to different political constituencies, to smugglers, to migrants, to right-wing and left-wing government coalition members, to the military-surveillance industry, to segments of the state bureaucracy, and to humanitarian critics, with many variations within each group. The Mare Nostrum 2013–14 operation, following two major shipwrecks (Chapter 5), is conspicuously notable because of its methodical search-and-rescue effort, the size and number of aero-naval means deployed, the number of people it has brought into Italy, its visibility in southern Italian ports and European media. But it is a "military-humanitarian" operation, as intended by the Italian government. To Italian citizens it was presented as a response to the ongoing "humanitarian emergency," as strengthening "the existing apparatus of immigration influxes control," as "bringing to justice those who profit from illegal trafficking with migrants,"[49] and as having a "deterrent effect" on "merchants of death."[50] Mare Nostrum is not an exception to sovereignty, but a particular, temporally defined exemplar of the humanitarian facet of military-humanitarian sovereignty.

Many among the governors and citizens of liberal democracies believe—I have to adopt this working hypothesis—that individuals in distress ought to be rescued, simply because they are human beings, even if outside the confines of territorial waters and national membership. The Libyan (and Egyptian) maritime patrols that bring back to their ports, detain, and possibly deport migrants do just that, they *save lives* also on behalf of the Italian and EU polity. In this logic, the EU, its member states, and their non-EU partners are indeed doing much to safeguard human rights. Further, it would be in the best interest of migrants' human rights not to risk their lives to reach the EU in the first place. It is precisely such a self-serving and limited understanding of human rights and safe ports that lends authority and credibility to the EU border apparatus not only as it rescues lives at sea but also in its restrictive and preemptive aspirations. Crimes of peace bank on such limited understanding of human rights. The administration of rights is outsourced or suspended, and justice preempted. Conversely, if taken seriously both a safe port and human rights imply and entail much more than rescue and the provision of food, shelter, and personal safety. Both a safe port and human rights entail, at the very least, the promise and the legal, bureaucratic, and political capability for implementing civil and political rights.

Impossible Sovereignty: Governing with the Drowned

When a liberal-democratic state or supranational entity lets someone die, or leaves someone to die, it does so in the name and on behalf of a territory, population, or value to be protected. The creation of the EU as an "area

Figure 5. Altare della Patria (Altar of the Fatherland), Rome. Photo: Maurizio Albahari.

of freedom, security, and justice" with relatively free internal mobility is inextricably related to the management of migration and to the perceived need to fight unauthorized migration as a criminal and threatening phenomenon. The object of surveillance is not territory but the bodies of migrants and would-be migrants, their distribution in space, their management, the optimization of their usability and productivity as talent or labor, and their inscription in a regime of visibility and regulation. Symbolically and materially, borders and their maintenance become indispensable to the state or supranational entity. Borders are a prerogative and a form of sovereignty, but also its means. They help reinforce sovereignty, as something else from society and even the nation (Mitchell 1991), detached but not extraneous or separate. The death of migrants serves as a ritualized spectacle through which the state or supranational entity reinforces its power also over its own citizen subjects.[51]

State sovereignty's claim to the monopoly on the lawful use of violence noted by Weber (1948) also consists of the right to kill or to leave to die certain categories of people without the actual commission of homicide, to adapt Agamben's concepts (1998). But here the issue is not necessarily a literal one or a judicial one. And it is not metaphorical, or symbolic. It is an empirical and political question. Does *each* new death in the Mediterranean interrogate current immigration policies and whether (or for whom) they are working? Does it interrogate the polity regarding the social relationships of the person who was left to die? Does it interrogate the polity regarding its members' own hierarchical relationships to the drowned migrants, to their places of origin, their loved ones, and their histories? With Agamben, we might think about the many ways in which people—persons who are put in the position of having to cross the Mediterranean, and at its longest stretches—are categorized as excluded from the group of those who ought not to be left to die. At the same time, it is fundamental to note that such categorization does not entail their expulsion from humanity, from a sovereign point of view. In other words, they still need to be saved, and therefore they need sovereign saviors.

This is crucial. For while *any* kind of sovereignty ascribes to itself the right and power "to make live and let die," as Foucault (2003 [1997]:241) would put it, it is the capability, power, and authority to foster life, to "make live," that legitimizes liberal democracies, including the EU and member states as they try to govern migration. Maritime and would-be migrants are subject to both the sovereign power that leaves them to die and the sovereign power that makes them live—or better, that rescues their lives. Sovereign humanitarianism, which renders migrants as victims of trafficking and speechless bodies awaiting salvation, is functional to the incontestability of sovereign policies of immigration regulation, even when these turn lethal.

Death, a prerogative of sovereignty, is one of the instruments by which liberal democratic society is purportedly defended, and its life and common good fostered. Military techniques, surveillance, and death are brought "back home," in the coastal Mediterranean and in the public sphere, to the normality of civilian, everyday life. While the death of migrants is not hidden, it is sometimes traceless, white noise to quiet subsistence. A muted crime of peace. But migrant death is also a politically productive crime of peace, in the sense of its co-optation into the indispensability of sovereignty to the common good. Paradoxically, this sovereign ideology of the common good is inclusionary—it includes migrants, who need to be freed from the grip of "human traffickers" and of "slavery," by deterrence and rescue.[52]

State and EU power and legitimacy are unstable projects. States are not the only organizations that can "dispense violence as well as justice with impunity" (Hansen and Stepputat 2005:36). They compete with other forms and authorities of power, including Mafia-like criminal organizations. In this sense, the state and the EU face a paradoxical dilemma: on the one hand they have to ensure the visibility of their sovereign legitimacy, including through the claimed monopoly on violence. On the other hand, they must abide by their own universalist proclamations, including on humanitarianism as an absolute and guiding value.[53] Thus, the state claims a monopoly not only on violence but also on migrants' rescue at sea and on their secular salvation.

Border humanitarianism nourishes the grandiose sovereign project of human mobility regulation. Border humanitarianism generates calls for more sovereignty rather than sovereignty's radical and emancipatory critique. The vast majority of humanitarian and international organizations, including nongovernmental ones, routinely call on "Europe" and its member states to "do more" to prevent further loss of life at sea—rarely to do less or to stop doing what they are doing (bilateral agreements, externalization, militarization of straits, carrier sanctions, unrealistic quotas, and making asylum inaccessible). These organizations demand more funds for the Triton Frontex operation, so that more lives can be rescued; more search-and-rescue vessels and manpower; more funds for the people brought to Italian, Greek, or Maltese safety; more legal channels for economic and forced migrants. What they are obtaining is the promise of more military-humanitarian sovereignty. EU and national officials do often reply by deploying the power of numbers—the redemptive number of the lives saved at sea; the escalating figures of new investments in surveillance technology instrumental to "saving lives"; the funds allotted to transit countries, contingent on the implementation of "human rights" for the migrants they readmit, detain, and deport.

Sovereign salvation is expected to solve the entrenched contradictions of "impossible sovereignty"[54] that keep reemerging. Such impossible sovereignty demands an excruciating toll. It explains the detention abuses, the tragedies, the illegalities, and the costs it manufactures by demanding more of itself and for itself, more of what has already proven inadequate and contradictory: externalization and accountability; maritime containment and salvation; hospitality and confinement; razor-wire fences and rights; democracy, inequality, and state violence.

The overarching policy aspiration is that eventually technology and intelligence will prevent undesired and unauthorized arrivals. As unauthorized travelers do arrive, their disquieting presence intersects with proclamations on human rights and the rule of law, and with the exercise of preemptive power and knowledge.

Chapter 4

Sovereignty as Preemption:
Undocumented States

Travelers into Immigrants: Life Behind Bars

It is an unusually bright, crisp January day in Otranto, the small tourist and fishing town at the easternmost promontory of southern Italy, in the Apulia region. When I arrive at the national Center for the Identification of Asylum Seekers for my first day as a volunteer,[1] I am tensely unsure about what to expect, as these facilities are off-limits to journalists, researchers, and even parliamentarians. In the neon-lit hall I notice watercolor pictures of Kurdistan, a legacy of the many Kurdish persons transited here, and a colorful "Welcome! Benvenuti! Bienvenidos!" handwritten poster. Checkered paper tablecloths adorn the patio-style plastic tables. Six young men are playing poker, others foosball, and a few are sitting on flimsy chairs in front of a television tuned to an Arabic cable channel. About ten soldiers of the finance guard,[2] easily recognizable by their gray fatigues, ensure "order and security," as an agent puts it. Through the large window you can see the pine trees, the ten-foot concrete wall, and the guarded gate I have just been let through.[3]

The center's permanent personnel—the *avvocato* (lawyer), the psychologist, and the interpreter—are in their mid-thirties. They welcome me into their shared office: a small room with a desk, a discolored personal computer, and a closet with personal hygiene items for guests. Thick folders fill the room. Everybody sounds enthusiastic about working in the center. Lucio, the lawyer, emphatically explains that this is not a detention center and that there is no judicial or police order requiring the detention of asylum seekers. It is "just" that "while they present their asylum claim, the state requires them to be traceable at the center." I restate that I am looking forward to assisting guests and personnel while observing the social dynamics at play.

Holding centers like this in Otranto, which originated in the 1990s as an "emergency" and temporary response to maritime migration, are structural nodes in the architecture of the national and EU network of migrant-processing facilities. But some informants have advised me not to "waste my time" at this specific facility in Otranto. It is not a detention facility, they point out, but merely a center for the identification of asylum seekers.[4] What these local informants suggest is that nothing extraordinary is really going on besides routine bureaucratic practices. Precisely: I intend to scrutinize the ordinary exercise of these practices and of the legal power informing them. What do they accomplish, in addition to their own bureaucratic reproduction? Are guests detained or not? How is information about them collected?

This facility was institutionalized in 1999 as a "humanitarian response" to the large number of people arriving via the strait at the coastal areas north and south of Otranto. It replaced the excruciatingly warm and excruciatingly cold metal trailers in the harbor, and a campsite. In 2002 the center—run by the local municipality in cooperation with the Misericordia Catholic lay brotherhood—became a state-regulated and state-financed institution. Its official legal function is to "identify" and host, for up to two months, non-EU would-be asylum seekers. During this time the police verify guests' names, criminal backgrounds, nationalities, and foreign ports of departure and transit by collecting photos and fingerprints and then using transnational databases. Police officers interview guests, compile their asylum applications, and grant temporary permits for residence in Italy,[5] which allow them to leave the center. The center is essential to carrying out EU migration policy, especially to the enforcement of the controversial Dublin Regulation: as lawyer Lucio tells me, most of the guests I will meet have in fact been "sent back" to Italy by countries such as Germany and Sweden, where often they had started a family and found a rewarding job. The reason for such deportations is that Italy, as the country where they first entered the EU (often disembarking on these Apulian beaches) is the country responsible for accepting and examining their asylum applications. In addition, the police occasionally use the center, at their discretion, as a last resort for "sheltering" (and keeping in custody) non-EU unauthorized migrants until "expulsion" from Italy can be implemented. During my presence there, guests in Otranto's de facto multifunctional center included people who intended to apply for asylum, asylum seekers who had been returned to Italy from northern Europe, stowaways who arrived on Greek ferries, and people who were awaiting repatriation or an expulsion decree (and who in theory should not be here, but in a center for identification and expulsion or CIE). Countries of origin included Afghanistan, Belarus, Brazil, China, Iran, Iraq, Moldova, Palestine, Romania, Serbia, Somalia, Tunisia, Turkey, and the Ukraine.

As I enter the center early Friday morning, January 14, 2005, there is a new group of about thirty guests in the hall. Luigi, a finance guard soldier, confides they might be *Zingari* from eastern Europe ("Gypsies," i.e., Romany). Quite obviously they are not understanding the center's interpreter, who is trying to communicate in English, German, French, and Spanish. It is my turn to try. In light of what Luigi said, I ask them in Serbian—my third language—where they are from. We manage to understand each other: they are from Bulgaria.[6] They gather around me while the interpreter hastily leaves. Women are crying, asking when *we* will let them go, for they are "just tourists." Some of them have already been given socks and slippers, as guests are not allowed to wear shoes in the center. Others ask me for basic personal hygiene items. Unexpectedly, I become the unofficial and only mediator between the staff and soldiers and these Bulgarian guests. The "technical director" of the center, whom I am told is very rarely here, abruptly summons me into the office and says that until my arrival everything had been working just fine, and that I am putting the staff's unity at risk. Moreover, the staff thinks that these new arrivals are just being intransigent: they could find "ways to communicate" if they wanted to. I am warned not to believe everything they say, as it is not even certain that they are Bulgarian nationals; this claim, I am told, will need to be verified.

The new guests are unapologetically being deprived of the relevance and credibility of their speech.[7] I should not even listen to them. My translation into Serbian, on the other hand, is thought of as a necessary tool of "order and security," or the moral and practical governance of the center. Thus, one of the first statements I am asked to translate is intended to clarify to the new guests that they "are now in Italy, and Italian law must be respected. Certain procedures need to be followed, no matter what [they] have to say."

Tundjel is wearing blue jeans and a denim jacket, and seems a few years younger than me, in his mid-twenties. Next to him, Bilgin says they left the city of Ruse in northeastern Bulgaria on January 6, for a tourist trip to Italy during the national (Orthodox) holiday season. They traveled by their own rented minibus through Romania, Hungary, and Austria and finally throughout Italy, from north to south. In Brindisi, about thirty miles north of Otranto, they embarked on a ferry to Greece, on their way home to Ruse. However in Greece, some thirty miles east of the port town of Igoumenitsa, a highway patrol stopped them. Bilgin shows me a purple bruise on his leg, saying it was from a policeman's baton. The Greek police escorted the group to a ferry and sent them back to Brindisi. They were subsequently brought here to the Otranto center by the Brindisi police.

I cannot think of any reason, other than perhaps expired visa stamps for someone in the group, for their expulsion from Greece and their arrest by the Italian police. But Bilgin reminds me that as Bulgarian citizens they may enter and stay in the EU as tourists for up to three months without the need for a visa. Tundjel repeats that they "are not criminals or terrorists, but tourists from another European country." I optimistically suspect that both the Greek and Italian police have made a mistake, perhaps due to the chronic scarcity of translators. Lucio, the center's lawyer, might be the only person able to clarify the situation. Can he just persuade Brindisi's police, who are holding the guests' passports and vehicle, to reconsider the arrest and release them immediately? However, it's already Friday afternoon; he is on holiday and will not return for another four days.

The weekend has gone by. There seems to be no mistake. Lucio, finally back from his shortened vacation, explains that "the Bulgarians" have been sent back from Greece because they failed to present adequate evidence of financial support there. Still, why these travelers would need any evidence of financial support in the first place remains unanswered, since they said they were just transiting through Greece on their way back to Bulgaria.

Bulgarian tourists have not needed a visa for the Schengen area, which includes Greece and Italy, since 2001, just as Bilgin told me. But border officers of Schengen countries are entitled to discretionally request evidence of financial support. Furthermore, the lawyer says they "will have to exit the EU from where they entered it—Austria,"[8] and that they will have to stay at the center while the Italian Ministry of the Interior "contacts Austria" to ensure authorization for their transit there.

It is already the third day of their detention. Disappointed and angry, they skip breakfast. They explain to me that at the Brindisi police station a Russian interpreter told them—in Russian—they would have to stay here for two days. But Lucio, perhaps on the basis of prior experiences, tells me that "these kinds of procedures develop nearly automatically, and once they start there is a whole machinery that has to conclude its cycle, despite the actual situation of the people involved." As I picture this anonymous, automated, and unstoppable bureaucratic machinery, the holding facility's prior function comes to mind; prior to its 1999 renovation, this was Otranto's municipal meat-processing plant.

The Bulgarian guests have been skipping all meals for two days now, bodily expressing their frustration and actively seeking recognition for the injustice they perceive. Giuseppina, one of the psychologists, takes pains to let them appreciate, through my translation, that the staff here "has nothing to do with the police," and that their job is simply to provide food and shelter. The guests, however, have made it evident that they do not want their survival to be a matter of charity or pity, but of right.[9] They are referring not only to the continuation of their journey, but also to the right to know what their rights are in the midst of this ambiguous situation.

According to the local police regulations, no guest may leave the center—not even to go to the local post office—without a two- to three-day advance request and police escort. Would-be asylum seekers may leave without notice "if they so desire," but this is a pricey freedom. They are told, either as a threat based on mistaken belief or as an outright lie, that they would lose the right to claim asylum in Italy and the EU. The Bulgarian guests, on the other hand, would be "forcibly brought back to the center and possibly prosecuted." Neither the lawyer nor the finance guard soldiers say on what grounds. Through my translation, these guests have effectively explained to Lucio and the soldiers that they do not intend to apply for asylum, and are just looking forward to returning to their country, their children, and their work. Days go by. The only direct assistance I can offer is to run their errands, as I also do for other guests: buying cigarettes, sending and receiving money to and from their families at the local Western Union, and printing out reading materials in their native languages.

Early on the morning of January 19, it's chilly and the situation is very tense. All the Bulgarian detainees have carried their baggage to the hall and are standing there, asserting they "are leaving, with or without permission," which they ask me to translate to the guards. About fifteen soldiers and additional police patrols guard the exit, their batons in hand. I tell Tundjel that the policemen could possibly press criminal charges against them if they attempt to exit, and that they are clearly going to use force. As I stand between the two groups, trying to prevent physical confrontation, I am hesitantly relieved when people give up and go back to their dormitory. By now it's clear that they are detainees, not guests.

A bit shaken, I walk a few yards down the corridor, stopping in front of the large map of Italy to chat with other detainees I have come to know. Viktor, a Ukrainian carpenter, shows me the town in the Calabria region where he lives with his wife and child. He says he is "waiting" here for his residence permit. The map is a reminder of the legal and geopolitical location of this center within state and EU migration regulation. In this sense, the map functions like the dogmatic statement I am often asked to translate not only by Lucio but also by the finance guard soldiers, and by police officers: "We are in Italy, and therefore you [guests] must respect the Italian law." Trying to prevent further tension, the lawyer has phoned the police in Brindisi and tells us all that they should be allowed to leave in a couple of days, on January 21—that is, not after forty-eight hours, but after a full week of detention.

Don Ciro is a Catholic priest and the director of the only NGO allowed to send volunteers, that is, external personnel, to the center. It was he who, taking care of the necessary paperwork with the police, originally enabled me to have access to the center. I had to resort to membership in his NGO and to the volunteer badge that comes with it in order to be granted access. Don Ciro advised me not to spend too much time with the soldiers and the staff, warning me that I would end up "thinking like them" and resenting the guests. In fact, I do feel enraged, but certainly not toward the guests—why isn't the staff at the very least pressuring the police to accelerate its bureaucracy?

Processing and detention centers like this one manage to physically exclude detainees from citizens' critical eye, and from a potential web of legal, political, and social interventions. Should I call the media, and report such an egregious violation of civil, legal, and human rights? Would it speed things up, or perhaps just make the police spiteful? Don Ciro, whom I have briefed about the situation, has warned me that I would definitely be kicked out of the center if I were to call the media; furthermore, his NGO might not be allowed to send volunteers anymore, so the center would be left "abandoned in the soldiers' hands," with no external, independent oversight. Lucio has also informed me that calling the media would be "illegal." It would "violate the guests' *privacy*." The unintended irony of his warning, together with that of the "impossible freedom"[10] accorded to the asylum seekers to leave the center without notice "if they so desire," provides a cursory example of how the idiom of neoliberalism pervades Italian migration governance.

On January 20, they are finally having breakfast, for it is Kurban Bajram (Eid al-Adha), the sacrifice feast celebrated by Muslims worldwide. Over lunch, Bilgin explains that they are Turks of Bulgaria, contrary to everyone's assumption about their Romany ethnicity. A question emerges: *Should I recast my account and refer to them simply as "Muslims" or "Muslim immigrants"*? For the festive occasion the staff offers panettone, a slice per person, and spumante in plastic cups, which many refuse on religious grounds. Gianni, a finance guard soldier, in a gesture of friendliness has phoned the Brindisi police, who have phoned the Ministry of the Interior in Rome. The soldier reports that "verification" of their IDs began on January 17.[11] This verification is routinely conducted through EU databases, such as the Schengen Information System and the European Dactylographic System. The latter keeps track of non-EU asylum seekers' and irregular border crossers' fingerprints. They are both functional to the implementation of the Dublin Regulation. For these Bulgarian travelers, "ID verification should take one week," Gianni says.

One more week? I can no longer bear my position as the transmission wheel of this machinery lubricated by inaccuracy. Why are they even in the center? Has there ever been any genuine basis for the police to promise they would go after two days, then one week, and now two weeks? I stagger between revolt and investigation, between the denunciation of individuals—the staff members, the police officers—and of larger mechanisms of structural injustice inherent to these practices of detention, verification, territorial rejection, and police discretion. I am tempted to just desert the center, for I feel powerless and I cannot really look my Bulgarian friends in the eyes anymore. I could easily smash a window, or bang my head against the wall. Only now, feeling an incarnated resonance, do I appreciate why I need to collect razor blades after the men are done shaving each morning. I might prevent self-mutilation, but I cannot do much about their gastritis (or mine) and high blood pressure. Anelia, a petite woman in her early forties, has to be hospitalized for a few days.

The center's psychologists are fully aware that guests are brought to a situation of frustration and psychophysiological uneasiness by their very detention. In this vicious cycle, though, they only patch up pharmaceutically the pathologies engendered by administrative detention. Detainees are given palliative care by the very institutions that create pathologies of injustice. In the process, sovereign institutions also numb citizens' awareness and procrastinate confronting their own contradictions.

Everyday life in (Italian) immigration holding facilities is inherently difficult. This is the case not only in CIEs (discussed in Chapter 1) but also in facilities dedicated to asylum seekers but still locked and closed to public oversight. Each day, structured around the bureaucratic needs of the institution and the basic needs of inmates, reduces those needs to their physiological and individual dimension, nicely exemplified by Oleg's words. For this thirty-five-year-old Ukrainian male, "all you do is eat and sleep, and you cannot but ruminate all the time." He laments the emptiness of daily routine, cyclical and uneventful. It is a structured boredom. As grasped by Herzfeld in the very different context of Cretan apprentices (2004:118), boredom has two facets. On the one hand, it is a "means of control," allowing the staff and surveillance apparatus to force people into routines that make it hard for detainees "to be overtly insubordinate." On the other, boredom provides a safe cover for "artful" ways to observe guards' habits and to enact insubordination.

In such a situation of structural boredom and overarching tension, conflict with agents and among migrants can materialize at any moment. It is often sparked by mundane inconveniences, related to poor sleeping conditions in crowded rooms, low quality and lack of variation in food, and poor sanitation in bathrooms. Such inconveniences are not single events or accidents, but conditions multiplied by hundreds of instances and encounters. And smoking within centers is not allowed. Migrants need to ask soldiers permission to go out in the gated courtyard for a smoke. Given this chance to exercise power, soldiers do take advantage of their prerogative and might deny a smoke to collectively punish detainees after escape attempts or minor disturbances. In short, there is a structural situation that makes possible psychological, verbal, legal and potentially physical abuse, often regardless of the actual intentions of the management.

In one example I observed, a small group of young Kurdish-Iraqi men, stowaways from Greece, were brought to the Otranto center. In a very tense environment a high-ranking police officer threatened them that if they kept refusing to have their fingerprints taken (an administrative procedure) they would be charged as Islamic terrorists and thrown into jail. Elsewhere in Italy, the coerced collection of fingerprints is a situation often resulting in riots. There have been cases of young men mutilating their fingers with acid or hot oil. Like them, the new Kurdish arrivals know that being fingerprinted in Italy means that their record will be entered in the European Dactylographic System database, making it almost impossible, for years to come, to legally travel to their intended destination (the United Kingdom, in this case) because of the Dublin Regulation. A few days after this verbal incident with the police, I saw Amir's left arm covered in blood. He had managed to find a piece of glass and scar himself in multiple spots. Long awaiting deportation, interviews, the outcome of legal appeals, or even basic information about their rights and legal prospects, inmates experience boredom, resignation, frustration, vandalism, and even self-destruction, including biopolitical gestures of protest such as scarring oneself, as in Amir's case. Others sew their lips shut, using the wires they find inside cigarette lighters. In overcrowded and often unsanitary conditions, tensions, riots, and conflictual relations with the staff, armed forces, and fellow migrants are routine. Moreover, guards are often inexperienced and unmotivated as they go about their duties dealing with unarmed civilians with whom they are often unable to speak. Some migrants do end up looking forward to the day of their forced removal. Others ingest batteries, nails, shampoo, and shattered glass. Authorities and staff members explain they do this because they know they will be taken to local hospitals, from where they can then try to escape. In this somewhat neofunctionalist explanation, there is no room to account for the structural causes that routinely bring migrants to effect such drastic acts, or for the political will they are expressing.

Lucio has finally clarified to me that his duty as the center's "lawyer" is limited to providing legal information, rather than direct counsel or advocacy as his title of *avvocato* suggests. After much debate Tundjel, Bilgin, and their friends have asked Lucio whether they have the right to a "real" lawyer then, by which they mean one who can actually help them get out as soon as possible. They do have this right. Lucio tells them that "the Italian state" will even pay for his or her services. For since they were not able to demonstrate sufficient funds to the Greek authorities, the Italian state has classified them as *indigenti* (poor). These Bulgarian citizens are poor. They are not to be left wandering in Italy without money, food, and shelter. Austrian authorities have to agree to their transit; otherwise they could reject them and send them back to Italy. Sovereign detention is equated with a form of governmental humanitarian assistance.

The Bulgarian Embassy in Rome, which the detainees and I have now contacted several times for assistance, has told us to call "later today," "at another time," and "in a week." The perception is that it has abandoned its citizens, perhaps concerned not to spoil Italian-Bulgarian relations. Indeed, EU candidates and recent members remain unequal outposts of EU labor recruiting and border control. In this light, one of the concerns underlined in the EU Commission's reports about Bulgaria prior to its 2007 full accession was that the country needed to make progress toward the joint management of non-EU migrants, including by building detention centers on its territory.

Tundjel, always freshly shaven and with short, gel-styled hair, has written many letters to his girlfriend in Ruse. Still wearing his denim jacket, he confides in me that he thinks they are here because Greek and Italian police suspected they wanted to work or settle in their respective countries. At any rate, he asks in disbelief, "even if in Greece they suspected we wanted to remain there, is it possible that all this [Greek expulsion and Italian detention] is based only on some policeman's thought, with no evidence, and no piece of paper?"

Two policemen from the local station have arrived looking for somebody among the Bulgarians who can speak English. Tundjel is quite happy to volunteer, even if he only speaks a few words. Without any hint of irony he is required to submit a "spontaneous statement" at the station. He tells me he welcomes this opportunity, because so far no Italian or Greek judicial or police authority has heard what they have to say. After a short ride in the police car we sit on faux-leather chairs at the station. Tundjel explains the group's journey, indicating the dates, the tourism purpose of the trip, and the route. He tells me he would have never imagined being taken and interrogated by the police, "like in American movies." I would have never imagined myself translating for police business—and certainly not using Bulgarian, Serbian, English, and Italian in one sentence.

It is already February 3, week three of their detention. The avvocato has recommended a certain Marco as a lawyer for the Bulgarian detainees. They have accepted, and I visit with him at his private practice in Otranto. He explains he is going to send an official *certified* letter to Brindisi police, simply asking for a *written* statement explaining the reason for such a "restriction of their personal liberty." Legally, the police have three days to reply. Until now, there has not been any actual judicial measure defining these Bulgarian citizens' status in Italy or requiring their detention in the center. I have also learned from Marco that there is another problem. He says that while he intends to help them out of the center, he has to be careful this is not accomplished through a decree of expulsion from Italy. Though it would be faster, a decree of expulsion would entail the confiscation of their minibus and the prohibition from reentering Italy for the next ten years (as is the case with any undocumented migrant expelled or removed from the country). He speculates that they are still here because the police in Brindisi lack the funds to escort them to Austria.

At lunchtime, Luigi, the finance guard soldier, tells me "the Bulgarians" are to leave tomorrow, February 10, and I convey this to Bilgin. After a month of such reassurances, it is difficult to believe this new information to be reliable. In the afternoon police officers and the Russian interpreter from Brindisi do arrive, with a bunch of folders. They hand each Bulgarian citizen a document to sign. Tundjel and Bilgin ask me to translate it for everybody, making sure the police interpreter is not "tricking them again." In English and Italian—again, not in Bulgarian—the paper states that, on the basis of preexisting bilateral agreements with Italy, Austria has agreed to their transit toward their Bulgarian hometown. The police will escort them to Austria tomorrow, and Austrian police forces should escort them to Hungary, from where they can return home on their own. Hugging and thanking me for being "the only one helping" them, Bilgin has made me feel just a bit less inadequate. He has asked me to let "everybody" know about their story.

It is the day of their departure. I am assisting them in requesting the items they were asked to deposit in the soldiers' office upon arrival, to avoid "acts of self-harm." We retrieve lighters, razors, homemade *rakija* (plum brandy), trouser belts, nail clippers, cameras, and perfumes. A luxury bus, ironically rented by the police from a local tourist agency, finally appears in front of the gate, escorted by three police Jeeps.[12] There are about thirty-five policemen in riot gear, vigilant and disquietingly jumpy with their batons and hard helmets. My friends are body-searched one by one, and asked to get on the bus. I am anxious, for they have to share an eight-hundred-mile ride to the Austrian border with these agents.

Reading Intentions: Preemptive Power and Preemptive Knowledge

Documentary accumulation, medicine, psychiatry, anthropology, photography, and bureaucracy can traditionally gain access to certain individuals and social groups precisely because they are placed in various forms of camps.[13] These are facilities conceived for humans in general, or for particular groups—not for actual, specific persons. Their routines and their spaces are functional for the perpetuation of a certain order of things, more than of public order. They are functional for their own maintenance, for surveillance, and for the pretenses of sovereignty. Occasionally they are functional for the work of specific categories, such as staff, guards, and the police. They are rarely functional for the life of their occupants. They are never functional for humans in general.

Migrants, in particular, often become special objects of knowledge and management.[14] And yet migrants and other types of essentialized social groups are not simply held in various types of camps, they are manufactured there through biopolitical and bureaucratic processes such as the ones I am illustrating. Migrant holding facilities allow for people to be fed and sheltered, and by doing that also to be fingerprinted, identified, confined, and deported. Indeed, material and legal mechanisms of administration of territory and bodies across it constitute the fulcrum of Italian and EU power to "allocate, classify, categorize, and formalize categories of the human" (Ong 2003:17). Law and police practices produce immigrants, immigration, illicit travel, and "even the state," argues Coutin (2000:10).[15] Still, Tundjel's interrogation remains unaddressed: "is it possible that all this is based only on some policeman's thought, with no evidence, or no piece of paper?"[16] To address Tundjel's query, I need to attend to mechanisms and power relations enabling such authoritative governmental "thought."

But first, you might be wondering: did Tundjel, Bilgin, Zhivko, Emil, Mitko, Marijana, Asija, and the rest of the group want to "immigrate" to Greece, as everybody in the center took for granted?[17] Probably not. Some of them have children and jobs in Bulgaria. Well then, did they intend to temporarily work in Greece, perhaps in agriculture? To suspect they intended to sneak into and work in Greece (or Italy), rather than going back home to Bulgaria after a few days of sightseeing, is precisely what the Italian and Greek police did. For in the racialized and racializing state and EU logics at work here, tourism is a compartmentalized prerogative of middle-class individuals meeting phenotypical and nationality expectations. In this logic, Bulgarians and especially Romany citizens from southeastern Europe cannot possibly be tourists. Conversely, as Heyman puts it discussing the moral evaluative work of U.S. immigration officers, the exhibition of "signs of wealth" entrusts certain travelers with the supposition that they "are 'obviously' not coming . . . to toil in the underground labor market" (2000:645). More broadly, social class "gives content to the imaginative pondering of officers, even if they label it 'national citizenship'" (645). Still, Italian and Greek police and border authorities would have no suspicions about Swiss travelers, for example, taking for granted *their very citizenship* as a sign of wealth. But in this case the police were dealing with people from eastern Europe, understood stereotypically as a container of cheap labor.[18] Moreover, these travelers' phenotype is tremendously heterogeneous, with one underlying characteristic precisely in its illegibility: the impossibility of being neatly categorized into any reliable container of ethnicity. This illegibility might have also worked as an alerting feature generating suspicion over their claimed Bulgarian citizenship and tourism purposes.

Admittedly, border and immigration officers often find themselves operating and reasoning "through fractured documentary and behavioral clues under tight time constraints" (Heyman 2000:643). In other words, officers often have to resort to their power of attribution of intention[19] in order to reject and admit at the border. In our case, they attributed to these "indigent" Bulgarian-Turks the intention to work, and more generally to engage in something other than tourism. Yet attribution and more broadly preemptive[20] knowledge production can be consequential only if enabled by the authority position of the agent vis-à-vis the traveler. Power of attribution, in turn, is an important constituent of state actors' authority and "right to be right," as Oberweis and Musheno (2001:6) put it.

Attribution of behaviors and intentions may or may not be deliberate. Arguably, it reflects the goal of "reasonable accuracy of causal understanding through inference economy" (Harvey and Weary 1985:6), and perhaps the ostensible desire to make the world predictable and controllable. Complex situations might require the "attributor" to pursue further investigation of his or her own first judgment, looking for "self-evaluative feedback" (Olson and Ross 1985:304). In our case, though, the border officers' first judgment—*these Gypsies are sneaking into the EU to settle and work illegally*— and further comparisons are informed not by individual cognitive guesswork, but by a hegemonic "paradigm of suspicion" (Shamir 2005). Such a hegemonic paradigm shapes seemingly commonsensical association rules: expectations of how certain phenotypes, citizenships, signs of poverty, and intentions correlate. When somebody becomes alien as a result of certain

moral, religious, racial, social, or legal taxonomies, one of the fundamental
pillars of the structure of racist fantasies, as Žižek (1989) would call them,
is precisely that this alien's actions are suspected of being guided by a hidden motive. Once performed, the suspicion of the Bulgarian travelers being
"immigrants" reconfirms what sociologist Abdelmalek Sayad critically calls
the "original sin" of "immigration" as a "latent, camouflaged offence" to
the nation-state logic (2004 [1999]:282). The burden of proof, then, is
shifted from the police onto the alleged immigrants, who can then be
rejected at a border or detained preemptively, in advance of unauthorized
activities. In this sense, Tundjel's question on the ungrounded nature of
their detention is a rhetorical question, I suggest below. In practice, the very
state that produces categories of (un)lawful and (un)documented aliens can
afford to be itself undocumented in its preemptive procedures.[21]

Liberal democracies normatively associate themselves with legality and
accountability, with rule-driven decision making and paper trails. This is
the case also "in a recession" when predictive policing, based on established
regional crime patterns and computer algorithms, is globally being promoted as "the next era in policing" and police chiefs supporting it are
asking, "What Can We Learn from Wal-Mart and Amazon About Fighting
Crime" (Beck and McCue 2009). Neuroscience and "new truth verification
technology," epitomized by the name and approach of No Lie MRI Inc.,
increasingly seek to identify brain evidence and to detect lies and deception
in legal and national security contexts (Aronson 2010). "Security threats"
posed by potential travelers are assessed in advance of arrival and of the
threats' materialization. "White" and "black" lists are compiled by governments, transportation civil authorities, and private contractors. And the
criminal justice system is more and more aimed at detecting "risky" groups
of persons as soon as possible.[22]

At the interstices of digital borders, checkpoints, airports, detention
facilities, international waters, and wireless spaces of communication, the
immediate objects of surveillance are fingerprints, irises, names, financial
transactions, biometric passports. In such a global nexus of security and
identification, prediction and attribution of intention (business travel, terrorist mission, labor, tourism, and so forth) enable the routine regulation
of mobility. In summary, techniques and technologies of preemptive
knowledge are clearly intertwined with the power and authority that both
enable them and make them authoritative and consequential. One of the
measures and constituents of sovereignty, both at the EU and member state

levels, is the ability and the prerogative to summon and enforce preemptive power and preemptive knowledge.

The overarching goal of these predictive efforts is to assess in advance thought and behavior while ostensibly transcending the "subjectivity and uncertainty of more traditional methods" (Aronson 2010:105) and bypassing other labor-intensive processes. An evaluation of the scientific merit and ethical-legal implications of such technologies is beyond the scope of these pages. It is legitimate to ask, though: "Are data-driven hunches any more reliable than personal hunches traditionally deemed insufficient to justify reasonable suspicion?" (Ferguson 2012:262). Generalizing Ferguson's discussion of predictive policing,[23] what I intend to highlight is that "blind reliance on the forecast, divorced from the reason for the forecast, may lead to inappropriate reliance on the technology" (Ferguson 2012: 269).[24] Additionally, we may note that "proving a future risk" is not so different from establishing past facts, since "both are processes of actively constructing, rather than passively discovering, knowledge" (Sweeney 2009:725).

The EU is heavily investing in situational awareness through networks such as Eurosur and through biometrics and "smart border" technology that recognize individualized "registered travelers" and their socioeconomic class.[25] Civilian institutions, like Frontex, engage in crafting "risk analyses" with military and humanitarian facets and implications. Scholars and practitioners are called to attend to the methods and processes behind the various results, findings, and conclusions that are presented for public consumption, and that affect the lives of the subjects they seek to make legible and apprehend. Conclusions, in both governmental and epistemological mechanisms, are not detached from the actors, unequal relationships, and situations that fashion them.

Undocumented States

The question as to why the Bulgarian travelers were detained, and for one month rather than forty-eight hours, cannot be indisputably answered—in light of ethnography, of legislative or bureaucratic norms, and of precedent. Indeed, the lawyer's certified letter to the police in Brindisi asked precisely why they were being deprived of their "personal liberty." The letter was soon followed by an act—they were liberated—but never by a reply. It is plausible

police officers found themselves unable to provide *any* legal written[26] explanation, any "paper." The police were undocumented. Unable, unwilling, or
unmotivated to ground their "hunches" about the Bulgarian citizens' intentions and subsequent detention, the police eventually opened the gate.

Perhaps never before as in this "age of total information awareness"
(Murray 2010) the secular, liberal-democratic state (and the EU) has
defined itself, its authority, and its laws as the privileged domains of transparency, absolute meaning, rationality, and certain belief.[27] There is seemingly no room for state actors' agency and discretion, and the "predictive
analytics" sketched above are marketed as bypassing human discretion. As
the Otranto center's lawyer phrased it, certain procedures "develop nearly
automatically, and once they start there is a whole machinery that has to
conclude its cycle." Or as Olivia Harris puts it, "legal processes can easily
take on a life of their own, in a nightmare of papers" (1996:10). Still, the
improvisation, discretion, "uncontrollable humanness,"[28] and "vernacular
expertise"[29] of state agents, whether simply unacknowledged or actively
concealed, are integral to the functioning of liberal democracies, and more
specifically to their governance of mobility. Law, as a system of codification,
constitutes a continuous attempt at fixity and closure into which actual life
situations can fit only imperfectly (Harris 1996:10). It is therefore inevitable
for legality-enforcing actors to resort to "institutional creativity" and to the
"fictions and presumptions" that assist in making decisions in conditions
of uncertainty (Pottage 2004:12). This is true at a border checkpoint, in a
detention center, and on the open sea.

More generally, state and EU border and migration management practices, enabled and sanctioned by Italian and EU policies, are not necessarily
or exclusively the outcome of documented, intentional, transparent, and
economically viable choices. From a postulated "clue," such as phenotype
or country of citizenship, and within a structurally racialized framework,
the "immigrant" is formed. He or she is made into an ideal type, an ostensibly legible subject in a hierarchical taxonomy. The lack of context and
particularity that forms this subject, then, "is not an oversight" (Scott
1998:346). On the contrary, it is a fundamental albeit unacknowledged
necessity in the economy of knowledge production that manages migration.
How else could the time-consuming, costly, grandiose, and never-ending
state and EU project of human mobility regulation be effected—think of
maritime pushbacks and summary removals—if not by crass simplification,
quantification, and depersonalization?

As suggested by Talal Asad (2004), the state's abstract character does not hide any essential core of coherence. "Confusion," to use Geertz's wording, is a fundamental state feature: "the confusion that surrounds it, the confusion it confronts, the confusion it causes, the confusion it responds to" (2004:580). Improvisation, discretion, and undocumented-ness play a major role in state agents' decision making—not only in Geertz's "complicated places," for *all* states are complicated. In other words, there is not necessarily a core of coherence and purposefulness to be "unveiled" behind the border practices of inspection, detention, and deportation detailed above. Ironically though, this very absence, emptiness, or nothing-ness at the core of state practices helps support the state's "verticality"[30] and distinctiveness "as an apparatus that stands apart from the rest of the social world" (Mitchell 1991:93).[31] Improvised, discretionary, and mun-dane procedures become thus anonymous but sovereign "nightmares of papers."

Discretionary, extrajudicial, and undocumented border practices of inspection, detention, and deportation are fundamental tools in state and EU production of information about "immigrants." Nevertheless, informa-tion does not necessarily coincide with factual data to be retrieved and transmitted. It is also in-*formation*. Certain bureaucratic and epistemologi-cal procedures do form and shape the people they are supposed to detachedly examine. In turn, the state and the EU can be understood as complementary networks that form and maintain themselves precisely through structurally improvised practices of knowledge production at their borders. And the establishment and policing of borders is highly significant in the spectacle of enforcement that renders the rule of law and migrant illegality visible and ostensibly natural.[32]

The ability to deport, for example, *whether exercised or not*, remains "one of the essential prerogatives of national sovereignty," in the same way in which liability to deportation is a main constituent of "foreignness" (Sayad 2004 [1999]:293). At border checkpoints, in ports and airports, at sea, and on highways, a single state agent enjoys the authority to enforce, or more accurately to effect, the state's prerogative to expel from its terri-tory certain categories of people—illegal immigrants, bogus asylum seekers, poor travelers, terrorists, and so forth—that the act of rejection retroac-tively reifies.

The Bulgarian travelers' ejection, detention, and deportation did not need to be legitimized by any law, regulation, decree, or other "piece of paper"—other than Greece-Italy-Austria preexisting bilateral agreements. As they were "pushed back" by Greece and "removed" by Italy, they were not owed any sovereign explanation.

The situation, while it happened, was grounded in "nothing," as Tundjel insightfully pointed out. As Mary Douglas (1966) suggested long ago, it is not only what is being separated (deterred, detained, deported, pushed back, executed) that matters but rather the power, practice, and habit of order and separation in itself, without the need to document or justify such practices. Such procedural undocumentedness stands as a measure and a constituent of sovereign power. Sovereign power does not owe explanations to its noncitizen subjects. Still, critical citizens, news agencies, national prosecutors, and the ECHR may demand explanations.

In light of the practices of law, attribution, and discretion that I have illustrated, what happened at the Otranto center—and routinely happens in the larger network of holding facilities—is not an exception to an otherwise democratic implementation of legal mechanisms, but an integral constituent of such mechanisms. In matters of security and surveillance, in particular, seamless tracking software but also "internment camps, secret trials, DNA profiles, border walls and fences, erosion of the line between internal security and external military action" constitute what Connolly calls a "national security machine" that threatens the survival of any "robust pluralist democracy" (2005:53–54).

Police measures, enabled by the executive's policies, are allowed to count as "enough." They become adequate not only for the undocumented detention of non-EU nationals but also for (Italian) citizens' deprivation of critical capabilities and political initiative. Holding centers are off-limits. At the EU level, Frontex activities are grounded in the existing infrastructure of EU agencies and legislation, prompting little mainstream political discussion—similarly to bilateral and so-called technical international agreements. Regardless of sanitary issues, complaints about the food ("it's pasta again, like each and every day!"), and architectural or design limitations, the *very existence* of an EU and global spectrum of administrative detention and of extralegislative and extrajudicial tools poses pressing questions. Routine forms of mobility management—including detention, whether in Europe or outsourced—constitute and sustain disquietingly undemocratic practices. Indeed, border practices too often "escape the sight of the democratic citizenry in the name of whom and for the protection of whom they are exercised" (Benhabib 2001:62). Democratic scrutiny is essential. But in light of ethnographic research, democratization of this kind of mobility governance might prove a contradiction in terms.

Resisting Preemption and Redemption: Trusting Ethnography

"You didn't ask the Bulgarians whether they were really immigrants?" "Why did you censor yourself?" "Oh, you will need a whole book to justify why you didn't ask them!" These and similar multidisciplinary interjections of unmet *expectation* have contributed to the scholarly formation of these pages. With questions that do not intend to be rhetorical, but rather empirical and epistemological, I may then ask: would these Bulgarian citizens, as "real tourists," deserve more ethnographic attention, and perhaps empathy? Would detention be more warranted if these were undocumented Muslim immigrants? Would the state appear more or less rational, and its extrajudicial and discretionary practices more or less legitimate? Would a police-based explanation of their one-month detention make it more democratic and ethnographically (ir)relevant?

In a reflection on her own predicament, anthropologist Asale Angel-Ajani (2004:135) writes that "as much as representation and the practice of fieldwork have been debated, the anthropologist has not entirely rid herself of the role of 'recovering the truth,' the role of being the one who assembles evidence and then testifies in a (court)room of her 'peers.'" I could have "testified." I could have asked them. I would have probably received an honest answer, made possible not by any identity between us[33]—relatively young males, south-Slavic speakers,[34] the sincere but debatable "friends" I employ above—but rather by a relationship of trust developed through engagement, glances, and silences. Long hours were spent gossiping, playing foosball, negotiating a smoke with the guards, looking for solutions, cursing, and listening to each other's stories, even if we were fully aware of the overarching asymmetry of power structuring that relationship.

And so I could have asked them. But it is analytically necessary to unpack not why I did not ask but why others think I should have asked. State agents did not make any effort to "really," empirically "know." They "connected the dots"[35] tracing the anticipated association rules between phenotype, citizenship, signs of poverty, and intentions. That undocumented and paperless assumption worked de facto as an indisputable certainty, drawing on and reinforcing governmental authority and power. For my interlocutors to get to the ostensible "real nature" of these travelers would not change the empirical, political, and analytical substance and unfolding of that governmental process. To put it differently: in these pages, as in the rest of the book, I have not analyzed a group of travelers or immigrants in isolation, but rather the situations, mechanisms, and relationships that have allowed one month of extrajudicial detention, the very manufacturing of immigrants, and practices of border control, confinement, and deportation. I sought to account for the governmental labor that manufactures various faits accomplis and makes possible the work of predicting, identifying, detaining, and deporting enemies, bogus refugees, poor migrants, and other undesirables. When dealing with migration holding facilities, in particular, there is no way to "know" the conclusion of these migrants' cases—*and therefore to account for it*—in advance of the process that generated it. For people held in such facilities, and even for members of the staff, the only known "conclusion" is that they will leave the facility at some point. They will know when, to which destination, under which legal classification (their presumed "real nature"), and in which psychophysiological conditions only immediately before departure. Intending to produce consequential knowledge we can thus analyze contexts, situations, and relations, in addition to identities; mobility, legibility, and confinement, in addition to immigrants. It is precisely by eschewing a focus on entities in isolation—such as immigrants, Muslims, policemen—that we might produce a more "realist" and empowered scholarship.

An attentive discussant once remarked that my analysis "attributes [something] to the state too!" Indeed, these pages suggest that attribution is a pervasive albeit often unspoken tool of knowledge production. As any other such tool, it is to be scrutinized, especially in its intersections with power and authority, rather than idealistically banned. More broadly, many assumptions inform our intellectual paradigms and actions as social scientists.[36] As Rabinow puts it, we address and analyze new (and familiar) problems using the Weberian device of the "ideal type" (2003:36). In particular, it seems to me that we do so when we treat immigrants as ontologically given, as starting points. But in so doing, we work as a "cooperative audience" (Duranti 1993:233) in sovereign taxonomies of mobility regulation, and like them we develop and deploy preemptive knowledge.

I understand my conference interlocutors' curiosity about the "real nature" of the Bulgarian travelers as pointing to a disciplined urge to attribute identities, intentions, and rationales in advance of ethnographic and research-based knowledge of actual subjects, relations, and situations. Fellow scholars might also pursue intellectual and moral comfort in meeting expectations, in finding and demonstrating closure and incontestable meaning, in the "presumed adequacy of a representation to its realities," to use Maurer's words (2005:53). State mechanisms also pursue and claim the teleological certainty of preemptive knowledge, and claim it as a marker of their liberal-democratic and secular nature.

Preemptive knowledge, then, also entails redemptive knowledge. Both preemptive and morally redemptive knowledge are informed by power and authority. They both "know" their end and the object of knowledge in advance of their relationship to it. Both preemptive and redemptive knowledge risk accepting as inevitable what is not inevitable. They ostensibly know the conclusion, whether dread or desired, and risk marginalizing ethnographic and procedural experience in pursuit of transcendent rationales, certainties, and story lines. Redemption and preemption are not interested in the mundane, in the situation, and in the ephemeral. They discount holding centers' motorized gates; the discretion that inhabits them; their musty sleeping quarters; their doorless restrooms; their empty routine; the lighters and the razors; the vagaries and uncertainties of sovereignty—in the name of closure. What is discounted, then, is the stuff of sovereign practice, and also the stuff of life and of ethnography. This is not context and scenery, the backdrop that illustrates border enforcement. This *is* border enforcement; the context and the situation are the story. This is how the governance of mobility routinely looks and feels like in a liberal democracy, not a parenthetical experience. And this is not a parenthesis in the life of people. It is their life. The ethnographic account, then, is not the colorful handmaid of analytical knowledge, but its constitutive body.

It is therefore crucial to resist the temptation to assemble a transcendent and teleological account that invokes the conclusion and temporal end of the process it describes as a "purpose" and therefore as an explanation of the very same process.[37] What is seemingly ephemeral might not be just a short-lived event or accident. As I am illustrating in this work, the ephemeral, the mundane, is deeply related to structured improvisations, injustice, and permanent states of emergency. Eliminating the ephemeral from our analyses is akin to analyzing hunger "believing I'll never again be hungry if I had a good meal" (Benasayag 2005 [2004]:132). In other words, we risk relegating beneath an immaculate lab coat of teleological fallacy multivariate relations and ultimately undisciplinable situations. Trusting ethnography, then, implies analytically sabotaging the expressway toward crystallized meanings, association rules, and identities too often laid out for public (and scholarly) consumption. Resistance also requires ethnographically meeting our interlocutors' plea to be taken seriously as they navigate—and sometimes set on fire, as we are soon to discover—old and new forms of discretion and inequality.

PART III

BORDERS ADRIFT

Chapter 5

Spring Uprisings, Fall Drownings

Torching the "Lampedusa Model"

Lo scoglio, "the rock." This is what Lampedusa's residents affectionately call the island, home to about six thousand. Migrants have long arrived at Lampedusa on boats, whether landing on their own or assisted by coast guard vessels. Fishermen, in particular, remember the arrivals of 1996, when some three thousand Tunisians were merely "asked" by state authorities to leave within two weeks. Historically, maritime arrivals from neighboring Tunisia were institutionally tolerated, and to this day Tunisian sailors staff many fishing boats in Sicily. Local residents also take pride in the history and position of the island.[1] They make a point of recommending a visit to the grotto and sanctuary aptly dedicated to the Madonna of Porto Salvo (safe port), historically open to the cult of both Christian and Muslim sailors and traders. A seasoned fisherman, always wearing his Juventus FC cap as he rides his Vespa, recalls that the Tunisian cities of Sfax and Sousse used to host Lampedusan communities.[2] Others brag about their fishing travels throughout the Mediterranean. Regulars at Bar dell'Amicizia (friendship café) discuss with a nostalgic tone how throughout the mid- to late 1990s newly arrived maritime travelers would stop there for refreshments and to ask for "directions" on how to get to Sicily.

Today, newly arrived migrants are brought to the local centro di primo soccorso e accoglienza, a center of first aid and reception. Since 2007, it has been officially intended for immediate assistance, limited to seventy-two hours. As typical elsewhere in Italy, the center is built in a somewhat remote and secluded location, known locally as Contrada Imbriacola. Migrants' short-term assistance in Lampedusa is to be followed by relocation to other centers in mainland Italy, or by repatriation. The "Lampedusa model," in institutional parlance, is that of an "efficient" and short-term "waiting room" where migrants are identified prior to being transferred to other holding facilities in Sicily and mainland Italy.[3] In such a situation, their presence on the island—confined behind the fence of the holding center—is tolerated, when not ignored. Prospective tourists are routinely reassured that there is no danger whatsoever, as migrants are locked in, unable to move freely on the island.

This seemingly well-oiled architecture of Italian border enforcement and migration management was built on bilateral agreements with Tunisia and Libya, curbing arrivals especially from the first country; pushback operations; Libyan detention of third-country nationals; short-term detention in Lampedusa; and immediate repatriation or deportation. But the Lampedusa model was shredded by the Arab Uprisings of 2011. In this chapter, I first trace the contradictions reemerging with the arrival of Tunisian citizens at Lampedusa and their transfer to a newly built tent camp in Apulia. I then draw the catalogue of institutional failures enabling the many maritime deaths of 2011, when during the war in Libya the Mediterranean was the most heavily patrolled sea in the world. The second part of the chapter focuses on the volatile situation in Egypt and Libya and the unresolved plight of Syrian and Eritrean refugees there, with shipwrecks in 2013 resulting in the military-humanitarian Mare Nostrum mission.

Tunisian president Zine El Abidine Ben Ali fled his country on January 14, 2011. His demise followed almost twenty-four years as the leader of an undemocratic, censoring, and kleptocratic regime. Quite interestingly, Ben Ali's bloodless coup d'état in 1987 had allegedly been facilitated, if not orchestrated, by members of the Italian government, assisted by Italian intelligence services. As perceived by Italian politicians, in the mid-1980s Tunisia's stability was endangered by growing Islamic radicalism, by the violent response to it, and by turbulent relationships with Algeria. The Italian government had (and has) material stakes in the stability of the region, and in particular in protecting the Algeria-Italy gas pipeline, which crosses Tunisia. What is certain is that barely one month after Ben Ali's coup in 1987 Italian prime minister Bettino Craxi accompanied the Italian-based energy company ENI's director Franco Reviglio to Tunis, to sign an agreement on Tunisian-Italian energy trade with the new leadership.[4]

Ben Ali also offered reliable cooperation with Italian authorities in curbing unauthorized emigration of his country's citizens.[5] When his armed forces bloodily repressed labor and politically driven uprisings in the Gafsa mining area, between January and June 2008, there were massive illegal crossings into Libya—but not to Italy. Nevertheless, many people among the ill-treated Tunisian workers intended to work in Libya only to pay the smugglers, and to leave for Lampedusa from the coastal area between Tripoli and the Tunisian border. This is a longer, more expensive, and more perilous route than from Tunisia, whose coast is more heavily patrolled. Protesting workers could not even apply for a Tunisian passport—they would risk being arrested based on the presumed association with the antigovernment uprisings of 2008.[6] In that year, sixty-seven hundred Tunisian citizens did manage to land in Lampedusa.[7] Thirty-four among these applied for asylum. The committee handling such applications in Gorizia, in northern Italy, denied them on the basis of the fine detail with which the applicants' stories were told. They were so precise as to be implausible.[8] They were too truthful to be true. Some were repatriated to Tunis and immediately arrested at the airport, as Italian authorities had notified their Tunisian colleagues of the asylum applications. Others waited for the results of appeals and after four months of detention were liberated, and could travel to France.

The Tunisian economy finds its principal partner in the EU economy. Since 2008, the EU economic crisis has affected Tunisia, adding further insecurity, especially for local seasonal workers. Young people with little training and many university graduates without rewarding jobs constitute a large pool of potential emigrants: three-quarters of young people are thinking of emigrating.[9] In January 2009, Italian interior minister Roberto Maroni (2008–11) travels to Tunis to meet his Tunisian counterpart, Rafiq Belhaj Kacem. They sign a bilateral agreement that further facilitates Tunisian citizens' readmission after attempting to emigrate to Italy, fosters collaboration in "preventing and fighting" "illegal immigration," and intensifies the struggle against human "traffickers" and other criminal organizations that exploit "clandestine immigration."[10] The Tunisian government further criminalizes leaving the Tunisian territory in an unauthorized way, with heavy fines and six-month prison sentences.

In February 2009, with the prospect of facilitated readmissions (expected to take at most two months for each new Tunisian arrival) allowed by Ben Ali's government, Maroni directs police forces to stop the routine transfer of newly arrived migrants from Lampedusa to the rest of Italy. Migrants stay confined on the island for weeks, essentially waiting to be repatriated to Tunisia. Designed for a maximum of 381 people, but somehow able to accommodate up to 800 if need be, the holding center holds up to 1,600 migrants for several days.[11] Faced with the prospect of repatriation, and following a hunger strike, some Tunisians within the holding center revolt against the police. They also torch the structure, built with extremely flammable materials and not up to code. A substantial part is permanently damaged, and the number of available beds is considerably reduced. Twenty-two agents and two migrants are injured as a result of the toxic fumes. Lampedusa's mayor Bernardino De Rubeis (2007–12) publicly blames the potential disaster on Maroni for having transformed the center into a *"lager,"* a long-term concentration camp.[12]

In Tunisia democratic aspirations, integral to the 2011 uprisings, are not confined to electoral representation. They imply the right to self-determination, to define one's own life without having to debase one's dignity—domestically to the demands of conniving clientelism and internationally to hierarchical relations with Italy, France, and the EU.[13] As several migrants have told me, many of their Tunisian friends at home perceive those relations, including the various migration-related bilateral agreements, as hierarchical and degrading.

In Sidi Bouzid, the city in central Tunisia where the self-immolation of Mohamed Bouazizi became the catalyst for the 2011 Arab Uprisings, people are not starving. What I see in Sicily is mirrored by what journalist Alexander Smoltczyk sees in Sidi Bouzid: "the soil there is fertile. But they object to the fact that the olives they harvest and the tomato paste they make are sold for pennies to Sicily, where they are converted into Italian antipasti."[14] The Tunisian uprising finds its larger horizon in the Euro-Mediterranean area, with the aspiration to the right of mobility for study, travel, and work, whether one takes advantage of it or not. But the months following Ben Ali's demise in January 2011 are characterized by political uncertainty, and enable the arrival in Lampedusa of some twenty-three thousand Tunisian nationals. "You don't know who is with you and who is against you; who is with Ben Ali and who is against him," says young Adel, whom I met in Milan in June 2011.[15] He shows me a scar, from a bullet he says he received from somebody "on Ben Ali's paycheck," a few days before crossing to Lampedusa at a cost of 1,000 euros. Like many others, he left also because he did not think democracy was "real" in post–Ben Ali Tunisia. Corruption, clientelism, and misery had not magically disappeared—as they had not in post-Hoxha Albania, two decades earlier. "Hunger drove our revolution," he says, "but you cannot eat freedom."

Ahmed, a Tunisian artist, freelance journalist, and political activist in his midthirties, arrived at Lampedusa in early April 2011. He was "really *lucky* to have met *the right lawyer* and police agents" upon arrival.[16] He was given the opportunity to lodge an asylum application, and his refugee condition was quickly recognized. His case serves as a powerful reminder of the discretion often shaping migrants' *access* to rights, such as the right to apply for asylum. It also serves as an example of the impossibility of formulating empirically valid static "white lists" of safe countries—his asylum application was correctly assessed in light of his individual story, rather than taking for granted that postrevolutionary Tunisia is a "safe" country for everybody. Mohamed is another Tunisian artist and political activist, who also arrived at Lampedusa in April 2011. He applied for asylum, and in June 2011 was still in the holding center, with no information regarding the status of his application. He was routinely told that other facilities in mainland Italy were full. His wife, Amina, was terrified at the prospect of her husband's repatriation to Tunisia. "He'd be killed," she said.[17]

Between late January and March 2011 Lampedusans were convinced that Interior Minister Maroni was purposefully not organizing the prompt departure of Tunisian arrivals toward holding facilities elsewhere. Similar inaction had occurred two years earlier, when the holding facility was partly destroyed. In a Council of Europe[18] document on the subject, Rapporteur Christopher Chope writes that through this inaction Italy "wanted to send a message to its neighbouring countries and to the whole of Europe that it was not able to cope, and that Europe should act and share the burden."[19] Conversely, in Europe many point out that Germany, France, the United Kingdom, and Sweden consistently receive more asylum applications than Italy.[20] Between 2007 and 2013, about 250 million euros, half of the EU funds for Italy, were allotted by the Ministry of the Interior to support activities of border enforcement. Other funds were allocated for migrants' integration, migrants' repatriations, and refugees. No funds were used to repair Lampedusa's holding facility, damaged since the 2009 fire and as of 2011 capable of housing three hundred people at most.

In winter 2011, Lampedusa's holding center is full beyond capacity. For a few days more than six thousand Tunisians outnumber local residents. On the island there is a sense of disruption of social order and morality more than a concern with personal safety. Indeed there are no serious incidents, except for a couple of break-ins by people looking for shelter. But "faces one has never seen" make it impossible to leave the keys in the

parked motorcycle and to leave house doors ajar as usual. A local grocery
posts a sign that advises "extra-communitarian [non-EU] sirs not to enter
in groups larger than two; selling alcohol to extra-communitarians is for-
bidden." Tunisian migrants have to sleep at the disused ferry station, next
to the local turtle conservation center. They share two restrooms. A truck
with the local sanitation department delivers some food.

Some people rest out in the elements, on the promontory between the
airport runway and the ferry station. Concerned locals call that "the hill of
shame." Rosario, a young resident, explains what he means by that.[21] It is a
shame for "the state," he says, and more precisely for "the government,"
unable to prevent, during those "ugly days," migrants' "violation of human
rights" and locals' "deprivation of spaces." Those more than six thousand
people, he says, were received "with no organization." It is only after several
days of growing tensions that the Ministry of Interior eventually ships to
the island basic facilities such as tents and portable toilets. And Rosario,
like many other Lampedusans, sees that lack of organized reception as a
political strategy, part of the governmental decision to stop transfers to
Sicily and to the mainland. But the hill of shame is also a "mountain of
solidarity," as Rosario calls it. Several Lampedusans bring warm tea, fruit
juice, clean clothes, and meals. In Lampedusa, fish couscous is a local spe-
cialty, just as in nearby Tunisia; local youth and women prepare about ten
kilograms of the dish, aware of its symbolic value. And Tunisian migrants
understand that their situation is not to be ascribed to local residents. They
always say "*grazie*" (thanks), says Rosario. These are hectic but "memorable
days." New friendships are made. Some of the local youth share a feeling
of "enthusiasm" and *festa* (joviality) with their Tunisian counterparts, as
they make an effort to welcome the new arrivals in the absence of an intelligible language. Prior social networking relationships become face-to-face
relationships, as Tunisian Facebook "friends" say that they will arrive to
visit Lampedusa shortly.

Many migrants spend their day strolling along Via Roma. They hang
around the town's Piazza Libertà, nearby, and the Church of San Gerlando,
also nearby—as is everything in the tiny residential part of the island.
Father Stefano, the parish priest, makes available parish spaces. National
Caritas delivers a truckload of clothes. Mayor De Rubeis is hosting some
families and minors in his family's empty villas. Routinely interviewed by
national media, he declares that "if all residents did this, there wouldn't be
migrants on the street." Families had been routinely hosted by private

citizens in the past, in Lampedusa as in coastal Apulia. This is now something that to most citizens sounds utopian and unfeasible, in Apulia as in
Lampedusa. The understanding is that hospitality needs to be extended by
state or religious institutions. Many Lampedusa residents, benefiting in the
past from fishing and more recently from tourism, have built a second or
third house, eventually to be left to their children. Lampedusa has housing
available for an estimated sixty thousand seasonal tourists. In 2011, most
of those accommodations stay unoccupied until summer.

On March 14, 2011, charismatic French politician Marine Le Pen travels
to Lampedusa, ostensibly to show her support for local residents over-
whelmed by immigration. She has just succeeded her father, Jean-Marie Le
Pen, as the president of the Front National, the restrictionist right-wing
French political party. She is accompanied by Mario Borghezio, a Northern
League Italian politician best known for his routinely racist remarks. On
March 17 there are demonstrations by a handful of local residents. They
feel "abandoned by the state," to borrow their wording. A few banners,
hanging in the piazza, read as follows: "No more taxation," "Solution?
Centers of reception on ships," and "Push them back now." A few residents
on the dock shout, "go away!" and "drop them in Malta!" toward Tunisian
migrants approaching on board a coast guard patrol boat. The vessel is
unable to dock because of the protesters. Hours later, riot police have to
physically block them to allow a safe landing.

In Lampedusa, in 2011, no one admits antipathy toward migrants. But
everyone tellingly brings up the same phrase: Rome and the EU have
"dumped this" on Lampedusa. Italian authorities have "fooled" its residents for years. The disruption of the small daily routines of civility and
propriety is only the latest source of frustration with the regional Sicilian
government and the national Italian one. In Lampedusa residents complain
about the absence of a delivery room in the local clinic; the lack of mean-
ingful employment prospects for the youth; the lack of entertainment venues, such as a cinema; the fact that, except during summer, distributors
refuse to ship magazines and newspapers to the island; the exorbitant price
of utilities and fuel, including the one necessary for the local fishing fleet;
the militarization of the island.[22] And "on top of all this" there are the
unceasing unregulated arrivals and the logistical inability and political
unwillingness to "dispose of" the migrants efficiently. There is also a perceived threat to the image and the economy of the island. Giovanna, owner
of a small, family-run hotel, explains that prospective tourists in northern

Italy and northern Europe start making reservations in March, and a vacation in Lampedusa might now seem a scary prospect.[23]

Two hundred migrants are flown elsewhere in Italy daily, but this still seems "too slow," as more Tunisians arrive. Voices can be heard of provocateurs suggesting they should be shot at or let drown. Other residents do pity these people behind a fence, and their mind goes to World War II "concentration camps." Despite their differing opinions, residents demand a political intervention. On March 27 Raffaele Lombardo, governor of Sicily (2008–12), visits the island and meets the mayor and local residents. A few days later, on March 30, it is Prime Minister (2008–11) Silvio Berlusconi's turn. As he has done for almost two decades, he anoints himself a redeemer and performs the role of the fatherland's savior, while failing to acknowledge his cabinet's responsibilities for the situation. He promises to evacuate some sixty-two hundred migrants and to "free Lampedusa and leave the island to local Lampedusans" within a matter of days, as six large boats will take the migrants away.

The Death of Abderrazak Madmoudi . . .

Starting at the end of March 2011, the Italian navy warship *San Marco* takes hundreds of Tunisian citizens—all males—from Lampedusa to the port of Taranto in the Apulia region. From there, they are taken to a new holding facility nearby. They carry no belongings: just a plastic grocery bag with bottled water and perhaps some food. The tent city, still unfinished at the time of the first arrivals, is located in a rural setting, between the towns of Manduria and Oria. There are no trees, as this used to be a runway. During World War II, the site hosted planes from the Italian, German, and eventually U.S. air forces. National politicians publicly define it as a "temporary CIE," a center for the detention and "identification and expulsion" of migrants. In reality its status and categorization remain undetermined, even when a hybrid phrase is coined: "center of reception and identification"—a concept that has not been administratively substantiated.

Local and regional authorities are first told they need to expect some five hundred people, then fifteen hundred, and finally up to thirty-five hundred. The region of Apulia's governor Nichi Vendola (2005–15) and council members had expressed their interest and enthusiasm in hosting and assisting refugees on Apulian territory, but in smaller, dispersed, and integrated locations—I am reminded of Don Giuseppe and his idea of (Albanians') diffuse reception back in 1997, not far from here. The large camp structure instead concerns local administrators in regard to the dignity and rights of people who face the prospect of long-term confinement. Nearby small towns including Andria, Minervino Murge, Torchiarolo, Fasano, and Gravina extend hospitality and host about eighty Tunisians. In Gravina Tunisian arrivals are warmly received by the mayor and city council, and invited to city hall for a public welcome featuring the Tunisian national anthem. The supporters of Taranto F.C. organize a memorable soccer match against the Manduria camp's "Tunisian Migrants' National Team." Local soccer enthusiasts lose 11–4, but are happy to use soccer "for liberty" and "against racism," as Giorgio, a local resident, puts it to me.[24]

In this situation, political commentators write that the right-wing Berlusconi government cannot afford to appear soft on immigration, as Italian local elections are scheduled for May 2011. This consideration might help explain both the confinement "solution," once again deemed a viable bureaucratic and humanitarian solution to a manufactured emergency, and the location of the tent city in southern Italy. This is seen as a way to avoid the redistribution of Tunisians on the entire national territory, which would allegedly disappoint the government coalition's Northern League constituents. In the meantime, Italy is enveloped in its *tricolore* national flag. Exhibits, mass media, schools, public administrations, and innovative artistic endeavors are celebrating in 2011 the 150th anniversary of the country's national unification.

By early April 2011, tension in the Manduria camp is palpable. As many as 500 people manage to escape on April 2, disappearing into the surrounding countryside but mostly headed to the railway stations of Oria and Taranto, where some are apprehended. There are 360 police agents guarding the camp, and dozens of others patrol the neighboring towns and countryside, especially to reassure local residents. Police agents are complemented by mounted guards of the National Forestry Department.

Even as the fence remains damaged for some time, many Tunisian citizens prefer to stay in the camp. But they sleep right outside the camp as a sign of protest, and organize a demonstration in front of the gate. They complain about conditions within the camp. At the same time, as with African refugees from Libya being hosted in hotels in Naples, the quality of the accommodations is not their primary concern. One of the Tunisian

protesters' signs reads as follows: "we did not come here to eat, but for
liberty and dignity." "*Liberté, liberté, liberté*" is the powerful chant that
resonates within the camp. With the fence wide open, it is clear that "liberty" for these Tunisian migrants does not mean merely personal safety and
freedom from confinement but also certainty about legal status and the
possibility of travel elsewhere. Police agents are unable and unwilling to
keep people locked in, and the camp essentially becomes an open camp.
But the agents still block local youth from entering for some time. Members
of Parliament would also like to enter to meet some of the remaining 1,600
migrants and to assess the facility's conditions.

The camp sits in the middle of a desolate rural area, halfway between
the historic towns of Manduria and Oria and between the administrative
provinces of Taranto and Brindisi. It is close to the road that links the two
towns. Migrants routinely walk to either town, out of curiosity but also for
espresso, cigarettes, drinks, and phone credit. Most importantly, the towns
constitute the only escape from the boredom of the camp and the frustration of the legal limbo. Traffic on the Manduria-Oria road is heavy. There
are no sidewalks and no public illumination. To minimize the hazard originating from such a situation, administrators with the province of Brindisi
decide to provide a free shuttle service linking the camp with Oria in their
jurisdiction. Local residents are generally happy about the availability of
new customers for their small businesses. Others spare some change and
do not mind chatting. But as there is no shuttle from the camp to Manduria, this becomes a contentious issue. Days go by and the Tunisian presence in Oria's hilly center increases in numbers and duration, with less
lingering presences in Manduria. A handful of citizens, newly organized
in a Committee for Security and the Protection of Quiet Life, and Oria's
Confartigianato (artisans' and small businesses' association, located, haunt-
ingly, in Via Tripoli) ask cafes not to administer alcohol to Tunisian customers in order to maintain "order and security"; to routinely sanitize
premises, utensils, and equipment; and to promptly report (Tunisians') acts
of "incivility," violence, and harassment.

Implicitly responding to such vocal but limited protests, the province
of Brindisi terminates its shuttle service between the camp and Oria. The
absence of an authorized and safe carrier, underpinned by the political
decision to bend to the pressure of a handful of vocal citizens, does not
prevent people from leaving the camp anyway and spending the day in the
town. Among them is Abderrazak Madmoudi, fifty-one.[25] The man has

left behind two children and his wife in Tunisia and reached Italy on a boat, intending to continue to the Netherlands, where his oldest son resides. Abderrazak had already been living in the Netherlands, but was expelled and repatriated—a decision he intends to challenge in court. On Friday night, April 15, 2011, he is walking back to the camp. The roadside is dark. He is run over by a car. The driver is charged with manslaughter. His wife and children, from Tunisia and the Netherlands, may now legally reach him. The Italian Ministry of Foreign Affairs offers to pay for the repatriation of the corpse, to be received by Abderrazak Madmoudi's elderly parents back in Tunisia.

The Boat That Was Left to Die . . .

In mid-February 2011, in Lampedusa and in EU governmental circles there is also growing concern with the situation in Libya. The Arab Uprising there is taking the shape of armed unrest. The Gaddafi regime and the unity of the country seem seriously challenged. Franco Frattini, foreign minister in Berlusconi's fourth cabinet, tells domestic and international media that Italy needs to brace itself for a "biblical exodus"—in 2011 the phrase of choice among Italian ministers—which will be "ten times bigger" than the number of Albanians who fled to Italy in the 1990s: "We know what to expect when the Libyan national system falls—a wave of 200,000 to 300,000 immigrants," Frattini says publicly. He estimates a third of Libya's population to be immigrants from sub-Saharan Africa, ready to flee the unstable country.[26] Interior Minister Roberto Maroni of the Northern League warns of Italy "ending up like Constantinople," a reference to the Islamic component of the North African unrest and emigration. There are no Libyan authorities to enforce the country's borders. South of Sicily, Italy deploys its air force planes, together with navy, coast guard, and finance guard vessels to be complemented by Frontex. Northern European countries assert that Italy, "a country of 60 million people, cannot possibly have problems in facing a few thousand migrants."[27] And they invoke the Dublin Regulation, according to which it is the first EU receiving country that is expected to either repatriate migrants or process their asylum applications.

In light of the unrest in Libya, by February 25 thousands of non-Libyan citizens working there are repatriated or transported to safe neighboring

countries, such as Malta and Greece. Citizens are for the most part evacuated by their own governments, through military vessels and planes, ferries,
cruise ships, and commercial flights. Countries directly involved in the
evacuation effort include Austria, China, France, Germany, Greece, Italy,
Japan, the Netherlands, the Philippines, Portugal, Russia, South Korea,
Turkey, the United Kingdom, and the United States. Canadians are evacuated with the support of the United Kingdom, Spain, and the United
States.[28]

As of February 2011, the IOM estimates at 1.8 million the number of
migrant workers in Libya.[29] On February 22, 2011, the major Italian newspaper *Corriere della Sera* publishes the testimonies of an Italian NGO,
EveryOne, according to which Eritrean, Ethiopian, Somali, and Sudanese
citizens, possibly including refugees "pushed back" by Italy in 2009, are
being physically attacked by rebels throughout Libya, with knives and
machetes: on the street, in their own homes, in detention centers.[30] Rebels
accuse black Africans of being mercenaries employed by Gaddafi. On February 26, in the port of Benghazi Human Rights Watch (HRW) workers
witness "men in military and civilian clothing beat with sticks and knives
two Africans who tried to jump on a departing Tunisian ship." On February
28 the crews of two ferries deny a group of sub-Saharan Africans entry to
the ships, explaining that "certain governments had commissioned them to
evacuate only their nationals and that the crews did not have the authority
to take on other nationalities."[31] On the same day, Tripoli's Catholic
bishop, Giovanni Innocenzo Martinelli, vocally solicits a "wonderful gesture" toward about two thousand Eritreans: we "just need a ship to pick
them up," he pleads.[32] In his prayer he is joined by organizations such as
the Jesuit Refugee Service in Malta and Christian Solidarity Worldwide.
Also on February 28, the UNHCR urges an effort to actively evacuate people who intend to leave Libya. Quite explicitly, High Commissioner for
Refugees António Guterres acknowledges that there are "no planes and
boats to evacuate people originating from war-torn or very poor countries."[33] He urges governments to consider the needs of all vulnerable people and not just their own citizens.

Libya has long been a country of transit or destination for refugees,
displaced persons, and stateless persons, but the vast majority have no
access to UNHCR registration or protection, in particular due to the limits
imposed on the UNHCR's activities by the Libyan government, well before
the 2011 turmoil. The UNHCR has managed to recognize only eight

thousand refugees, including people of Palestinian, Iraqi, Sudanese, Ethiopian, Somali, and Eritrean origin. Of particular concern are people from sub-Saharan Africa, including refugees registered with the UNHCR, who are not able to reach safety in Egypt or Tunisia, and are "choosing to keep a low profile and stay at home; they say they are fearful of being targeted if they attempt to leave." Finally, the UNHCR appeals to all neighboring governments in North Africa and Europe to "maintain open land, air and sea borders for people forced to flee from Libya."[34] By the end of February, the UNHCR and global media such as *Al Jazeera* call attention to the scarcity of food and medical supplies in the North African country.[35]

By early March, researchers with HRW in Libya manage to interview displaced workers from countries such as Burkina Faso, Cameroon, Eritrea, Ethiopia, Ghana, Haiti, Ivory Coast, Mali, Niger, Nigeria, Somalia, and Sudan. They collect several stories of people who claim that they have been recently assaulted, harassed, threatened, forced to flee from homes and workplaces, and robbed of their belongings. Unconfirmed reports purport that Gaddafi had brought in sub-Saharan African mercenaries to attack anti-government protesters. African migrant workers—for a decade the object of racialized violence and resentment—become the target of numerous violent attacks. From Benghazi, Peter Bouckaert, emergencies director at HRW, solicits the governments who have successfully evacuated their own citizens to also assist in the evacuation of vulnerable and displaced non-Libyans, primarily from Asian and African countries, noting that their governments have apparently "been unable or unwilling to rescue them."[36] Fifty-seven Eritreans who have documents from the UNHCR in Libya are taken to Italy by plane. Regarding Eritreans, as well as other African nationals, humanitarian and religious organizations essentially argue that they face a considerable risk of persecution in Libya, by governmental and insurgent forces and by the general population. HRW, in particular, argues that "until they are able to avail themselves of the protection of their own governments they have essentially the same protection needs as any other refugees, and the international community is *obligated* to prevent their expulsion or return to a place where their lives or freedom would be threatened."[37] Amnesty International also calls for neighboring countries to allow entry to all arrivals from Libya, including non-Libyans; for those countries to assist in the repatriation of those who do not claim international protection; and for the "international community" to assist countries receiving those fleeing Libya.[38] But states rarely implement human rights out of moral obligations.

UN Security Council Resolution 1973 is adopted on March 17, 2011, establishing a no-fly zone over Libya and demanding the protection of civilians and a cease-fire between the forces loyal to Gaddafi and the various revolutionary militias who intend to oust him and his family. Two days later, a multistate coalition under the NATO umbrella begins military intervention. The coalition does not seem to have considered the preliminary questions an Italian navy officer says must be asked before starting any war: "Where do you put the prisoners? Where do you put the dead? What do you do with the refugees?"[39] Every European government has known for years that Libya hosts both a large immigrant population and thousands of refugees. It is also widely known that the Gaddafi regime does not think any African ought to be recognized as a genuine refugee, and that Gaddafi himself manipulates the issue of migration through Libya, often threatening to "flood" and "blacken" Europe with migrants. There are no unintended consequences in national politics and international relations. There is systematic negligence, at best. There are sovereign priorities and political choices.

The Mediterranean is one of the commercially busiest seas in the world, with thousands of fishing and cargo vessels sailing at any given moment. Especially following the attacks of September 11, 2001, it is also one of the best monitored. Since October 6, 2011, NATO has been present with an important, although relatively unpublicized, operation. Active Endeavour is aimed at demonstrating "NATO's [internal] solidarity and resolve in the fight against terrorism and to help deter and disrupt terrorist activity in the Mediterranean." This is particularly significant, according to NATO, as "some 65 per cent of the oil and natural gas consumed in Western Europe pass[es] through the Mediterranean each year, with major pipelines connecting Libya to Italy and Morocco to Spain."[40] The mission consists of a "balanced collection" of surface units, submarines, and aircrafts. The operation counts on the systematic collaboration of Greece, Italy, Spain, Turkey, Denmark, Germany, Norway, Israel, and Morocco.[41] As of October 2013, Italy has contributed 230 million euros to the NATO mission.[42] Active Endeavour seeks to improve what is known as "maritime situation awareness," meaning that a collection of networked sources, including intelligence, satellite, and radar facilities from a variety of countries and institutions, help in identifying trends and anomalies in the Mediterranean. Although vessels participating in Active Endeavour have occasionally contributed to rescue operations—as the law of the sea requires of any vessel able to do so—it is a military operation. As such, it does not routinely exchange information with civilian agencies, including Frontex. Admiral De Giorgi (2014), Italy's chief of naval operations, has recently suggested more integration of NATO's Mediterranean operations and its situational awareness with search-and-rescue activities.[43]

With the beginning of the war against the Libyan regime, the stretch between northwestern Libya, Tunisia, Lampedusa, Malta, and Sicily—already under surveillance by NATO vessels and aircrafts, radars, and satellites—becomes more heavily patrolled for military purposes. An Italian officer, discussing the prospect of maritime migration during the war, declares: "I expect that sailing from Libya towards Italy should be a bit like doing slalom between military ships."[44]

On March 25, 2011, a group of 68 people, mostly Somalis and Eritreans, leave the port of Tripoli seeking to escape the country. Their boat goes missing—it never makes it to Lampedusa, Malta, Sicily, or Tunisia. Another boat that left on March 22 with 335 people on board is also reported to be missing. On March 31, *Corriere della Sera* reports that some 70 bodies have washed up on Tripoli's beaches. As of September 2014, local acquaintances of mine confirm that this continues to happen.

On March 26, 2011, a small dinghy leaves the Libyan coast headed toward Italy. Upon passengers' embarkation, smugglers on land have taken their bags of food and water, in order to cram as many people as possible. The dinghy carries 70 young adults, including pregnant women, and two small children. Passengers originate from Ethiopia, Nigeria, Eritrea, Ghana, and Sudan. A Ghanaian citizen serves as the "captain." A passenger from Ethiopia declares: "it was completely overcrowded. Everyone was sitting on everybody else. I had someone sitting on top of me, and this person had someone sitting on top of him."[45] Abu Kurke Kebato, twenty-five, is also among the passengers. He fled his native Ethiopia as a result of political violence, trekking across the Sahara. The boat is "very small, very dangerous." He considers swimming back but his travel companion warns that Libyan forces might open fire.[46] Abu Kurke says that soon "the fuel ran out, the weather turned rough and with people squeezed in, sitting and standing, it was difficult to stay onboard." The captain has a Thuraya (telephone provider) satellite phone, and shortly before the batteries run out somebody manages to call Father Mussie Zerai, an Eritrean priest in Rome. He is well known among migrants from the Horn of Africa for his humanitarian work. They tell him babies and adults are sick and have no water.[47]

He contacts Italian authorities. The Maritime Rescue Coordination Centre in Rome is able to pinpoint the boat's position based on Thuraya's records and sends out a distress call for any close-by vessel to help. The center keeps sending distress calls every four hours for ten days. For fourteen days the boat is adrift in the Mediterranean. There are a number of direct contacts between the dinghy in distress and other vessels, and with an unidentified military helicopter that drops biscuits and water. "We saved one bottle of water from the helicopter for the two babies, and kept feeding them even after their parents had passed," says Abu Kurke. He survived by drinking his own urine and eating toothpaste. "But after two days, the babies passed too, because they were so small."[48]

There is also an encounter with a warship. "Some [sailors] were looking through binoculars and others were taking pictures of us," says Ghirma, from Eritrea. But the ship remains at a distance, even as people in the dinghy hold up the dead babies and the empty fuel containers. Somebody jumps into the sea to push the dinghy toward the warship, in vain.[49] There is also direct contact with two fishing vessels, from Italy and from Tunisia, and with a Cypriot vessel. These three commercial vessels, the warship, and the military helicopter fail to provide substantial assistance and possibly to report the exact position of the dinghy in distress.

On April 10, 2011, the dinghy washes up on the rocks close to Zliten, 160 kilometers east of Tripoli. Of a group of seventy-two, only eleven people are alive. One woman dies in Libya. They are arrested. Their possessions are confiscated—wedding rings, necklaces, photos, documents, and SIM cards. Abu Kurke's friend is among the dead. Following detention, Abu Kurke is forced by the Libyan military onto a boat to Italy. "Going back to sea, after my experience, was like a death sentence," he says. "On board, I hid, I didn't want to look at the sea. I thought I was going to die." He makes it to Lampedusa. From there he is relocated to a facility in mainland Italy and reaches the Netherlands, where he applies for asylum and lives with his wife and child, trying to build a future but also coping with injuries from sun exposure and with his sleepless nights.[50] On April 5, 2012, the Dutch police act on an expulsion order and remove the couple from an asylum center.[51] Abu Kurke "entered" Europe in Italy, as possibly proved by the collection of his fingerprints there, and Italy is where his application needs to be adjudicated and where he needs to be deported, according to the Dublin Regulation. The Dutch Council of State, to which Abu Kurke's lawyer appeals, suspends the deportation order.[52]

We know about the story of Abu Kurke's "left to die" boat, as it has come to be known, because of an independent investigation carried out by the *Guardian*, the British newspaper. Additionally, the Parliamentary Assembly of the Council of Europe sponsored a nine-month inquiry led by Tineke Strik (2012), a Dutch parliamentarian and migration expert. In the report, we read that the boat in distress was in the Libyan SAR maritime area, but was "left floating in a responsibility vacuum" by Italian and Maltese rescue centers. Maltese and Italian personnel knew, or should have known, that Libyan authorities, fighting for their survival, did not have the ability or willingness to coordinate SAR operations in their area; on the contrary, some were forcing people to leave. Nevertheless, "neither felt an *obligation* to mount a full search and rescue operation." Maltese authorities ultimately claimed that the boat was just too far from their island—a recurrent challenge, as we will see. Regarding Italian authorities, "during the period in question their assets [patrol boats] were working around the clock, with between 20 to 25 incidents requiring attention on just one day. Between 26 and 28 March, the Italian authorities were engaged in incidents involving approximately 4,300 people. Over 2,200 of these people were assisted at sea and around 2,000 were rescued from distress situations. From the Rome MRCC's perspective, priority needed to be given to the large number of incidents occurring within Italy's SAR zone rather than incidents occurring elsewhere."[53]

Nevertheless, the report also critically points out that "not being responsible on the basis of SAR zones, doesn't relieve another State which is informed about an incident at sea of its responsibility to ensure the rescue operation." It is important to quote in detail the "catalogue of failures" that can help assess the mechanisms of this egregious crime of peace. No one among relevant rescue countries and NATO forces participating in the war claimed as theirs the helicopter and the warship that could have rescued the migrants or at least called for assistance, and instead acted as complicit bystanders, dropping cookies and bottled water and watching and photographing people as they were dying, from afar:

From this story, a catalogue of failures became apparent: the Libyan authorities failed to maintain responsibility for their Search and Rescue zone, the Italian and Maltese Maritime Rescue Coordination Centres failed to launch any search and rescue operation, and NATO failed to react to the distress calls, even though there were military vessels under its control in the boat's vicinity when the distress call was sent (including the [Spanish] *Mendez Núñez* which was estimated to have been 11 miles away, although this distance is disputed by Spain). The flag States of vessels close to the boat also failed to rescue the people in distress. Furthermore, two unidentified commercial fishing vessels also failed to respond to the direct calls for assistance from the boat in distress. Alongside these failures, a number of shortcomings contributed to the distress calls not being answered, including gaps in the maritime legal framework and a failure by NATO and the individual States militarily involved in Libya to anticipate adequately . . . an exodus of asylum seekers and refugees.[54]

. . . And Another 2,290 Crimes of Peace

In May 2011, maritime arrivals from Libya to Lampedusa are continuous. Shortly following the arrival of a boat with 800 people, including 138 women and 12 children, early on Sunday morning, May 8, 2011, the coast guard, the finance guard, and local citizens rescue 528 people whose boat has crashed on the cliffs. It is a day of celebration and gratefulness. On Monday, though, scuba divers find the corpses of three young men, between twenty and twenty-five years old, who had not been seen.

On May 10, 2011, CNN, among others, reports that a boat has capsized off the coast of Tripoli. It carries "more than 600 asylum seekers of various Arab and African nationalities," including 240 Somalis. UNHCR spokeswoman Laura Boldrini declares that, based on refugees' testimonies, "Libyan authorities are facilitating the departures of non-Libyan citizens from Libyan coasts."[55] IOM officials point out that many refugees say they did not have to pay for their passage to Lampedusa, although they were stripped of their savings and belongings by Libyan officials.

In mid-May 2011, Melissa Fleming, a spokeswoman for the UNHCR, declares that since the conflict began, 12,000 people have arrived in Italy or Malta. Also, up to 1,200 people fleeing Libya have died in the Mediterranean Sea since mid-February.[56]

By late spring 2011, to most residents in Lampedusa the presence of newly arrived migrants is barely noticeable. "Sub-Saharan" Africans, as they are routinely referred to, are hosted in the local facility for a short

Figure 6. The *Flaminia* ferry, Lampedusa, taking migrants to mainland Italy. Photo: Maurizio Albahari.

time. Organizations such as the IOM and Doctors Without Borders are present with their workers to inform the migrants about asylum and immigration laws and to assist families. The *Flaminia* and other ferries of the Tirrenia shipping company are contracted by the government to regularly take migrants—up to 900 each time—to mainland Italy. For some migrants the journey takes several days, as the ferry needs to stop in different Italian ports on the same trip. Ports of destination include first Cagliari, in Sardinia, and then Naples and Genoa. From there, migrants will be transported to different facilities, including hotels reimbursed by the state administration. Most often, they are not aware of their destination. Some, waiting for asylum adjudication, will be exploited in a variety of ways in Italian cities, and by a variety of people, including migrant residents with a longer presence. Others pursue seasonal opportunities in agriculture.[57] Their working and living conditions are excruciating. Off the book, pay is discretionary and abysmally low. Italians have been subjected to similar conditions for decades (although at least they have received temporary shelter during the picking season). But it is migrants' strikes and mobilization against Mafia-like organized crime—in Rosarno[58] and Nardò in southern Italy, in particular—that help foster legislative answers in this respect.[59]

On June 2, 2011, the Tunisian Press Agency, or TAP, reports that between 200 and 270 people are missing in the Mediterranean off the Tunisian Kerkennah Islands, on their way to Lampedusa. The nationals of Ivory Coast, Cameroon, Tunisia, and other African countries die following an engine failure, as in hectic moments they try to reach the Tunisian coast guard's and army's rescue vessels. In all, 570 people are rescued.[60]

Authorities of the new, post–Ben Ali Tunisia are also dealing with the arrival of Libyans and other nationals displaced by the war in Libya. Eritrean, Somalian, Sudanese, Nigerian, Iraqi, Palestinian, Pakistani, Ghanaian, and Malian citizens are hosted in the tent city of Choucha, Tunisia, very close to the border with Libya in the vicinity of the coast. Some are unwilling to "return" to their regions of origin—they originally left because of political violence. Together with other humanitarian organizations, UNHCR solicits the relocation of these refugees to "Western countries," but between July and December 2011 only Norway and Belgium agree to resettle hundreds of refugees. Thousands of others spend months in the camp. In front of his tent, Abdullah Mohamed has grown wheat to spell out the message, "I love to live in the U.S.A."[61] Smugglers help some of the camps' displaced persons to once again cross the border to Libya, and eventually to the port of Zuwara, from where other smugglers will provide the unauthorized and perilous journey to Lampedusa. Tunisian and Libyan smugglers cannot directly facilitate the transatlantic passage toward the American Dream, but they are efficient salespersons of the European Dream.

On June 17, 2011, Minister of the Interior Maroni, following a conference in a northern Italian university, creatively proposes a possible new way to implement pushback operations off the Libyan coast. He proposes that "NATO, which keeps its warships north of the Libyan coast to prevent the delivery of goods to the country, could be asked to implement a naval blockade also for people exiting the country. This would already be a solution to the [clandestine immigration] problem."[62] On August 1, 2011, a boat in distress is safely escorted to the port of Lampedusa. There are 271 occupants, including 36 women and 21 children. But in the hold, where the old engine is located, rescue workers find 25 bodies. Twenty-five people died of asphyxiation. As they tried to climb out through a tiny trapdoor, they were pushed back by those on the deck,[63] usually able to pay a little more than those in the hold.

On August 6, 2011, the Italian newspaper *La Repubblica* covered "the umpteenth maritime tragedy." People died of thirst and hunger. Unlike others whom he saw getting sick, Robert, a young Nigerian survivor, resisted drinking seawater.[64] For many maritime travelers the Mediterranean journey is the very first close contact with the sea: perhaps they do not know that excessive seawater makes your blood pressure plummet, augments your thirst and further dehydrates you, and makes you delusional. It causes renal failure and death, robbing you of a little extra time—should help ever arrive.

I was born and raised in a coastal town. I think I know better: you shouldn't drink seawater. But this is not about normative, standardized, and disembodied knowledge. It is about a situation in which I cannot anticipate whether I would have done as Robert did or not. Together with some of his companions, he had to throw into the sea about 100 corpses, including his cousin's. Crossing himself, he asks out loud the question that quietly torments the life of maritime survivors: "what else could we have done?" He is also interrogating the shipmasters, naval captains, and other military and rescue forces that were unable or unwilling to help: "we have been seen by many big ships, with cannons and radars, but none have come closer."[65] The crew of a Cypriot tugboat, at a distance, threw some rafts that proved impossible for the migrants to reach. The coast guard forwarded the distress call to "NATO headquarters." But there was no rescue intervention. There was no salvation. In all, 376 people survived the week-long crossing. Talking to journalist Francesco Viviano, an anonymous member of the Italian armed forces long involved in rescue operations bitterly asks: "This war [NATO's Operation Unified Protector] is supposed to save thousands and thousands of people from the Gaddafi regime. But among these people to be saved aren't there all those who managed to flee Libya by embarking on a wreck, risking their life to get to Lampedusa? . . . We want to save them in Libya by bombing Tripoli, but once hundreds manage to leave they are abandoned. What does it mean? It's an incredible paradox, we want to save them in Libya and we let them die in the sea?"[66]

By the end of September 2011, the IOM claims to have completed the evacuation of 40,000 migrants "trapped in Misrata, Sabha, Gatroun, Tripoli and Benghazi," bringing them—on ferries, buses, and planes—to safer places within Libya, taking them across the border into Tunisia and Egypt, and facilitating repatriations to African neighboring countries. But the IOM has been unable to significantly repatriate sub-Saharan African citizens, claiming difficulty in locating those countries' diplomatic representatives.[67]

Muammar Gaddafi is killed on October 20, 2011, and NATO terminates its military activities a week later. Also in October, Amnesty International publishes a compelling report on the dreadful situation of black Libyans and African third-country nationals in Libya, including massive use of extrajudicial detention, beatings, other ill treatment, and torture. For the organization, detention abuses are "staining the new Libya."[68]

By the end of 2011, a total of 56,000 people landed in Italy (including 28,000 Tunisian citizens). Malta and Greece also received 1,574 and 1,030 people, respectively. At the end of January, 2012, the UNHCR released figures based on "interviews with people who reached Europe on boats, telephone calls and e-mails from relatives, as well as reports from Libya and Tunisia from survivors whose boats either sank or were in distress in the early stages of the journey." The data pointed to at least 1,500 migrants who drowned or went missing in the Mediterranean in 2011. Senior communications officer Sybella Wilkes told journalists that this "makes 2011 the deadliest year for this region since UNHCR started to record these statistics in 2006."[69] Gabriele Del Grande of the blog *Fortress Europe*, basing his figures on the daily scrutiny of news items published by media around the Mediterranean, put at 2,352 the number of recorded deaths in the Mediterranean for the year 2011.[70]

On October 12, 2012, the Norway-based Nobel Committee announces that the Nobel Peace Prize for 2012 is to be awarded to the European Union. The EU, an area of freedom, security, and justice, receives the prize for over six decades of contribution to "the advancement of peace and reconciliation, democracy and human rights in Europe."[71]

Floating Sovereignty

Following the fall of Ben Ali and of his state apparatus, in early April 2011 the Tunisian political and institutional architecture appears fragile, under pressure from popular discontent and vibrant legal and constitutional discussions. As elections are still to be held, various political figures occupy for brief periods the offices of president and prime minister. On April 5, 2011, the prime minister is Béji Caïd Essebsi. This Tuesday is a mildly warm day, like most other days at this time of the year in Tunis. And there happens to be a beautiful waxing crescent moon. Italian interior minister Maroni and Tunisian authorities sign yet another bilateral "technical agreement of cooperation." The agreement stipulates that Tunisian migrants who arrived at Lampedusa between January 15 and April 5 will be granted a temporary residence permit in Italy, valid for six months. Italy will also provide "technical" assistance to strengthen its neighbor's border enforcement capabilities, in the form of patrol boats and about a hundred off-road vehicles. Tunisian citizens who happen to arrive in Italy starting on Wednesday, April 6, will be considered "clandestine economic immigrants" and will be pushed back at sea or speedily repatriated (just as happened to Albanian arrivals following the April 3, 1997, bilateral agreement with Italy). Tunisian officials agree to up to one hundred repatriations per day. Mirroring the Italian-Egyptian bilateral agreement signed in 2007 (in the Mubarak era, and still in force), for newly arrived Tunisians simplified return procedures will amount to collective summary removal.

In the Manduria tent camp, in the meantime, many Tunisian migrants express the desire to reach relatives and friends in France and elsewhere in Europe. Influential government officials in France and Germany critically discuss the basic tenets of the Schengen Agreement, which since 1995 have gradually abolished passport and immigration controls at common, internal borders. France, in particular, decides to implement border enforcement in its coastal southeastern region, in order to stop Tunisian arrivals on trains from neighboring Italy. The French Ministry of the Interior asks France's prefects of police to fully assess the status of new arrivals from Italy, including checking their passport, residence permit, and assets, ideally at least sixty-two euros for each day of intended sojourn in France.[72] Indeed, out of 23,500 Tunisian citizens who arrived at Lampedusa between January and the end of February 2011, as many as 11,700 have managed to "escape" from various facilities and become "invisible" to Italian bureaucracy.[73] Italian and international commentators suggest that the Ministry of the Interior is essentially allowing Tunisians to leave Manduria and other facilities, knowing most of them seek to reach France, Belgium, and other EU countries; such "dispersion" of an essentially unwanted population might also be instrumental in putting France under pressure, and fostering a reform of the Dublin Regulation, seen as penalizing Italy (with Greece and Malta) as a central Mediterranean location that is also a an EU frontier.[74]

In Lampedusa, as I said, some residents believe the challenge of immigration has been methodically "dumped" on them through active governmental strategies of emergency. Following the establishment of the camp in Manduria, local politicians there argue that, in a country of 60 million people, immigration is not and should not be merely a "problem of Apulia and of the Italian south," and that all Italian regions should take a quota of migrants.[75] National politicians and prominent institutional figures routinely argue that this is not just an Italian issue, but a European one. And European governments reply with figures, citing funds allotted to Italy and the sizable refugee populations they already host. Tunisia—a country of about 10.5 million citizens—is emerging from the uprising and revolution. For the most part, authorities leave the border with war-ravaged Libya open, receiving by the end of April 2011 some 276,000 people, mostly non-Libyan migrant workers. In the southern part of Tunisia, in particular, local families—some descended from Libyan families who fled Italian colonialism exactly a century earlier—share their homes and whatever food they have with as many as 27,000 Libyan refugees. There, only 3,000 Libyans need to be assisted in temporary camps, rather than in homes.[76]

In the meantime, Prime Minister Berlusconi tells the media that the prospect of deportation facing Tunisians, following the April 5, 2011, bilateral agreement, should work as a deterrent against the "human tsunami."[77] Whether he is seriously convinced of this, hopeful, or simply performing certainty for the consumption of Italian voters is another question. While arrivals do slow down, Tunisians still attempt to reach Italy, especially with calm weather conditions.

As routinely happens throughout Italian holding facilities, on September 20, 2012, Tunisian inmates in Lampedusa set some mattresses on fire—they are trying to resist the prospect of repatriation. A substantial part of the facility, already damaged by the 2009 revolt, is further damaged. Hundreds of young men thus spend a night of vigil on the soccer field and on a small square close to the port. The next day, some journalists are harassed by local residents, and Mayor De Rubeis threatens force against the migrants. Riot police intervene against a group of young Tunisian men who have taken a propane tank from a nearby restaurant—allegedly threatening to kill themselves, or as a defense against angry residents, as suggested by a local eyewitness. The next day, September 22, Lampedusa conspicuously celebrates its religious patron, Madonna di Porto Salvo—Madonna of "safe ports," patron and protector of sailors. Some citizens wonder whether there

Figure 7. Madonna di Porto Salvo (and coast guard station), facing the sea in Lampedusa. Photo: Maurizio Albahari.

is anything to celebrate, following such "shameful" events. Others are openly wary of Tunisians. The Catholic bishop of Tunis, Maroun Lahham, serves as the honorary guest of the civil and religious celebrations. But he is not allowed to visit his fellow citizens in the holding facility.

Both physically and politically, there is no more room for Tunisian migrants on the island. Mistral Air planes fly them to CIEs in mainland Italy, and eventually to Tunis. Others are taken away on ferries. Some six hundred people are held for days in the Sicilian port of Palermo, waiting for deportation flights or for accommodations to become available elsewhere. The *Moby Vincent* ferry serves as a de facto floating CIE. Its side is painted in bright cartoonish colors, with the friendly faces of Sylvester the cat, Bugs Bunny, and Tweety Bird. Its Tunisian passengers are confined away from cameras, journalists, and activists, but also from lawyers and judges, who normally warrant migrants' detention. As also happens through the deployment of bilateral agreements, physical, administrative, and documentary borders emigrate to follow and physically envelop would-be migrants' bodies.

Confinement in the ferry, with Tweety's face, exemplifies the resilient, adaptive, just-in-time qualities of sovereignty in the early twenty-first century.

A large EU flag adorns the entrance of a brand-new migrant detention center in Albania, since 2009 a candidate for entry into the EU. The flag acknowledges EU funding. Similar "model" facilities, also funded by the EU, are planned for Turkey.[78] The flag serves also as a visual reminder of the "externalization" trend of EU migration management, including detention. After the fall of the authoritarian gatekeeper regimes in North Africa, EU institutional actors and Italian authorities are hard at work to refashion containment between Africa and Europe. But agreements with Libya and Egypt prove much more unrealistic than the ones with Tunisia. Both countries face extremely volatile situations, and the continuing arrivals of refugees from Eritrea and Syria.

Lining up the Coffins

Mustafa Abdul Jalil, chairman of the Libyan National Transitional Council (de facto head of state between 2011 and 2012, following Gaddafi's demise), visits Rome and Prime Minister Mario Monti (2011–13) on December 15, 2011.[79] The Treaty of Friendship, Partnership, and Cooperation signed in 2008 by Gaddafi and Berlusconi is reactivated after suspension during the war. Its newly enforced provisions are expected to include migration management. On April 3, 2012, Annamaria Cancellieri is the first interior minister in Europe to visit postrevolutionary Libya. In Tripoli the Italian politician meets her counterpart, Fawzi Al-Taher Adulali; Minister of Foreign Affairs Ashour Ben Khayal; and Prime Minister Abdel Rahim Al-Keeb. They sign a bilateral agreement "in the field of security, in particular regarding the contrast to human trafficking," which envisions police training, strengthening of Libyan coastal border patrol activity, and facilitation of voluntary readmission of third-country nationals.[80] Speaking to Amnesty International, a Libyan official claims that the country receives about one thousand new migrants daily. Arrests are the norm, and people—not charged with any crimes—cannot challenge the legality of their detention, as has happened for years. As Amnesty puts it, "The options for refugees and asylum-seekers arriving in Libya from countries where they faced conflict and persecution, such as Eritrea, Ethiopia, Somalia and Sudan, are limited. None of Libya's neighbouring states has effective refugee protection systems in place. Italy has made agreements which accept that people in need of international protection remain effectively trapped. They are left in a country where they are not recognized as refugees, and where they are at risk of human rights abuses, including forced return to a country where they would face further threats to their lives."[81] In July 2012, the Italian Foundation IntegrA/Azione publishes a similar report based on testimonies from African migrants in Libyan detention. In addition to denouncing forced labor, inmates report that those among them who hold a passport are bought out of detention by locals who need cheap laborers. Employers keep their passports to make sure they do not flee.[82]

During 2012, the UNHCR in Libya manages to visit some eighty-five hundred people of concern held in thirty-three migration detention centers. It facilitates the release of more than one thousand refugees, implicitly pointing to unfair detention criteria and practices. Its workers note that prospects for the local integration of refugees are very limited. They also note that sub-Saharan Africans and other nationals are arrested and detained by local militias, and estimate that ten thousand more persons in need of international protection in Libya could have applied for asylum with the UNHCR in 2012 if given the opportunity. Indeed, at this time the UNHCR still operates in Libya "cautiously," as there is no official agreement on its presence. Additionally, the anticipated financial costs for its activities in Libya for 2012 amount to $31.4 million, but the actually available expenditure amounts to only $12.7 million.[83]

By mid-2012 there are growing concerns over the vulnerability of Eritrean refugees not only in Libya but also throughout northeastern Africa. A variety of humanitarian reports, journalistic investigations, police investigations, criminal prosecutions, doctors' testimonies, trafficked people's testimonies, and mutilated bodies speak of the brutal and harrowing routine of kidnapping, torture, violence, degradation, organ extraction for transplants, and death to which traffickers subject their victims (especially but not exclusively in the troubled Sinai peninsula of Egypt). Often, torturers act while on the phone with Eritrean relatives in Israel and the United States to solicit ransom payment. What was originally a smugglers' trade, out of Ethiopian and Sudanese refugee camps toward Israel and North Africa, has become an entrenched trafficking network with many levels of transnational corruption, negligence, and administrative involvement. These kidnappings are confirmed by multiple forms of evidence.[84] Father Mussie Zerai, other members of the Catholic Church, and groups including

HRW and the Italian association EveryOne have been trying for years to transform this information into consequential knowledge at relevant policy levels.

Until mid-2012, Eritrean nationals and others who escaped their homicidal traffickers and Egyptian border guards managed to reach Israel.[85] By June 2012, however, "Israel had nearly finished its 240-kilometer border fence with Egypt and the numbers dipped."[86] The *Los Angeles Times* reports that, speaking at a ceremony marking the completion of the main section of the fence, Israeli prime minister Benjamin Netanyahu "praised the effort to curb the illegal entry of migrants from Africa, reduced from more than 2,000 a month in January 2012 to fewer than 40 in December [2012]."[87]

In May 2013, EU leaders authorize the implementation of the European Union Integrated Border Management Assistance Mission in Libya. The initial mandate is for two years, with an annual budget of 30 million euros. Modeled on similar activities since 2005 in (non-EU) Moldova and Ukraine, the mission is to support and train the Libyan authorities in improving the security of the country's porous borders[88]—it is worth noting again that Libya's land border alone, largely in the desert, amounts to about 4,400 kilometers.

In early July 2013, following the "continuing flow" of mostly Eritrean migrants to its country, newly elected Maltese prime minister Joseph Muscat, national leader of the Labour Party, threatens to fly "a planeload of freshly-landed boat people back to Libya," their transit country to Europe. Muscat "would not call this a push-back," but a message that "we are not pushovers."[89] The small Mediterranean country is pressing EU authorities for assistance and wants Libya to prevent departures. The following month, Maltese authorities deny entry to a Liberian-flagged tanker, *MT Salamis*, which has rescued 102 migrants and is heading to Malta. They reroute it to Siracusa, Sicily, and even there Italian authorities initially do not grant permission to land.

In August 2013, UNHCR officers in Libya "remain concerned about the lack of safety and security" for refugees and asylum seekers in the country, and in particular about the punitive use of detention for irregular arrivals, in conditions of food deprivation and physical abuse. The UNHCR has managed to register 13,319 refugees from Syria.[90] Libyan sources estimate the number of Syrian refugees in Libya as close to 110,000. Nevertheless, UNHCR activities in Benghazi—closer to Egypt, where most Syrian refugees arrive from—have to be suspended for security reasons, in light of a series of attacks targeting the international community, the surging instability in the east of the country, and confrontations among militias.

In September 2013, UNHCR reports that many persons—including Ethiopians, Eritreans, and Somalis—face "widespread and ongoing mistreatment in detention." Persons with medical conditions and pregnant women and children are detained. The UNHCR also notes the dramatic increase in the number of boats embarking for southern Europe, carrying mainly Eritreans, Ethiopians, Palestinians, Syrians, Somalis, Sudanese, Malians, Nigerians, and Egyptians. During the month of September 2013, a total of 4,619 people leave Libya by boat, compared to 775 people in September 2012. Three of thirty-two boats are intercepted by the Libyan coast guard; upon apprehension travelers are typically detained for unauthorized exit.[91]

Authorities in Tripoli actively check the health and paperwork of refugees and migrant workers, including by setting up several checkpoints across the city. A holding center is located at the edge of the local zoo. Some of the detainees do maintenance work in the zoo—presumably without compensation—as their documents and health are checked over a period of one to three days. The head of the "illegal immigration unit" based at the zoo, Abdul Razag Al-Gerjame, says that they undergo blood tests, and that if they are ill—he says 20 percent of those arrested test positive for HIV or hepatitis—they will be deported. He admits that workers from Syria, Eritrea, Ethiopia, and Somalia (all refugees) cannot be deported, though, and this is "Libya's biggest problem." But he is keen to point out that his unit respects the human rights of those arrested, including by feeding them the same sandwiches his soldiers eat, paid for by members of the underfunded brigade themselves.[92]

In neighboring Egypt, the armed forces seem less concerned with the "human rights" of migrants, including refugees. Toward Syrian refugees, in particular, there is a major shift in policy and public opinion following the July 3, 2013, ouster of President Mohamed Morsi. Syrians must now obtain a visa and security clearance before entering the country. In what is a profoundly split and increasingly unstable political environment, some Egyptians believe Syrian refugees sympathize with former president Morsi's Muslim Brotherhood, and thus are increasingly wary of them. Many Syrians opt to seek refuge elsewhere, including Europe. On September 19, 2013, a communique of the Alexandria police admits that two Palestinians (that is, Palestinian refugees first displaced in Syria, and then displaced from

Syria by the protracted civil war) have been killed by authorities as their
boat set sail toward Italy from the port of Abu Qir, close to Alexandria. The
Egyptian coast guard "shot into the air in an effort to intercept the boat"
carrying 50 Syrians, 122 Palestinians, 2 Egyptians, 1 Moroccan, and 8 Egyptian crew members, asserts the communique. Fadwa Taha, in her fifties,
and Omar Delol, who is traveling with his pregnant wife and child, have
been killed. Survivors are taken into police custody in Alexandria.[93] There,
they meet another 300 Syrian and Palestinian refugees, detained for
attempting to emigrate to Italy illegally (intending to reach northern
Europe).[94] At the end of September 2013, there are 250,000 to 300,000
Syrian refugees in Egypt. UNHCR notes the massive use of administrative
detention and deportation to third countries.[95] Tirana Hassan, a senior
researcher at HRW, puts it like this to *Ahram Online*: "It is a matter of
semantics; refugees face 'forced return' or 'forced voluntary return'" to
Gaza, Lebanon, Syria, or Turkey.[96]

Despite the active efforts by Libyan and Egyptian political and military
authorities, during summer 2013 boats with Syrian and Eritrean refugees
from the two countries do regularly arrive in southern Italy. And there are
casualties. On August 8, 2013, Italian president Giorgio Napolitano (2006–
2015) calls attention to the issue of "immigrants' integration and workplace
security" as Italy honors the memory of the 262 people, including 136 Italian emigrants, who died in a fire in the mines of Marcinelle, Belgium, the
morning of October 8, 1956. On the occasion Laura Boldrini, former
spokeswoman for the UNHCR and president of the Chamber of Deputies
(2013-present), mentions the deadly effects of the lack of rights, and hints
at creeping racism as "we [Italians] neglect to see that migrants arriving at
Lampedusa have the same eyes as our fathers who arrived at Marcinelle."[97]
Two days later, on August 10, a fishing boat carrying about 100 Syrian
refugees, including women, minors, and children, runs aground in front of
a beach in Catania, eastern Sicily. People have to swim to safety. The bodies
of 5 young men and a minor, presumably from Syria, wash up on the
beach. Local mayor Enzo Bianco proclaims an official day of mourning. A
similar scene takes place on the beach of Scicli, close to Ragusa in southern
Sicily. On September 30, at least 13 young men from Eritrea die as their
crowded boat, with some 250 people, runs aground. Local mayor Francesco
Susino proclaims an official day of mourning.

Hundreds of Syrians and Eritreans also arrive at Lampedusa. On October 2, 2013, Lampedusa's holding center is full, overcrowded with almost

1,000 people. In the evening, coast guard and finance guard vessels rescue 463 Syrian passengers on two fishing boats. Health-care workers are up all night. Sailing from Libya, migrants have paid between $1,500 and $2,000. Some have been in the center for almost three weeks, with no idea about their prospects. Many have to sleep outdoors.

Early in the morning of October 3, 2013, off Lampedusa there is a fishing boat overcrowded with migrants. It's a scirocco day, and some residents report hearing something in the distance, like the lament of seagulls. The boat is adrift in the vicinity of the "Rabbits' Island" tiny tourist paradise. It has made it undetected from the Libyan coast. It is in distress from an engine failure, with water seeping on board and possibly a gasoline leak. After about two and a half hours in the absence of assistance, and with no phones on board, the boat's driver or a passenger ignites a blanket to generate smoke and thus call for help.[98] Many people on board do not realize what is going on, panicking. The boat capsizes. Around 7 A.M., amateur fishermen sailing in the area see dozens of people barely keeping afloat, clinging to life however they can, and calling for help. Some people are rescued. Their skin is slick with gasoline. It is difficult to pull them on board. They are cold and debilitated. They vomit seawater and gasoline. There are too many passengers floating; it is difficult to sail. Some are face down. People don't let them go. Others go down in front of the rescuers. When all bodies are recovered, weeks later, the world learns that at least 366 young men, women, and children, most if not all Eritreans, lost their lives. Vessels of the coast guard, finance guard, army police, and firefighters, with two military helicopters and additional fishing vessels, reach the scene around 7:45 A.M., rescuing more people. The drowned and the 155 people saved travel next to each other on coast guard boats *CP 301*, *CP 303*, and *CP 312*, among other vessels. Bodies are lined up on the dock. Next to fishing nets needing repair there are now dozens of black, green, and white body bags. Coffins will need to be shipped from Sicily. Eventually 366 of them are lined up in the local airport hangar. Some coffins are smaller, white. The wreckage lies at a depth of about fifty meters. To smugglers, the fatal trip has brought about 1 million euros.

In discussing the shipwreck national media use the word *strage* (massacre; carnage)—until now mostly reserved for international and domestic terrorism. *Strage* is added to the repertoire of "tragedy," "shipwreck," and "rickety boat." Differently from such routinized words, though, it does evoke human responsibility. Visiting Lampedusa, Deputy Prime Minister

(2013–14) and Minister of the Interior (2013–present) Angelino Alfano speaks of a "shame" of Europe and the West, as these are "European, not merely Italian" frontiers. Speaking to the Italian Parliament, on October 4 he also solicits further international cooperation among police forces to fight the "traffickers of death," and warns that tragedies such as this will repeat themselves. To the media, he also says that "there has never been a state, or a union of states, which does not protect its border. If it doesn't, then it is not a state."[99] With these brief words, he summons the military-humanitarian nexus of sovereignty. More crucially, he inadvertently implies that the enforcement of the external borders of the EU is in some way related to the 366 deaths.

In an official statement following the "tragic accident," European commissioner for home affairs Cecilia Malmström (2010–14) emphasizes—as has been done in Italy and Europe for two decades—"the need to intensify our efforts to fight criminal networks exploiting human despair so that they cannot continue to put people's lives at risk in small, overcrowded and unseaworthy vessels." But smugglers are the agents of irregular transportation, not the reason—at least not the only reason—explaining why people intend to cross the Mediterranean. Malmström also invites EU countries to "engage more in the resettlement of people in need of international protection. This would demonstrate an increased and much needed commitment to solidarity and the sharing of responsibility and would help to reduce the number of people putting their lives at risk in the hopes of reaching European shores."[100]

The Italian Parliament suspends its October 3 session as a sign of mourning. In the afternoon, the Council of Ministers decides that the following day, October 4, is to be observed as a national day of mourning, to include a minute of silence in all public schools. On the fourth, Prime Minister Enrico Letta (2013–14) declares that the dead of Lampedusa are honorary "Italian citizens." The 155 survivors, according to the immigration law, are prosecuted for the crime of illegal immigration, like every single maritime or otherwise unauthorized migrant.[101] That Friday all shops are closed in Lampedusa. In the evening there is a silent march and candlelight vigil—Via Roma and the small square overlooking the port are full of residents, led in their thoughts and prayers by Father Stefano and by local high school students. Vigils are also held in Valletta, Tel Aviv, and Rome, as solicited by Mayor Ignazio Marino, with the participation of members of the Eritrean diaspora and other residents.

All survivors declare Eritrean nationality. They share harrowing stories preceding their departure from Misrata, in northwestern Libya. A group was kidnapped for ransom in the area around Sabha in southern Libya, after having crossed from Sudan. Sudanese and Somali criminals tortured and raped their victims.[102] Anbessa, twenty-four, from Asmara had been conscripted into the Eritrean Army as a minor. He deserted and intended to reach his brother Freselam, a naturalized Swedish citizen, in Sweden. In the absence of a legal opportunity for family reunification, he used the unauthorized route to Europe.[103] Isaias's father is in prison in Eritrea because of his Pentecostal affiliation—a denomination not recognized by the regime. His mother and two brothers are in Khartoum, Sudan, and his sister is a refugee in London. He was able to escape from detention in Tripoli. Others paid the guards $2,000.[104] Bodies are slowly pulled from the sea by scuba divers and recovery teams. Lampedusa's doctor, Pietro Bartolo, inspects them. A young woman and the preterm child she gave birth to are still attached through the umbilical cord. Doctor Bartolo thinks the woman delivered in the moments of terror preceding her drowning.[105]

On October 6, at least fifty-one people are killed and hundreds are injured as street clashes between supporters of ousted President Morsi and supporters of the new authorities erupt in several Egyptian cities.[106]

On October 8, Commissioner Malmström adds her wish that "what happened in Lampedusa will be a wakeup call to increase solidarity and mutual support and to prevent similar tragedies in the future." In the short term, Malmström advocates for the importance of Eurosur and Frontex. In particular, she proposes that EU governments "deploy an extensive Frontex search and rescue operation that will cover the Mediterranean from Cyprus to Spain."[107] But Frontex's 85 million euro funding for 2013 is already depleted.[108] Two million euros therefore need to be reallocated, giving priority to the extension until November 2013 of Operation Hermes, south of Sicily and Lampedusa, while another Frontex operation is also ongoing in the Ionian Sea, between Greece and Italy.[109] During the week between October 7 and October 12, police experts with the Italian Ministry of the Interior are dispatched to Libya to "obtain" the cooperation of the local police forces in monitoring the coast and "stop the departures organized by smugglers."[110]

On October 9, Italian prime minister Letta visits Lampedusa together with Alfano; President of the European Commission José Manuel Barroso (2004–14); and Malmström. President Barroso promises an additional 30 million euros to support Italy.[111] Prime Minister Letta extends Italy's apologies for the country's *"inadempienze"* (negligence; default) regarding this and similar tragedies.[112] It is an unprecedented public acknowledgment. He also announces state funerals.

The Italian government delivers a memorial service on October 21 in the port of Agrigento, Sicily. But people have already been buried, in Agrigento and elsewhere in Sicily, where many city councils and private citizens have offered spaces in local cemeteries. The request of survivors to attend is not accommodated, as they are still detained in Lampedusa. And many in the Eritrean diaspora cannot understand why Italian authorities have invited to the memorial the Eritrean ambassador to Italy—as it is precisely from the authoritarian Eritrean government that their deceased brothers and sisters sought refuge. "The presence of the Eritrean regime offends the dead and puts in danger the living," reads a banner held at the ceremony by Eritrean nationals living in Italy.[113] Lampedusa's mayor, Giusi Nicolini (2012–present), does not attend the ceremony, in disagreement with the government's decision to hold the memorial far from the island, far from survivors, and far from the bodies of the deceased.

On October 10, the EU Parliament approves the "operating rules" of Eurosur, the pan-European border surveillance system. Members of Parliament insist that "it must also be used to help save migrants' lives." Its infrastructure is constituted by drones, offshore maritime sensors, intelligence equipment, and satellite search systems, supporting an EU network of knowledge sharing. The objective is to survey the Mediterranean in its entirety, providing member states with "situational pictures" of border activities and maritime dynamics. It focuses on enhancing border surveillance in order to "contribute to the management of migration flows by reducing the number of irregular migrants entering the Schengen area undetected; protect and save lives at the external borders by considerably diminishing the unacceptable death toll of migrants at sea; increase the internal security of the European Union by preventing serious crime at the external borders of the Schengen area."[114]

The official cost estimates for Eurosur amount to 244 million euros for 2014–20, including costs for setup, maintenance, and personnel. Critical voices are numerous and to the point. They are grounded in a detailed study by the Heinrich Böll Foundation—which, incidentally, estimates the cost at 874 million euros.[115] The decision to establish Eurosur has not been subjected to discussion by national legislators, civil society, or the EU

Parliament—which has been essentially presented with a fait accompli to be ratified. A salvational and humanitarian discourse seeks to make the military and surveillance project more palatable to public opinion and politicians increasingly concerned with the "shame" of death at sea, especially following the October 3 shipwreck. Eurosur is intended primarily as a border enforcement mechanism—exactly like Frontex. It is not a Euro-Mediterranean, supranational coast guard, which could be one way to more effectively conduct search-and-rescue operations. In addition, it does not solve the thorny issue that has characterized interstate relationships for years, especially between Italy and Malta: when a boat in distress is located in international waters, who should intervene? Where should people be taken? Who will be responsible for them?

The EU Commission emphasizes that Eurosur will be implemented with full respect for human rights and the principle of nonrefoulement.[116] This is a significant and welcome aspiration. But when it comes to the external borders of the EU and the human rights of migrants, there is ample evidence that the inclusion of rights in the policy framework is not necessarily implemented on the ground.[117] And how will biometric and other data be shared with possibly undemocratic countries of origin and transit? The authors of the Heinrich Böll Foundation's study voice their concerns:

> The [EU] Commission has repeatedly stressed EUROSUR's future role in "protecting and saving lives of migrants," but nowhere in the proposed Regulation and numerous assessments, studies, and R&D projects is it defined how exactly this will be done, nor are there any procedures laid out for what should be done with the "rescued." In this context, and despite the humanitarian crisis in the Mediterranean among migrants and refugees bound for Europe, EUROSUR is more likely to be used alongside the long-standing European policy of preventing these people reaching EU territory (including so-called push back operations, where migrant boats are taken back to the state of departure) rather than as a genuine life-saving tool.[118]

Indeed, in May 2014 Gil Aria Fernández, Frontex's deputy director, declares that "for the time being" Eurosur is not helping in preventing migrant boats from sinking. And even when the system finally incorporates satellite images, "this would not be even useful for preventing tragedies because satellite images will be available to the border authorities hours or even days after."[119]

EU policymakers, Frontex leaders and agents, and EU member states' armed forces need to clarify, to themselves and to their constituencies, whether they monitor and patrol the Mediterranean to deter migration, to rescue people, or to intercept and deport them to countries of origin and transit. The main challenge of maritime migration is often not invisibility in a deserted stretch of sea, but a problem of decision making, of coordination, and of political will to accept people in the rescuers' country's "safe port." A fundamental problem lies also in the liberal-democratic expectation that North African patrols can somehow safely, humanely, and without the use of force deter, dissuade, and reroute Europe-bound migrant boats—a challenge widely appreciated at least since the *Sibilla–Kater i Radës* 1997 collision. Finally, there is the challenge of vessels ignoring distress calls and even direct encounters. Fishermen and shipmasters, in particular, should never have to fear that rescuing people will result in criminal charges for aiding and abetting undocumented immigration. In the hectic moments following the October 3, 2013, Lampedusa shipwreck, Mayor Giusi Nicolini spoke of three vessels that allegedly ignored the boat's call for help. To my knowledge, Italian prosecutors have yet to follow up.

Between Nobody's Sea and Our Sea: A Lost Generation

Early in the morning of October 11, 2013, a fishing boat is in distress some 60 nautical miles (113 kilometers) south of Lampedusa—118 nautical miles southwest of Malta. For $3,000, smugglers in Zuwara, Libya, have promised their Syrian clients that they would embark fewer passengers than usual. African passengers are therefore locked in the hold, far from Syrians' sight.[120] Smugglers take some of the life vests Syrian passengers have bought for themselves. During the night, an undetermined boat chases them from the Libyan coast, opening fire and damaging the hull.[121] In the morning, water is leaking in. The boat driver—a twenty-one-year-old Tunisian citizen—asks for a volunteer who speaks English. By 12:39 P.M. a Syrian doctor borrows the driver's satellite phone to alert Italian authorities. He gives them the boat's position, after double-checking GPS phones of several passengers. He alerts the authorities regarding the number of people on board, engine failure, and the fact that water is leaking in. Italian personnel tell the doctor that the boat is in the Maltese SAR area (this is the case even if actually closer to Lampedusa than to Malta), dictate a Maltese phone number, and alert their Maltese counterparts.[122] At 1:05 P.M., Maltese authorities take responsibility for coordinating the search-and-rescue operation, including how best to coordinate vessels in the area. What happens for the next two to three hours "remains under wraps."[123] At 1:34 P.M., a message to mariners ("hydrolant") calling for assistance is sent to boats in the Mediterranean. An Italian navy vessel, the *Libra*, is sailing only 27 nautical miles (50 kilometers) from the boat in distress. It slowly gets closer, allegedly to within 10 miles (18 kilometers).[124] But the ship has only been "instructed [by whom is not clear] to go around in circles at slow speed."[125] All bystanders are potential good Samaritans, but "being there," without legal legitimation and political will, is not always enough to warrant action.

Two merchant ships in the vicinity—the *Stadt Bremerhaven* (Antigua and Barbuda) and the *Tyrusland* (United Kingdom)—fail to respond to the maritime warning.[126] More importantly, it appears they have not been formally requested to divert to the area, as an efficient (Italian or Maltese) search-and-rescue coordination would require. A King Air search-and-rescue plane leaves Malta at around 3 P.M. The plane spots the migrant boat around 4 P.M. According to the Armed Forces of Malta, the boat capsizes a few minutes later. According to Admiral Felicio Angrisano, head of the Italian coast guard, the boat capsizes at 5:07 P.M. As the *Malta Independent* puts it, "this could either mean that someone in Italy or Malta got the time all mixed up or that Malta waited for a whole hour before finally asking for [Italian] help." Further testimonies record the time of the boat capsizing at 5:07 P.M.[127] Around 5:20 P.M., Malta's plane and a military helicopter (Maltese or Italian) drop life rafts and vests. Maltese patrol boat *P61* is first to arrive on the scene at 5:51 P.M., followed by the Italian *Libra* and later by vessels of the Italian coast guard and finance guard, whose navigation time from Lampedusa is two hours at most.[128] They manage to save 212 Syrian refugees. Sailors on board the small rescue boats sent by the *Libra* have to throw out corpses to make room for the Syrians rescued. No African passenger is rescued. They drown more quickly than others, trapped in the hold. Their unauthorized ticket to Europe was cheaper. Between 212 and 270 people lose their lives, including some 60 children. The depth of the sea—eighty to one hundred meters—makes it improbable they will be recovered, although technically that depth would be accessible by scuba divers.[129]

Admiral Giuseppe De Giorgi, Italy's chief of naval operations, "refuses to answer" the question posed by the Italian magazine *L'Espresso* (whose investigation is conducted primarily by journalist Fabrizio Gatti) regarding the delay in the arrival of the *Libra*.[130] Similarly, the Armed Forces of Malta have refused without an explanation a freedom-of-information request made by the *Malta Today* newspaper. The Armed Forces of Malta and the Maltese Home Affairs Ministry also have refused to answer questions sent by the *Malta Independent* as well as by *L'Espresso*.[131] Speaking to members of the Italian Parliament's lower Chamber, Deputy Minister of Defense Gioacchino Alfano asserts that the coordination of rescue operations was Malta's duty, and that the Italian navy and coast guard could not have intervened prior to Malta's request for assistance.[132] As clearly explained to me by Lampedusa's former coast guard commander, Antonio Morana, it is quite common for Lampedusa search-and-rescue vessels to intervene in rescue operations in the vast Maltese SAR area. This can happen only after Maltese colleagues coordinating the operations call him though. In turn, Lampedusa's coast guard station needs to call "Palermo" (Sicily) and "Rome" (Maritime Rescue Coordination Centre) to ask for authorization.[133]

The issue of where precisely the boundaries of the Italian and Maltese SAR areas are is contentious, and arguably detrimental to swift and efficient search-and-rescue coordination activities. Moreover, Italian and Maltese authorities often disagree regarding what should be done with migrants rescued in the Maltese SAR area. In principle, Maltese authorities claim that military and merchant vessels intervening in the Maltese SAR area must take rescued migrants to the nearest safe port—which is often Lampedusa. This would also entail that persons should be identified and given the possibility of applying for asylum in Italy. Italy, conversely, insists that it is the country responsible for the SAR region that should take in those rescued in the area. But Malta's vast SAR area, with some 250,000 square kilometers, spans from the sea immediately to the east of Tunisia to the south of Greece, and even encompasses Lampedusa.

In light of such contradictions, critical voices in Malta have suggested relinquishing responsibility for substantial portions of the area (to Italy and Greece), at least until adequate resources are allotted to effectively coordinate search-and-rescue operations in such a vast stretch. In response to these calls, in a 2009 interview Maltese minister for justice and home affairs Carmelo Mifsud Bonnici said: "It is true we are a small country but the large SAR area could be considered to be part of the bonus we inherited from our [British] Colonial past. It is an asset for our country and I don't think a country should simply give up its assets."[134] More specifically, benefits of a large SAR area, for either Italy or Malta, include funding for the coast guard, fishing interests, and prospects of oil exploration. In addition, the *Times of Malta* notes that giving up a portion of the SAR area "would cost Malta, since the country earns millions of euros a year from air traffic control charges on aircraft using the area, known as the flight information region."[135]

Maltese prime minister Joseph Muscat visits his Libyan counterpart, Ali Zeidan, in Tripoli on October 13, 2013. They vow that improved training and the strengthening of marine patrols, along with greater surveillance, will "narrow the opportunities for the smugglers who trade in human beings, so often with tragic consequences."[136] In a news conference the Libyan prime minister says that from preliminary inquiries, the Libyan military was not involved in the alleged shooting of the boat sunk on October 11.[137] The meeting between Muscat and Zeidan comes just a few days after Zeidan's brief abduction by a group of armed militiamen who stormed the Corinthia Hotel, where Zeidan was staying. On October 13, the *Libya Herald* reports that a Libyan oil tanker has rescued 174 Syrian migrants in international waters "off the Italian coast." As confirmed by a Libyan naval spokesman, Colonel Ayoub Omar Qassem, the operation has been conducted in cooperation with the Italian coast guard. All migrants are returned to Libya, where they will be "handed over to the immigration authorities."[138] Speaking to Reuters and indirectly objecting to such practices, prefect of police Riccardo Compagnucci, a top official with the Italian Interior Ministry's immigration office, rules out Libya as a safe port because of its "poor security and human rights situation." Compagnucci says some rescued migrants could be taken to Malta and Greece when this facilitates rescue operations, but certainly not Libya: "Libya isn't safe even for its prime minister."[139]

During a news conference just a few days after the largely nonpublicized return of the 174 Syrian refugees to Libya, Reuters's Steve Scherer asks Italian prime minister Letta whether Libya can be considered a safe port. This is indeed the fundamental question to be asked at this time, because if there is a consensus that Libya is not a safe port, then people cannot be returned there, just as prefect Compagnucci has emphatically stated. But Letta is hesitant, defining the question as a "technical question" to which he "does not want [to] and cannot" answer on the spot.[140] Asked a second time, he does stress that the Libyan coast needs to be patrolled, and inadequacy on behalf of the Libyan authorities regarding their responsibilities will not be further tolerated.[141] By the end of the month it seems that Italian authorities are taking the matter of Libyan land borders in their own hands. In a news conference, Libyan prime minister Zeidan announces that "Italy will start the aerial and electronic surveillance of Libyan borders," from the area near the Egyptian-Sudanese border in the southeast to the western junction of the Libyan-Tunisian-Algerian border. Prime minister Zeidan adds that this border surveillance will have an important role in "reducing border incursions by illegal immigrants." The Italian Embassy in Tripoli, contacted by the *Libya Herald*, does not have further details to add.[142]

In mid-October 2013, Letta's government (2013–14) and in particular Ministers of Defense Mario Mauro and of the Interior Angelino Alfano announce the establishment of the "military and humanitarian" operation in the Mediterranean, to be named Mare Nostrum—the somewhat controversial phrase ("Our Sea") used to claim the Mediterranean not only by the ancient Romans but also by Italian nationalists. Despite the EU Commission's repeated calls for "EU solidarity" following the October shipwrecks, the mission remains essentially an Italian-operated enterprise.[143] Only Slovenia has dispatched to Sicily the military vessel *Triglav*, one of the only two warships at the disposal of Slovenia's navy. The *Triglav* is named for Slovenia's highest mountain: the small Alpine country has only some forty-seven kilometers (twenty-nine miles) of coastline, and is not directly affected by maritime migration.

Farther to the north, EU countries are not enthusiastic about the mission. Giovanni Pinto, the director of the Italian Interior Ministry's border police, explains to a parliamentary committee that northern European countries "look with diffidence to such policies of approaching the African coast," because they see it as a "travel insurance policy" and therefore an additional pull factor for would-be migrants. Pinto also says what all humanitarian organizations and governments of southern and southeastern Europe already know—or should know: "there are 2.5 million Syrian residents outside their own country, for the most part in Lebanon (about 800,000, possibly one million), with substantial numbers in Jordan, Turkey, and Egypt."[144]

Asylum by Swimming and Citizenship for Sale
(a Preferential Option for the Rich)

The northern European concern with unregulated migration through the Mediterranean is not incongruous with the fact that countries such as Belgium and Latvia, and also Bulgaria, Cyprus, Greece, Malta, Portugal, and Spain, among others, are in various forms offering or considering offering to wealthy non-EU citizens the opportunity to purchase residence permits and citizenship "by investment." Private websites offer legal assistance only to applicants who can dispose of at least $300,000. Critics, including members of the EU Parliament, refer to these practices as "citizenship for sale." Criticizing the Maltese government and referring to the plight of refugees in the country, Herman Grech, the head of media at the *Times of Malta*, asserts provocatively: "At least have the guts to give passports to everyone. It is completely xenophobic and cynical to only give it to rich people."[145] At the EU level, a "blue card" is in the early phases of implementation. Essentially a permanent residence permit, it is aimed at "migrants of high economic or educational capital" (Feldman 2012:174) with higher professional qualifications and a job offer with a salary threshold of at least 1.5 times the average gross annual salary paid in the relevant EU member state.

EU member states Greece and Bulgaria are building fences and otherwise fortifying portions of their borders. As a Bulgarian news outlet puts it, in October 2013 Bulgaria's army began "the construction of a fence that will be used to restrict the number of refugees entering the country from Turkey."[146] Unprepared Bulgarian authorities, by the end of 2013, had received some ten thousand Syrian refugees, often in extremely poor conditions. They plan to extend considerably the 33-kilometer (20-mile) fence at the border with Turkey. Turkey, at the end of 2013, was hosting at least four hundred thousand to six hundred thousand Syrian refugees. Bulgaria's decision to build a fence and to dispatch additional border guards has not been well received there. Speaking with *Hürriyet*'s reporters in the early stages of the fence planning (2011), Edirne Commodity Exchange deputy chairman Serdar Yalçıner complained: "Bulgaria wants to build a 143-kilometer fence along the border with Turkey under the pretext of foot and mouth disease. It is asking the EU to pay for the costs. It means the EU is building a 'Berlin Wall' along our borders. Let's say they managed to stop boars with a fence—what about birds and moles? The EU is marking its borders."[147]

Greece has also completed a 10.5-kilometer barbed wire fence at its border with Turkey "to prevent a wave of unregistered immigrants from flowing into the country," as a Greek news outlet reports, at a cost of 3 million euros. But a drop in arrivals through the now fortified Evros River area has been accompanied by a spike in the "illegal influx" from Turkey via the islands of the Aegean Sea.[148]

In turn, Turkish authorities are building a fence in the ancient city of Nusaybin, of which Qamishli, across the border in Syria, is basically an extension. Ismail Boubi, like many others in the local, mostly Kurdish community extending across the international boundary, demands "that the wall be halted, the [Turkish] minefields cleared and the barbed wire dismantled." He declares to the *Guardian*: "Refugees scramble through dangerous territory to get here. It is extremely hard to get aid into the northeastern part of Syria. If the border was open, people would not have to resort to smuggling, and they would also go back to their own towns much faster. The construction of the wall demolishes democracy. This is not what we need. We need more trust, more freedom, and more co-operation."[149]

Farther south, upon completion of the border fence with Egypt in the Sinai desert, Israeli prime minister Netanyahu is reported by the *Los Angeles Times* as saying that "just as we have stopped infiltration into Israeli cities, so too we shall succeed in the next mission, repatriating the tens of thousands of infiltrators [unauthorized migrants] to their countries of origin."[150] In addition to extremely low rates of asylum acceptance, Eritrean and Sudanese refugees, among others, face the prospect of indefinite confinement in the Negev desert. *Haaretz* reports that the Israeli state "has been putting a lot of pressure on them to leave voluntarily, in exchange for a $3,500 grant. Under pressure of detention, the number of African asylum seekers leaving Israel reached 773 in January [2014] (up from 325 in December and 63 in November)."[151] A growing number of countries, including India and the United States, "are flocking to Israel to study border security," and especially its long-distance radar capabilities.[152]

Early in 2014 Italian deputy interior minister Filippo Bubbico provided news agencies the figures of maritime immigration to Italy for 2013. Most people at sea were assisted to the mainland or rescued and brought there; they did not land undetected. In 2013, maritime arrivals totaled 42,925 persons. This is up 325 percent over 2012 (and less than one-third of 2014 arrivals), and it indicates an upward trend *preceding* Mare Nostrum. The majority of migrants set off from Libya, followed by Egypt, Turkey, Greece, and Syria. The main country of origin based on declarations made on arrival was war-torn Syria (11,307 arrivals in 2013, compared with 582 in 2012). It was followed by Eritrea (9,834 arrivals in 2013, up more than 400 percent over 2012), Somalia, Egypt, Mali, and Afghanistan.[153] According to prefect of police Riccardo Compagnucci—one of the top immigration officers in Italy—some 75 percent of all 2013 arrivals were in need of humanitarian protection.[154] The 2013 upward trend in arrivals continued in 2014 (and dramatic decreases in 2015 seem unlikely, given the geopolitical situation). Arrivals were constituted in roughly the same percentage by people entitled to humanitarian protection. As of September 2014, Eritrean citizens constituted about 70 percent of arrivals, followed by Syrian refugees, and then by people from Mali, Nigeria, Gambia, Somalia, Pakistan, Senegal, and Egypt.[155] In such a scenario, in the short term EU and member states implementing or envisioning readmission agreements with countries of origin and transit would need, at the very least, to reassess and continuously monitor whether those countries offer a democratic state apparatus in the first place, a functioning asylum system, and the legal, financial, and humanitarian resources to adequately implement human rights for both citizens and third-country nationals or stateless persons.

The Italian Ministry of Labor has estimated that until 2015 the country, especially in light of its dramatically aging citizenry, was in need of an average of 100,000 additional workers per year. This is true, according to the ministry, even considering the escalating unemployment plaguing Italy and the 80,000 to 100,000 citizens who leave the country yearly (not necessarily permanently). Between 2016 and 2020 the demand for workers per year is estimated at some 260,000.[156] At the same time, for 2014 the quota of non-EU workers the Italian government accepted was 17,850 persons (excluding seasonal laborers, highly skilled workers, and specialized workers such as nurses).[157] Also to be noted: migrants' contributions in taxes and social security funding in Italy are generally higher than migration-related public spending: for 2011, the figure was 1.4 billion euros higher.[158] These are admittedly complicated and fluctuating matters. Rather than being taken at face value, they need to be scrutinized and to be factored into larger discussions on (manufactured) immigrant illegality[159] and on the sustainability of refugee reception, at the level of member states and of the EU.

"Developing countries," it is also to be noted, host some 80 percent of the world's refugees, even if this does not necessarily imply the safety, dignity, and civil and political rights of those hosted.[160] And the criteria to clearly differentiate between forced and voluntary migrants, elaborated after World War II and in the Cold War, are increasingly blurred by terrorist activities, short-term military campaigns with long term consequences, corruption, border disputes, trafficking, soil and water depletion, land grabbing, droughts, sectarianism, and even certain development projects[161] that displace people south and east of the EU.

Giusi Nicolini knows this. She knows this not as aggregate data but based on her experience, first as an active citizen of Lampedusa and then as its mayor. Like other residents, she has opted to experience material, social, and emotional proximity to the drowned, to the saved, and to their families. She asks: "Why in a country such as Italy and in Europe does the right to asylum need to be asked by swimming? Why do we need to let mothers with their children embark in the Mediterranean? Why do we need to care only about the survivors that make it? Is it not a crime, to wait for migrants to be decimated at sea?"[162] But Italy, Europe, and several international actors have done much more than merely "wait" with indifference, as I have demonstrated. They *actively* design their sovereign architecture with digital and material thresholds, bilateral agreements, contradictory bureaucracies and unenforceable policies and then, at best, respond with search-and-rescue operations.

At the end of October 2013, the EU's twenty-eight heads of state and government dedicated a segment of their European Council meeting to Mediterranean migrations, in light of the recent shipwrecks. In their December meeting, they discussed more concrete proposals, formulated by a specific Task Force Mediterranean. These include cracking down on organized crime; boosting search-and-rescue and Frontex border patrol activities; implementing Eurosur as part of a more comprehensive effort at Mediterranean situational awareness; cooperating with countries of origin and transit, especially in preventing migrants from "embark[ing] on hazardous journeys toward the European Union" and crafting "an effective return policy"; and collaborating with international agencies on the resettlement of persons in need of protection.[163] Regarding the last point, the task force recognizes resettlement as "an important mean[s] by which persons in need of protection can arrive safely [at] the European Union without going on hazardous journeys over the Mediterranean," and suggests that the use of this instrument should "be encouraged alongside actions that improve access to self-reliance for refugees in third countries which [is a] key precursor to a durable solution." Additionally, the task force suggests that "more legal mobility opportunities for study and work should also be considered including by offering alternative avenues of entry to potential asylum-seekers."[164]

Maritime migrants are often referred to as "desperate" people—including by sympathetic media and citizens. No: they may need rescue, but not salvation. They are not "deprived of hope." Perhaps this is best embodied by the many women carrying to a better place the promise of a child; by passengers taking turns to bail water out with buckets; by acts of escape; by prayers, tears, and palms open to the sky, once people feel rescued; by tales of desire to reunite with families even in the absence of a legal hence cheap and safe way to do so. If and when they are listened to, these persons opt for the prospect not only of material wealth but also of belonging to a community that accepts them and their children for who they are and who they become; of participating in civic and democratic life as persons with rights and duties—rather than as *sudditi*, passive "subjects" in their country of origin or temporary guests in a country where their labor happens to be needed. Some are convinced Europe has this to offer. Opaque technocracy, self-serving and generic humanitarianism, rescue operations, and militarization cannot alone provide answers to their demands. For every single day we postpone knowledge, discussion, and action on human rights, justice, equality, solidarity, and sovereignty, "freedom, security, and justice" and the "European Dream" they underpin remain a lethal scam, marketed by smugglers and by conniving dream-dealers.

Chapter 6

Public Aesthetics Amid Seas

To the boat that flew to the sky
While the children were still playing;
I would have given the whole sea
Just to see them landing.
　　　—From Roberto Vecchioni's song
　　　　"Chiamami Ancora Amore"

Otranto: Tears of Glass

Following years of abandonment in a military area close to the port of Brindisi, Italy, the rusty wreck of the *Kater i Radës* is destined for the junkyard. The ship was recovered from the seabed approximately six months after the 1997 "Good Friday Tragedy" in the Strait of Otranto. Italian prosecutors inspected every inch of it—as if to confirm that the explanations and responsibilities for the egregious crime of peace that caused the deaths of at least eighty-one people were situated on the vessel itself. Meanwhile, the passengers' remains found a resting place in Albania, in a dedicated section of Vlorë's cemetery.

In 2011, following the conviction of both the *Sibilla*'s and the *Kater i Radës*'s captains, the Court of Appeals in Lecce ordered the wreck to be demolished. But Klodiana Çuka, founder of the nonprofit NGO Integra Onlus, feared that demolition would inevitably translate into oblivion. She obtained the necessary authorization from Lecce's tribunal, and the upper part of the wreck was taken to the coastal town of Otranto, with the support of local mayor Luciano Cariddi. There, the *Kater i Radës* wreck was crafted into a "monument to the humanity that migrates," L'Approdo (the landing place). L'Approdo stands on a concrete platform a few meters from the harbor. The *Kater i Radës's* upper part is sealed into the ground. Gray concrete binds what remains of the vessel to a place from which it had unceremoniously been turned back on that Good Friday night of 1997.

Several institutions have enabled and sponsored this artistic initiative, including the municipality of Otranto, the province of Lecce, the region of Apulia, the United Nations Educational, Scientific, and Cultural Organization, the UNHCR, the IOM, and the Albanian Diplomatic Mission in Italy. Firms in the region have also offered their financial and logistical help in transforming the wreck into a monument, for example by providing paint and cement, services, and a qualified workforce. One multinational company donated twelve tons of glass. What remained of the rusty and corroded hull was enveloped in piles of thin sheets of glass. On a sunny day, they shine with a beautiful turquoise. On cloudy days, they resemble dark waves. Greek sculptor Costas Varotsos is the artist who envisioned L'Approdo and worked on it in Otranto, together with young artists from Albania, Syria, Egypt, Montenegro, France, Cyprus, and Italy. He says that he intended to let the *Kater i Radës* "emerge and sail once again," and so it sits in the middle of a storm, "as if the sea exploded on it."[1] He adds that, for him, glass does not work as a material that separates, but rather as something transparent that "forces you to look across it and beyond—helping the Adriatic Sea to regain its fluidity as a route of communication."[2] L'Approdo was officially inaugurated on Sunday, January 29, 2012. The event built on a series of conferences and initiatives through which Otranto's administration engaged the continuing legacy of maritime migration. The tourist town is also interested in revitalizing its heritage as "the West's outpost" and "gateway to the East."[3]

March 28, 2014, marks the *Kater i Radës* shipwreck's seventeenth anniversary. Klodiana Çuka is again in Otranto, joining Mayor Cariddi and other local authorities. They take to the sea on a coast guard vessel. Eighty-one carnations are thrown overboard. Flowers are also left on the ship's memorial site. However, at the time of my latest visit in June 2014, the monument has become dilapidated. There is still no plaque explaining what it stands for. Some of the glass sheets are damaged. An unnecessary hazard, in the eyes of concerned parents.

The structure is surrounded by rusty scaffolding and red tape. The larger harbor area is also under construction, and at present L'Approdo

Figure 8. The *Kater i Radës*'s prow, now part of L'Approdo, Otranto. Photo: Maurizio Albahari.

stands isolated from the old city nearby and from the daily perceptions and preoccupations of Otranto's residents. The wreck of the *Kater i Radës* was saved from the depths of the Mediterranean, and later from disposal. But L'Approdo also needs to be inspected, maintained, discussed, made mean-ingful. This is true for all known Mediterranean crimes of peace, if these are to become incarnated into an irrepressible memory. The ongoing migrant landings along the nearby coast, in Sicily, and elsewhere in southern Italy are not by themselves enough to nourish this kind of memory.[4] In bringing back to light the *Kater i Radës*, artist Costas Varotsos intended to promote a "message of balance between past and present."[5] Particularly in light of the continuing arrivals and frequent shipwrecks, it is difficult—indeed, undesirable—to confine that paradigmatic shipwreck to the past.

In Brindisi, about an hour's drive north of Otranto, on September 15, 2014, port authorities are waiting for the coast guard vessel *Diciotti*. A local acquaintance gives me some details: the *Diciotti* carries almost 600 rescued north of Benghazi, Libya. The vast majority declare Syrian, Palestinian, and

Bangladeshi origin. There are about 100 minors and some pregnant women. Most passengers will be taken to reception facilities throughout Italy, while others will be taken to Bari's CIE—possibly awaiting an expulsion decree or deportation. In recent months, the procession of commercial, coast guard, and navy vessels involved in Mare Nostrum has brought to Italian ports 142,000 people, in 384 distinct search-and-rescue operations.[6] Smaller coast guard vessels participating in the operation are identified by a simple registration number (including *CP 906*, *CP 904*, and *CP 319*). Navy vessels feature names related to geography, constellations, history, religion, and winds, including *Bergamini, San Giorgio, Grecale, Chimera, Etna, Orione, Sirio, Aliseo, Scirocco, Borsini, San Giusto, Foscari*, and *Fenice*. The *Libra* is also part of the Mare Nostrum operation. This is the same warship that, a week prior to the launch of the operation, on October 11, 2013, allegedly did not receive orders to intervene, beyond monitoring the boat in distress. For many maritime travelers, *approdo*—a landing place, a haven, a truly safe port—remains only a costly probability. There are no comforting certainties. There is no conclusion.

Lampedusa: A Wide-Open Door

"Who is it, the pope?!" With this sharp, rhetorical comment, a retired fisherman questions the pomp, cameras, police forces, and hectic atmosphere in Lampedusa's small port. June 20, 2011, is World Refugee Day, and "a special day for Lampedusa," as some locals tell me. Several journalists, Mayor Bernardino De Rubeis, and officers of the various maritime and armed forces accompany the small group of visitors. These include António Guterres, UN high commissioner for refugees; Laura Boldrini, spokeswoman for the UNHCR; and Angelina Jolie, the actress and director who has come as a goodwill ambassador for the UNHCR. Boldrini and Guterres meet local finance guard, coast guard, and air force officers. There are several Italian and European journalists. Zeinab Badawi broadcasts for BBC on board the coast guard's *CP 309* search-and-rescue vessel. The visual background of scuba divers and rescuers resonates with the larger moral aesthetics of sovereign salvation and humanitarianism. In speaking to the BBC, Guterres admits that he understands the pressure on Lampedusa, a small island. But, implicitly, he also calls into question the governmental unpreparedness or simple lack of political will to properly receive maritime

Figure 9. The *CP 309* search-and-rescue vessel. World Refugee Day, Lampedusa. Photo: Maurizio Albahari.

arrivals. "With adequate forms of solidarity this challenge can be overcome," he says, pointing also to the fact that in 2011 "about one million people left Libya after the conflict started and less than 2 percent came to Europe."[7]

In the afternoon the delegation visits the monumental sculpture Porta di Lampedusa—Porta d'Europa (gateway to Lampedusa—gateway to Europe). The Porta was commissioned in 2008 by poet and artist Arnoldo Mosca Mondadori; by Amani Onlus, an Italian NGO;[8] by Pietro Veronese, journalist for *La Repubblica*; and by the local NGO Alternativa Giovani. The latter youth-driven NGO works on environmental and active citizenship issues drawing on members' visceral attachment to the island. Salvatore is one of its most active members, and explains the monument's genealogy.[9] A private tourism company from Palermo donated 35,000 euros to defray the costs of the work of art, and Lampedusa's civic administration and then-mayor De Rubeis supported the initiative with enthusiasm. Domenico "Mimmo" Paladino is the renowned artist who envisioned

Figure 10. Porta di Lampedusa—Porta d'Europa, Lampedusa. Photo: Maurizio Albahari.

and crafted the Porta, donating his time and skills. The idea was born out of the realization that no plaque or monument publicly marked migrant deaths elsewhere in Sicily.

The sculpture stands five meters tall on a promontory overlooking the coast, close to the port and a few meters from what remains of a World War II bunker. It has the structure of a memorial gate, decorated with clay, ceramic, and iron inserts. It emanates a warm, golden hue, which evokes both the arid rock around it and the deserts many maritime travelers have had to cross. Clay inserts represent faces, ears, hands, shoes, and dishes. They are not merely symbols, says artist Paladino, but "small fragments of life." They make of the Porta a "minimal thing," rather than a symbol or a monument.[10] For "the artist should never celebrate, but narrate," he says.[11] And there is no door—the sculpture cannot be closed.

There is no barrier around the Porta, and visitors are free to walk through it. It is, indeed, a physical and symbolic threshold. I understand the Porta as extending a visual invitation to not only look at it and study its many details but to actually cross it. It is, in this sense, a "minimal thing," a simple instrument that provisionally summons one's gaze only to focus it on what exists beyond itself—the open sea and, still farther, the Libyan port city of Zuwara. In 1912, Zuwara, not far from the Tunisian border, was brutally turned into the western outpost of Italian colonialism in North Africa. A century later, it serves as a migrant hub, promising arrival to Lampedusa, Italy, and Europe. Lampedusa's fishermen avoid this stretch of sea to the island's south—they know their fishing nets break easily there, torn by the many wrecks on the seabed. The random digits and numbers, in relief on the Porta, suddenly acquire a meaning. The Porta invites citizens to cross it and to look beyond it. But it has two facades and two sides, and, as any door, it allows for mobility in two directions. Its ceramic tiles, facing south, reflect moonlight and sunlight, and make it a steady lighthouse for returning fishermen and approaching travelers. Saber, from Tunisia, left his signature on the sculpture on March 30, 2011, together with a fading "*Viva Italia*" and "*Liberté*" in handwritten graffiti. I am reminded of his fellow Tunisians' chant "*Liberté, Liberté!*" in Manduria's tent city, and of the twenty thousand Albanian passengers on board the *Vlora* chanting "*Itali! Itali!*" that critical morning of August 8, 1991. Most of them were to be deported. There is no guarantee that crossing the geopolitical threshold of the Italian state and of the EU—by oneself; with the help of smugglers; or rescued by fishermen, sailors, the navy, or the coast guard—results in the right and ability to overcome the many legal, social, and moralized boundaries still ahead.

At Sea and in the Eternal City: Mare Nostrum and Mos Maiorum, Redux

The October 2013 shipwrecks publicly exposed the contradictions inherent in sovereign aspirations of salvation. In particular, their public drama exploded the *humanitarian* facet of the border apparatus, as unsustainably pretentious. Mare Nostrum was instituted in mid-October as a "military-humanitarian" response to such loss of life. Indeed, with the important number of people it brought to Italy, Mare Nostrum successfully addressed the humanitarian facet of the border apparatus, but in turn it exploded its *military* facet. This happened, perhaps ironically, through the use of warships.

Between October 2013 and September 2014 I scrutinized the inception of the Mare Nostrum mission, its operation, and the "exit strategy" that materialized out of news releases, media debates, EU documents, and statements by relevant politicians and navy officers. What I intend to highlight here is that, alongside the humanitarian dimension of the mission, members of the Italian government and of the navy have taken pains to emphasize also its policing dimension. This includes the collection of fingerprints on board,[12] the prosecution of some three hundred people as smugglers, the capture of four large ships, and the ostensible deterrent effect preventing terrorist arrivals, in comparison to undetected landings. Such emphasis on the policing dimension is tailored to those portions of the Italian and EU public and policymakers concerned that the mission is "purely" humanitarian. Indeed, Interior Minister Alfano has pointed out that a pan-EU intervention in the Mediterranean would be warranted not only by the fact that migrants intend to reach Europe rather than merely Italy, but also by the danger that Italy may become "an objective of Islamic extremists."[13]

Emphasis on policing is also appreciable in a more recent EU operation. Toward the end of their presidency of the Council of the EU (May–December 2014), Italian authorities launched a joint police operation, coordinated by the Italian Ministry of the Interior's Central Directorate for Immigration and Border Police in cooperation with Frontex. Other EU and Schengen countries were successfully invited to participate. The operation was intended to apprehend irregular migrants, disrupt smuggling organizations, and provide a situational picture of unauthorized routes and networks. These joint operations are customarily initiated by national governments as they take over the EU presidency. The 2014 operation was named Mos Maiorum. The phrase refers to the core "mores" of the "ancients," and more specifically to the unwritten code at the heart of personal and collective morality and social norms in ancient Rome. Mos Maiorum provides an etymological and political indication of the renewed centrality of public morality to sovereignty. At the heart of early twenty-first-century sovereign moralizing there is not only humanitarianism, then, but also military and police preemption and repression. This is important to note, once again. For there is the risk that a moralizing and somewhat humanitarian law of large numbers—25,500 drowned, but 142,000 saved—might strike from the record of justice both past and forthcoming crimes of peace.

When it comes to the termination of Mare Nostrum in 2014, I note that state and EU funding is rarely a matter of numbers, of scarcity and availability. It is a question of distribution, and of political will and priorities. Let us consider the massive spending allotted to Eurosur, the long-term commitment of countries around the Mediterranean to NATO's Active Endeavor, and the fact that since 2008 national navies *have* come together to participate in Operation Atalanta in the Indian Ocean. This multiyear, extensive operation is coordinated by and integrated into the EU Naval Force and substantially contributes to antipiracy activities.[14] In summary: I am suggesting that Mare Nostrum did not celebrate its second anniversary not because it was economically unsustainable, but for political reasons. While the Italian navy has strenuously defended Mare Nostrum from its critics, and routinely continues to rescue migrants on the high seas, certain Italian architects of the operation[15] and other European governments have come to see it as a state-owned ferry line for migrants, a "pull factor," an unwarranted humanitarian operation disfavored by voters. From such a point of view, the meticulous search-and-rescue activities effected through Mare Nostrum were too successful; implementing the law of the sea brought too many people to safety. Like Bari's mayor Enrico Dalfino attending to Albanian arrivals that warm morning of August 1991, Mare Nostrum is disparaged as "merely" humanitarian. Search-and-rescue activities became uncomfortably too close to what I call "sovereignty-as-responsibility" activities. Responding to such a contradiction, Operation

Mos Maiorum emphasizes the military, policing, and surveillance side of military-humanitarian sovereignty.

Trailing Behind the Ḥarrāga

Scholars are tracing a new historiography of sovereignty as responsibility, arguing that the conventional history of national sovereignty as inherently opposed to extranational responsibilities is a relatively recent cultural construct.[16] The practices and doctrines of sovereignty as responsibility can be pursued in a variety of ways, and have multifaceted applications. Those concerned with rights, democracy, and justice easily appreciate that sovereignty as responsibility is an ambivalent construct. Humanitarian wars, for example, are allegedly not "against" anyone but rather "for" the protection, rights, and liberation of people, notably in Kosovo-Serbia (1999) and Libya (2011). Sovereignty as responsibility can take the form of allotting funds to mitigate protracted refugee situations "provided that refugees don't go further than the developing world."[17] But sovereignty as responsibility can also prove a legitimation for refugee resettlement, and for redressing global inequality, injustice, and unsustainability. Mare Nostrum, as a hypothetical sustained search-and-rescue EU operation, could have de facto sabotaged, from within, EU technopolitical aspirations to the preemption and deterrence of unauthorized migration and asylum. It could have sabotaged the presuppositions of impossible sovereignty and engendered legal and political reconfigurations of territory, authority, and rights. Instead, any rigorous reconsideration of EU and national citizenship and of migration paradigms seems to have been suspended.

Vision, leadership, innovation, and ambition clearly emerge as national and EU leaders discuss regulatory and restrictive aspects of immigration and asylum. This is appreciable with programs such as Eurosur and Frontex, "smart borders," mobility partnerships, and the externalization of detention, processing, and border controls. In addition to ancient Roman morality (with Mos Maiorum), in recent years an inclusive pantheon of Greek, Norse, and Baltic gods has been ambitiously mobilized to name EU joint police operations seeking to disrupt unauthorized immigration: Perkūnas, Hermes, Mitras, Demeter, Balder, and Aphrodite. But a lack of vision, leadership, and ambition emerges when it comes to relatively modest political objectives such as the creation and implementation of a more integrated EU labor market and a single area of asylum recognition and migration. The EU's "strategic guidelines" for 2014–20 were defined at the European Council of June 2014.[18] On that occasion, European leaders reached a consensus on the need to enforce immigration and asylum policies already in place. As legal scholar Philippe De Bruycker (2014) puts it, in charting the 2014–20 EU vision it was "easy to build a consensus" because, other than proposing intergovernmental and administrative forms of "harmonization," leaders merely contributed to a "collection of previous general statements without commitment," lacking "real content."

National and EU policymakers trail behind the *ḥarrāga*, the people at sea who "burn" papers and frontiers. These are the Tunisian youth on a Zodiac dinghy, singing their lungs out as lights are in sight. The emigrating, precariously employed or never employed youth of southern Europe. Their siblings and friends, working-class men and women staffing navy vessels. Those who have to hope in these sailors' help, and in luck with the currents, the engine, the pump, the fuel, and the smuggler. Those in need of protection, actively confined in the interstices between responsible jurisdictions. Ḥarrāga are those whose labor is actively devalued, and the impoverished who share what they have got. Ḥarrāga of the early twenty-first century are all those who experience the border apparatus and its citizenship regime as not quite working for them and on their behalf.

Europe, write Karakayali and Rigo, exists as a legal and political space *"only to the extent that it is circulated whether this means the circulation of goods, people,* or *rights"* (2010:140; original emphasis). It is the embodied presence and "circulation" of people, in particular, that makes places meaningful and that substantiates discursive articulations of human rights. But circulation, when it comes to certain noncitizens, is preempted, intercepted, pushed back, measured, regulated, and tracked. Circulation, in EU institutional parlance, has also become a euphemism for seasonal, temporary migration. And circulation is taken hostage, south and north of the Mediterranean, as geopolitical tensions resurface, profiteers defend their smuggling monopoly, and well-financed terrorism ghastly reinvents itself.

Some think the legal, political, symbolic, and physical partition of people and spaces can actually be accomplished, humanely or otherwise: with a diplomatic handshake, with surveillance technology, with conditional aid, with militaristic discipline, with brutal fanaticism. However, once set at sea such "omnipotent rationalism" finds many obstacles to its deployment (Chambers 2010:679). It needs to be radically recalibrated, for the sea is something else: it is salt and matter, a vision and a stretch of water, a horizon, a route, gulfs, bays, and shores. You are small at sea, even when you are not a lost sailor.[19] Its liquid mobility exceeds sovereign pretensions, and the law of the sea is hard to breach.

In Italy, any *lido* (beach resort)—like all harbors, rivers, lakes, the entire coastline, and select public domain lands—sits on national state property, *demanio*. What is *demaniale* cannot be bought and sold, as it belongs to the citizenry. Private residents and corporations are allowed to administer public domain lands, including the lido, in the interest of the collectivity. They are entrusted with such lands' day-to-day maintenance and beautification, on behalf of citizens. Still, it is not uncommon to find portions of the coast left unadministered, unassigned to any private actor. There is no entry ticket to pay; people just bring their own beach umbrellas, in all sizes and colors. It can be expected that such a public beach neighbors a lido. Local children climb or swim around the rusty fence to take advantage of the lido's fresh-water showers, to take a stroll, buy gelato, or simply have fun with friends on the other side. They join other children in building a nice sand castle, with four observation towers, a central square, galleries, and plastic soldiers. As they work on the castle, they also tap down the moist sand into a beautiful, smooth wall that encircles it. Seawater soon appears in the holes they made when taking sand out, eroding its way into an expansive moat. Portions of the wall crumble. As always happens in the afternoon, waves begin to pick up. Children try hectically to add more and more sand and to fortify the walls, but more than the waves hitting the castle it is the backwash that is eating away the ambitious construction. I am not naturalizing, spatializing, or infantilizing migration and minimizing forced migration. On the contrary, I am playing with sovereignty's own spatialization to denaturalize its utopian pretense to wire the Mediterranean with digital, geopolitical, social, and documentary thresholds. I also want to hint at important political and legal discussions that, sparked for example by situated concerns with the way public domain lands are de facto administered, are reappropriating the larger vocabulary of popular sovereignty, responsibility, and economic justice, to make it relevant and inclusive.

Residents are working hard to take back their coastal places and seascapes from organized crime, from mass polluters, and from those who privatize profit and socialize risk. Workshops involving artists, constitutionalists, politicians, and old and new residents are busily at work so that what is ostensibly public and common good does not become, as it often does, a dilapidated and littered no-man's-land, or alternatively a de facto privatized and securitized space. The proliferation of these experimental laboratories of physical occupation, deliberative discussion, and organized action deserves its own book—I am working on it. Here, I note that these laboratories of public citizenship have taken up the challenge of actualizing the seemingly empty words of the Italian Constitution every child learns at school (Article 1): "Italy is a democratic Republic founded on labor. Sovereignty belongs to the people and is exercised by the people in the forms and within the limits of the Constitution."

Crucially, these laboratories bring together residents and migrants,[20] social networks with Italian and Mediterranean nodes, intent on mapping and unraveling the interrelation of geopolitical interests, neoliberalism, structural injustice, and displacement. Such a movement is necessary because people subjected to crimes of peace, including migrants, should not "wait for their time to come, and a good thing too—because it won't" (Honig 2009:131). In other words, the "goal" of a just, plural, democratic, and egalitarian society will never be handed down; it needs to be translated into a method, on the horizontal, situational, and antiteleological ethnographic map of daily practice.

These pages have examined the nexus between sovereignty and responsibility, military and humanitarian logic, hospitality and confinement, preemption and rule of law, democracy and state violence, legality and illegality, connivance and dissidence. What they have traced is a sovereignty that excludes as it feeds and shelters, that deports persons by rescuing lives: the gray area.

The Gray Area: Mafia, Democracy, Migration

The large image of Peppino Impastato, in black, is portrayed on the whitewashed exterior wall of a modest house in Lampedusa. To the right of Peppino's bearded profile sits a blue wooden plaque, carved out of a migrant boat's hull. The white, hand-painted inscription reads quite simply: "Peppino Impastato, born in Cinisi on January 5, 1948. Killed by the Mafia on May 9, 1978." Peppino was born near Palermo, Sicily, into a family with connections to the local Mafia.[21] But as a teenager he finds the courage to break off relations with his father, who in turn kicks him out of the house. Peppino becomes involved in various political movements, and participates in local feminist and antinuclear civic battles. It is the world's 1968, but it is also Cinisi's 1968, with its specific social issues and with the pressure to conform to be expected in a small town of twelve thousand. Peppino assumes an important role in the struggle of his town's peasants facing land expropriations. Much land has already been taken to build Palermo's Punta Raisi Airport, in the shade of the mount that dominates Cinisi. The unfavorable position between Montagna Longa and the sea soon warrants the construction of a third runway. The Mafia is allegedly involved.

Peppino's strong, radical anti-Mafia activism is shaped by an overarching urge for social justice. It is not confined to "peasants" as a group of victimized people in isolation, but is grounded in his daily method of not conniving with the Mafia and seeking just societal relationships. In 1976 Peppino is among the pioneers of the new Radio Aut station, and in the popular program *Crazy Waves* he uses humor and satire to expose the silences, phrases, manners, and crimes of local Mafiosi close to his own family. He accords them no respect. His brother, Giovanni, also becomes involved in these initiatives. Local elections are scheduled for May 14, 1978, and Peppino runs as a candidate for his town's council with the leftist Proletarian Democracy Party. His conclusive speech and rally is scheduled for May 10.

It is the morning of May 9, 1978. His body is found in Cinisi's countryside next to the railway tracks. These are the "lead years" of Italian political terrorism. Police forces purport that he died a terrorist in a failed attempt to detonate TNT and damage the tracks and commuter train. Some suggest he committed suicide. These are the facts emerging on television and printed media. That Tuesday, though, most citizens are intent on following the details of another dramatic event. Following a fifty-five-day kidnapping, preeminent politician Aldo Moro is found dead in a Renault 4 parked in Via Caetani, Rome. It appears he was assassinated by the Red Brigades. A few days later, many among Cinisi's citizens vote for the late Peppino, symbolically electing him to the city council.

Spanning many years, the efforts of Peppino's brother, Giovanni, his mother, Felicia, and fellow anti-Mafia activists and friends helped to illuminate the Mafia's responsibility for his assassination. In 2000, the Italian Parliament's Anti-Mafia Commission issued a report outlining the responsibilities of state officials in leading the investigations astray. In 2001 and

2002 his executioner and the instigator of his killing were convicted. The latter individual was the infamous "Don Tano," Gaetano Badalamenti, whose family's house sits a mere *cento passi*, one hundred footsteps, from Peppino's home.[22]

In Lampedusa, the whitewashed house with Peppino's face painted on the outside hosts Askavusa, a local association. The small, street-level apartment is not far from Piazza Libertà (Liberty Square), the main square. The name "askavusa," a feminine adjective in Sicilian, can be translated as "barefoot." Since 2009, the nonprofit association has been active in a broad range of activities, from the organization of successful summer film festivals centered on migration to the material solidarity with newly arrived and detained migrants, to the denunciation of environmental injustice. I ask Franca, a committed member of Askavusa, about Peppino's picture right outside the house. Why *him*, a "hero" of anti-Mafia struggles, as the recognizable face of an organization that seems concerned primarily with migrants' rights?

Her answer is laconic, and telling. "It's about civic engagement," she says.[23] But Franca is not there all day, every day, to explain to residents and visitors alike why the anti-Mafia citizen is so prominently featured. Peppino looks you in the eye. Passersby are urged to engage the portrait and find their answer. Or they can turn a blind eye.

The institutions that should have taken responsibility for the protection of Peppino's life from the Mafia's outreach, and that should have safeguarded his civil and political rights, failed to do so: first by negligence, second by removing evidence, and third by fabricating around his remains a story of terrorist illegality. Peppino is considered by many to be a "hero," together with Aldo Moro, dozens of police and carabinieri agents, priest Don Peppino Diana, migrant Jerry Masslo, and anti-Mafia judges such as Giovanni Falcone and Paolo Borsellino—both murdered by the Mafia in 1992. Palermo's airport was renamed and rededicated to the latter two judges' memory. For in Italy it is not uncommon to hear of anti-Mafia deaths as forms of *sacrificio*, or sacrifice. Many think of these dead as heroic victims of organized crime and terrorism. But in the daily and institutional encounters *of their lifetime* they were considered annoyances and burdens.

Peppino's name and life inspire and substantiate a variety of civic, institutional, and artistic enterprises, including those pertaining to Askavusa. One of the very first anti-Mafia public demonstrations in Italy was held in

Cinisi, Peppino's hometown, on the first anniversary of his death. Peppino's life was marked by the courage, anticonformism, persistence, and creativity he put into his battles of and for critical citizenship. While people arrived from every corner of Sicily to participate in his funeral, many of his own townspeople actively ignored the event, at best gazing from behind shutters and airy curtains—as they had done during his lifetime. His friends and comrades, in procession through Cinisi's streets, held a large banner: "The Mafia kills. Your silence, too."

Citizens' readiness to ignore what they see and hear, and their unwillingness to speak up, has long enabled the success of various criminal organizations, in southern Italy as elsewhere. The strength of the Mafia lies also in conniving, complicit, and conforming behaviors, says sociologist Nando dalla Chiesa (2014:40)—the son of General Carlo Alberto dalla Chiesa, assassinated by Mafia killers in Palermo together with his second wife and an agent of his escort in 1982. Without complicit institutions, implied or explicit threats of violence, and tacit popular acquiescence, the Mafia could never be what it is. Why would I cover my eyes, ears, and mouth? Perhaps in exchange for the promise of a quiet life, to protect the safety and freedom to which my family is entitled, when no one else does. There is hardly anything that stands further away from the ideal and substance of citizenship and rights in a democratic society. I might perhaps feel free and protected in my individual isolation, but at the price of my neighbor's freedom and of my liberty as a person. Liberty emerges in the company of equal others—in critical association, in participation, in engagement, in conflict and compromise, in challenge and change. It is when the sociopolitical sphere of life is destroyed that people are driven to the impasse of isolation (Arendt 1958 [1951]:474). The sociopolitical sphere that enables rights, citizenship, equality, and an always-precarious democracy is essential to the human experience. On the doorsteps of Europe, and on the threshold of liberty, this is relevant, with different modalities, to citizens as it is to maritime travelers and to migrants behind bars.

Mediterraneo: the sea "amid lands," the Great Sea, the White Sea, the Middle Sea, as some of its people call it. *Cosa Nostra*: "Our Thing," a widely used synonym for the Sicilian Mafia; a phrase that renders something—a system, a mechanism, a network—that cannot otherwise be reified. *Mare Nostrum*: "Our Sea." Which meaning do *we*—in our own situations as scholars, workers, "second-generation" citizens, unemployed, policymakers—want to emphasize and enforce, when thinking of our sea, the sea around which we live? Here the drowned and the saved, their families, their pro-bono lawyers, fishermen, activists, sailors, investigative reporters, judges and rescue workers are writing many pages of the social history of the present. Which legacy do we want to leave? Which Europe do I want to live in? We can make the Mediterranean "ours" by further privatizing it, taking advantage of the ensuing inequalities at an excruciating cost. But in doing so we risk also privatizing "us," under siege in a bastion of crumbling self-sufficiency and angst. "Great Teacher" and "Sole Force" Enver Hoxha colonized every corner of the public sphere with mobile defensive bunkers. That was his autarchic vision of liberty and security for the People's Socialist Republic of Albania.

Or we could demand something else, daily—with our examples, votes, relationships, and disobedience and by affording scholarly and public resonance to *already existing* social engagements and policy alternatives. We could demand that the fact that migrants often do not intend to stay in Italy or Greece be appreciated as a socioeconomic warning about the plight of these countries, rather than proclaimed with relief. That European social insecurity be addressed through the solidarity of fairer social and work relations, rather than through the creative use of digital barbed wire, the costly technocracy of austerity, and always fashionable scapegoating. That political disaffection be addressed through more honest and grounded politics, rather than through the infantilization of citizens and the xenophobic populism of self-anointed saviors. That the Italian south offset the prospects of the so-called human and industrial desertification (related also to sustained emigration and structural impoverishment). That Italian, Euro-Mediterranean, and postcolonial hierarchical relations between a majority of people put in the position of needing salvation and an elite of saviors—and between "South" and "North"—be redressed with daily pragmatism and sustainable politics of justice, rather than reproduced by predatory paternalism and moralizing racism. That migrants' queries be addressed with rights, respect, and justice, rather than with permissions, spectacle, and emergency. We may insist that increased public funding for the social inclusion of migrants and their children, currently averaging 123.8 million euros per year in Italy, makes it unnecessary to allocate an average of 247 million per year in rejection practices such as detention and deportation.[24] That Nadha—the baby born on August 24, 2013, to Syrian refugee parents at sea—be granted Italian citizenship. That "foreigners" born and raised in Italy do not have to wait eighteen years before having a confusing chance to apply for Italian citizenship.[25] I am inclined to believe some of these initiatives require more accountability in public funds allocations, and a redistribution of spending. But should they ultimately require additional public funds, we would need to ponder a tax increase, unimaginative and mundane as it sounds. We would then have the opportunity to assess, personally and as parties to democratic politics, the value we attach to human dignity, rights, justice, and a sustainable and egalitarian polity.

Six young men and one woman among the Eritrean survivors of the October 3, 2013, shipwreck are doing their part by supporting prosecutors in Sicily with the case against one of their suspected traffickers, who held them for ransom in Libya prior to the journey to Lampedusa. As a result, these survivors have been confined in the Lampedusa holding facility for 101 days, because of the needs of the justice system, as Interior Minister Alfano is reported to have put it.[26] Their travel companions were flown to Rome after "only" 45 days in the facility legally meant for short-term "assistance" of up to seventy-two hours. Six Syrians also left Lampedusa's holding facility to testify in the case against their smuggler.

The Lampedusa holding center—damaged by fires in 2009 and 2012—is being renovated. Island residents are also learning that new radars, with functions including NATO support and unauthorized vessel detection, are to be added to existing military infrastructure on the strategically located island. New migrant boats, and new coffins, are expected. Everything changed, after the October 3 shipwreck. And all stays the same, emergency after emergency. Emergencies do not last two decades. The political priorities, active policies, and structured negligence that perpetuate them as such do.

Diasporas of Migration

How many pages would it take to list the names of the 25,500 persons who perished at the borders of the EU? How long would it take to find out those names? To call them aloud? To look everyone in the eye, or to see everyone's picture?[27] To listen to 25,500 different variations of "push and pull" factors? To learn and say something about their religious practices, bustling villages, cities in ruins, tastes, fears, aspirations, mistakes, tortures, and journeys? How much space does it take to trace 25,500 kinship networks, with the faces and relationships of those who lost a loved one, but are still waiting for their phone call? How many square meters would 25,500 plaques take, in our cities? How much space, for 25,500 people to be properly buried?

In Lampedusa, dozens of boats that have survived the Mediterranean crossing lie relatively undisturbed in "the boats' cemetery," a fenced and guarded ground close to the harbor. On the boats' now-oblique decks one can see toys, clothes, gasoline containers, rusty extinguishers, shoes, and empty bottles. The exposed wood rots in the sun. Large holes in the white and blue hulls offer an opening into the sky—or toward the sea, depending on your vantage point. A fisherman shares rumors about locals routinely stealing usable electrical and mechanical parts, as the boats sit impounded for months. The destiny of these boats, or of what remains of them, is to end up in a wood chipper. Until recently, their "*smaltimento*" (disposal) has cost some 700,000 euros per year, a job awarded without invitations for multiple bids.[28] The perpetual state of emergency ostensibly has justified that nothing much has been taken apart, sold, or recycled. Mattresses, rubber dinghies, photographs, phone books, jackets, and batteries are all equally destined for the chipper unless "allegedly" stolen or unless Askavusa's members rescue them from the local dump.

In the tiny apartment rented by Askavusa there is a kitchenette, a living room-studio-library, and a room that initiates the organization's seminal attempt to create the island's Museum of Migrations. The idea was born in 2005, when Giacomo[29] found a copy of the Quran in the vicinity of a migrant boat. Life vests, volumes of the Bible and of the Quran, cigarette packages, scarves, shoes, letters, phone cards, fishing nets, dictionaries, olive oil from Sfax in Tunisia, pasta boxes, compact discs, and evil eye pendants hang on the wall and are assembled on tiny shelves. The ceiling of the one-room museum is covered with blue tarpaulin. Does it remind you of the sky, or are we under the sea?

Recently, Askavusa's members have further developed the museum, also relying on migrants' collection, translation, and dissemination of relevant materials. The museum has obtained the official *patrocinio* (sponsorship) of Lampedusa's civic administration and national and international organizations. Lampedusa, as a "node in Mediterranean migrations," intends to become "a place of memory and of reception," not of rejection and respingimento, as the town administrators put it.[30] Prominent art historian and restoration specialist Giuseppe Basile served as a consultant for the museum. In his words, the museum would simply be inadequate as a site of conservation and of memory of the past, even if that past is recent. What is needed, he suggested just days before passing away, is "a documentary monitoring activity" linking past and present, and clarifying their meaningful relationship.[31] The museum will eventually be visited, online and in person, also by migrants and their descendants. The activity will document, contextualize, analyze, and narrate the institutional offense and human defiance of Euro-Mediterranean crimes of peace. Still in the making, the museum promises to resist identitarian entrenchment, tourist marketing, spatial incarceration, and the redemptive boundaries of the past and of conservation—crimes of peace are ongoing.

The Museum of Migrations aspires to be lived as a *museo diffuso*, serving as the occasion for a diasporic, diffuse, scattered experience of public citizenship shared by old and new residents. For the experience of maritime journeys, of rescue, of assistance, of counting the bodies, of confinement, and of solidarity is not just the immigrants' and rescuers' experience. It is inseparable from the embodied time, the public square, the moral aesthetics, and the civil and political rights and duties that constitute the life of people in Lampedusa, in Otranto, and in Valletta.

In small coastal locations as in larger cities social actors are actively laboring with daily practices and overarching ideas. They demonstrate to administrators and others in the polity that the substance of rights is integral to the substance of democracy, and that there is more to politics than a club consultation and the electoral ratification of purported consensus. They labor to reconfigure the outposts of European sovereign salvation into nodes of a more just Euro-Mediterranean network. But the Euro-Mediterranean network exists only insofar as it is navigated. *Mare Nostrum*: the Great Sea, the Middle Sea, the White Sea, "Our Sea." It belongs to all and to no one. *Mediterraneo*: a public and common good "amid lands" made of bays, salt, water, people, routes, visions, and shores. Its seafarers are recharting Europe, as a land amid seas.

Notes

Introduction

1. Smugglers' names in this work are pseudonyms. Publicly available names, for example in the case of convicted smugglers, have been retained. Names of public figures (including politicians, journalists, members of armed forces, and priests) are real, unless otherwise noted. Names of migrants, residents, bureaucrats, armed forces members, and administrators whom I have personally interviewed are pseudonyms, unless otherwise noted. I have, for the most part, retained the names and pseudonyms already used in publicly available media coverage of migrants' stories. All translations into English are mine unless otherwise noted.

2. On Italian twentieth-century colonialism in Africa (Libya, Eritrea, Ethiopia, and Somalia) see Palumbo's (2003) and Ben-Ghiat and Fuller's (2005) comprehensive collections.

3. Maximilian Popp, "Europe's Deadly Borders: An Inside Look at EU's Shameful Immigration Policy," *Spiegel Online*, September 11, 2014, http://www.spiegel.de, accessed September 11, 2014. The European Agency for the Management of Operational Cooperation at the External Borders of the Member States of the European Union, known as Frontex (from "external borders" in French), is the EU agency for border security. It was established in 2004.

4. On the many difficulties facing non-Libyan citizens, including refugees, in Libya, see Chapters 2 and 5 and Jesuit Refugee Service Malta 2014.

5. Popp, "Europe's Deadly Borders."

6. Eurosur (see Chapter 5) is a network of border surveillance and "situation awareness" monitoring gradually implemented since 2013. Satellite, maritime, radar, and statistical sources detect, ostensibly in real time, trends and anomalies at Europe's external borders, including in the Mediterranean. On Eurosur, see also Feldman 2012:96.

7. For a specifically Italian and European focus, see Stolcke 1995; Carter 1997; Cole 1997; Holmes 2000; Sniderman et al. 2000; Calavita 2005; Lucht 2012. On Italian immigration laws and modalities of "integration," see Zincone 2006; Albahari 2008; Allievi 2010; Caneva 2014.

8. See the concern with "foreign" pathogens explored by Darian-Smith 1999.

9. Prior to its "civil war" (starting in 2011), Syria was the third largest refugee-hosting country in the world, with possibly a million Iraqi refugees, in addition to the protracted presence of at least half a million Palestinian refugees. See Paz 2011:3.

10. De Giorgi 2014. Up-to-date European immigration statistics are available in English. See, for example, Eurostat, "Migration and Migrant Population Statistics," http://ec.europa.eu/eurostat/statistics-explained/index.php/Migration_and_ migrant_population_statistics# and, for Italy in particular, Istat, "Immigrants," http://www.istat.it/en/archive/immigrants. Several organizations provide reports on asylum and refugee legal issues, including detailed statistics. See, in English, ECRE 2014. Residents of Italy, a country of roughly 60 million people, include more than 5 million foreign citizens (about 8.6 percent of the total population). These include almost a million noncitizen minors born or raised in Italy by foreign parents and about 3.8 million non-EU citizens holding a residence permit. The countries of origin include, in decreasing order of presences, Romania, Albania, Morocco, China, Ukraine, the Philippines, Moldova, India, Poland, and Tunisia. In 2011 there were some 18,000 "mixed" (citizen with noncitizen) marriages, 8.8 percent of the total number of marriages. Many migrants are employed as domestic workers and care-givers, in construction and agriculture, as truck drivers, in fishing and maritime transportation, in restaurants and catering, and in trade, or work as private entrepreneurs. Finally, it needs to be noted that prior to the war in Syria and the increased arrivals from Eritrea, most unauthorized migration (up to 90 percent) occurred through land borders and visa overstaying. IDOS 2013; Istat, "Non-EU Citizens Holding a Residence Permit," August 5, 2014, http://www.istat.it/en/archive/129859, accessed August 5, 2014.

11. "The Migrants' Files," https://www.detective.io/detective/the-migrants-files/, accessed September 14, 2014. In Chapter 3, I detail the methods grounding such complex figures. Building on the work of the Migrants' Files and including a comparative perspective and an extensive bibliography (see also Grant 2011a), a recent IOM report (2014) has noted that the Euro-Mediterranean area is consistently the deadliest border zone in the world, with an average fifteen hundreds deaths per year since 2000. During 2014, in particular, migrant deaths in the Mediterranean accounted for 75 percent of global migrant deaths. Other areas of particular concern include the United States–Mexico border, the Bay of Bengal, the Red Sea and Gulf of Aden, the Caribbean, the Sahara, and Southeast Asia.

12. IOM 2014. See also UNHCR *News Stories*, "UNHCR alarmed at death toll from boat sinkings in the Mediterranean," September 16, 2014, http://www.unhcr.org/ 54184ae76.html, accessed September 16, 2014.

13. Ali shared his experience of migration during a personal interview, February 3, 2005.

14. This practice has been documented up to August 2013.

15. Officers of CIR, the nonpartisan Italian Council for Refugees NGO, are on call at such maritime ports of entry. There, their primary task is to guarantee access to

the process of asylum application. Nevertheless, it appears they are called only at the discretion of the police.

16. This is a "customs and excise" armed force, and has an important role in maritime border patrol, as we will see.

17. The epistemological and material complexity of the gendered body's "ability" to narrate, explain, and critique forms of structural injustice, global hierarchy, and political violence is traced by an emerging body of scholarship. See, among others, Feldman 1991; Scheper-Hughes 1993; Rabinow 1999; Farmer 2003; Herzfeld 2004; Sayad 2004 [1999]; Braidotti 2011; Biehl 2013; Holmes 2013.

18. Teenagers saying they are minors but who are without identification documents are routinely subjected to such x-ray examinations. In pediatric medicine, skeletal maturity is sometimes assessed with complex x-rays of carpal and epiphyseal areas of the nondominant hand, complemented by automated mathematical processing. There exist several radiological methods to assess "bone age," and all have margins of error up to two years. Rather than bone ages, x-rays can thus indicate bone stages. They point to discrepancies (for example, due to hereditary diseases, fractures, and endocrinologic problems) between skeletal maturity and the *already known age* of children typically under ten (see Giordano et al. 2009). Thus, attributing an exact age—below or above eighteen—to a person whose health history is not known does not seem a valid procedure. Ethical concerns about radiation exposure and informed consent can also be raised. What is crucial here is that these practices often result in the opportunity to receive humanitarian protection for those defined as minors, and rejection at the border or deportation for "adults."

19. Such speedy "readmission" is made possible by a 1999 Greek-Italian bilateral agreement.

20. See, most recently, Cabot 2014.

21. This event is reported in Sciurba 2009:175.

22. Greece has a very high percentage of refugee application rejections, which creates a salient differential with Italy. In 2012, out of 11,195 first-instance decisions, 11,095 (99.1 percent) were rejections, typically after two years of legal limbo for applicants and the legal impossibility to seek employment. This means that out of one hundred applicants, only one, at best, is recognized as a genuine refugee or at any rate as needing subsidiary or humanitarian protection. When able to access (free) legal assistance, some among the other ninety-nine people may appeal the first-instance negative decision, and wait another two years. In contrast, in Italy, also in 2012, out of 22,165 first-instance decisions, 13,900 (62.7 percent) were rejections. This means that out of one hundred applicants, thirty-seven are recognized as refugees or as people needing subsidiary or humanitarian protection. (Eurostat, "Eurostat Asylum Applicants and First Instance Decisions on Asylum Applications: 2012," http://epp.eurostat .ec.europa.eu/cache/ity_offpub/ks-qa-13-005/en/ks-qa-13-005-en.pdf, accessed June 29, 2014.)

23. Detailed in Cabot 2014:23, 219.

24. This EU law establishes the criteria and mechanisms for determining which member state is responsible for examining asylum applications lodged by non-EU citizens and stateless persons.

25. UNHCR 2014. ECRE 2014 also provides an in-depth and comprehensive legal, political, and administrative contextualization of such figures.

26. On the many political uses of statistics, see Urla 1993; Asad 1994. On the genealogy of "populations" as objects of survey, intervention, and concern see Foucault 2003 [1997].

27. ANSAmed, "Bavaria minister slams Italy on refugees, EU law not applied," August 22, 2014, http://www.ansamed.info/ansamed/en/news/nations/italy/2014/08/22/bavaria-minister-slams-italy-on-refugees_c79cd352-0f83-46d0-beea-8976016e3d77.html, accessed August 22, 2014.

28. Bernd Riegert, "Maiziere: EU must help refugees at the source," Deutsche Welle, July 11, 2014, http://dw.de/p/1CZhQ, accessed July 11, 2014.

29. Nikolaj Nielsen, "France wants to create new EU migration post," *EUobserver.com*, September 2, 2014, https://euobserver.com/justice/125438, accessed September 2, 2014.

30. Gérard Bon, "Afflux de migrants à la frontière avec l'Italie," Reuters France, August 4, 2014, http://fr.reuters.com/article/topNews/idFRKBN0G41TI20140804, accessed August 5, 2014.

31. The Schengen Agreement of 1985, gradually enlarged to comprise twenty-six European countries, generally stipulates the abolition of passport and border controls at common ("internal") borders.

32. *La Repubblica*, "Immigrazione, migliaia di migranti 'respinti' dall'Austria al Brennero," September 18, 2014, http://www.repubblica.it/esteri/2014/09/18/news/emergenza_immigrazione_al_brennero_austria_rispedisce_in_italia_1400_stranieri-96098555/, accessed September 18, 2014.

33. See Save the Children 2014 and ECRE 2014. Note that these figures do not include people who entered Italy undetected.

34. On the difficult condition of migrant teenagers (in the United States) as objects of humanitarian and policing concerns, see Heidbrink 2014.

35. Based on ethnographic evidence, I agree with Cornelius and Rosenblum (2004:102) that "forced migrants" are often brought to "confront decision-making practices similar to those of voluntary migrants."

36. I follow, in this sense, established UN usage. For approaches on trafficking that bring together issues of human rights, policy, and social justice, see Brysk and Choi-Fitzpatrick 2012. For an analysis of the nexus between labor, trafficking, and immigration (in the United States), see Brennan 2014.

37. Green has recently (2013) provided a comprehensive survey of the anthropological scholarship on EU borders, with particular emphasis on the EU institutional architecture in light of the financial crisis. Fassin 2011 provides an equally comprehensive

review (with a larger geopolitical focus), and urges further analytical attention to the border–social boundaries nexus. This book contributes to meeting that demand.

38. Consequently, they also point to the potential inadequacy of policy models that ambitiously seek to deter arrivals and, upon failure, to swiftly deport them to the EU country of first arrival, to their "home" country, or to a "safe" transit country.

39. For an understanding of the "public sphere" as constituted by nuanced, fragmented, and asymmetrical encounters, see Fraser 1992.

40. For a Euro-Mediterranean comparative perspective, see Suárez-Navaz 2004; Zammit 2007; Lauth Bacas and Kavanagh 2013.

41. A phrase I borrow from Vicari's 2012 documentary on the subject, titled precisely *La Nave Dolce*.

42. Bari is the capital of the administrative region of Apulia. Apulia comprises the southeastern peninsular part (the "heel") of Italy, stretching into the Ionian and Adriatic Seas and facing the Balkan Peninsula. It has been at the forefront of the reception of maritime migration since 1990, because of its relative proximity to Albanian, Montenegrin, Greek, Egyptian, and Turkish ports. Calabria is the peninsular region (to the southwest of Apulia) opposite Sicily.

43. This is the region, incidentally, where anthropologist Ernesto de Martino grounded his *La Terra del Rimorso* (1996 [1961], "The Land of Remorse"). Giordano 2014 has recently contextualized his work (see also Albahari 2008).

44. As suggested by Sarat, Douglas, and Merrill Umphrey 2005:10.

45. In this book I use "legible" as developed by Scott 1998 and Torpey 2000.

46. On Frontex "risk analyses," see Feldman 2012.

47. To adapt Greenhouse 2002:27. This understanding resonates also with Asad 2004.

48. On spatialization, especially in its intersections with neoliberalism, see the seminal work by Gupta and Ferguson 1992 and Ferguson and Gupta 2002; and more recently Mezzadra and Neilson 2014.

49. In this work I use "pluralism" in the conflictual, processual, and polycentric sense developed by Connolly 2005.

50. Monsignor Giuseppe Betori, qtd. in "Cei, monsignor Giuseppe Betori: 'La Chiesa continuerà a parlare,'" *La Repubblica*, September 27, 2005, http://www.repub blica.it/2005/i/sezioni/politica/prodipacs1/ceiparla/ceiparla.html, accessed September 2, 2014.

51. Throughout this work, understanding religion as historically produced and therefore integral to social, legal, and political dynamics brings me (building on the work of Talal Asad, e.g., 1983) to resist the dichotomy between religion and secularism. In the European political setting, see Holmes 2000; Schlesinger and Foret 2006; Albahari 2007.

52. I am referring to the so-called Italian Southern Question, which I have tackled in detail elsewhere (Albahari 2008). On the shifting, relational, and "segmentary"

nature of the dynamics of marginalization, specifically in Italy, see also Gramsci 1957; Schneider 1998; Agnew 2002; Herzfeld 2007; Capussotti 2010; Forgacs 2014.

53. Dainotto 2007:13. See, more generally, Wolf's seminal work (1982).

54. For a recent analysis of the relevance of space in migration and asylum, see Mountz 2010. On the continuing global flourishing of walls and fences, see Brown 2010; Mezzadra and Neilson 2014.

55. On these aspects of fishing, see Feldman 2012:80; Lucht 2012; Andersson 2014.

56. For an explication of this logic, see Eliade 1959:20.

57. For such a political-theological genealogy, see Kantorowicz 1997 [1957].

58. European Council 2014:1.

59. See, for example, Chavez 2008; Chebel d'Appollonia 2012.

60. See the many relevant contributions in Pagden 2002.

61. See De Genova and Peutz 2010.

62. Expressed at an international conference I attended, October 28, 2011.

63. On migrant detention and human rights in Malta, see Debono 2011.

64. As recently noted more generally by Fassin and Pandolfi (2010b).

65. As argued by Mouffe 2005:75, among others.

66. See Austin 1962 and Mertz 1994.

67. Giordano 2014:73–79 offers a discussion of Basaglia's democratic-psychiatric work.

68. Including the Vatican's *L'Osservatore Romano*, August 25, 2014. In Albahari (forthcoming) I discuss Pope Francis's pastoral visit to Lampedusa in July 2013.

69. I am thinking, for example, of the Bhopal "disaster" (Fortun 2001).

70. On the death penalty, see Kaufman-Osborne 2002; Sarat 2014. The relevance of the death penalty to the issues examined here is mentioned in Chapter 3.

71. See Albahari n.d.

72. People are never speechless victims, as already argued by Malkki 1996 and James 2010. They might be made so, or represented as such.

73. Hastrup 2004 and Mertz 2002:361 further explicate the motives of such an approach.

74. The EU Commission is the executive body of the EU.

75. See Riles 2006.

76. On the very idea of "the field," see Gupta and Ferguson's critical work (1997). It should also be noted that it is not only that new factors such as supranational governance, technology, travel, and global finance and migration determine a different approach to fieldwork and to ethnography. What needs to be factored in is also a cultural and political change in how the social sciences, and their actors, perceive their object of study and their own geopolitical and epistemological location (Wolf 1982; Gupta and Ferguson 1992; Marcus 1995).

77. One might ask: what kind of democracy (e.g., technical, unpolitical, populist, or plebiscitary, as Urbinati 2014 would put it) emerges from a focus on the border apparatus?

78. As argued by Ticktin 2011; Fassin 2012.

79. See, among others, Merry 2005; Bornstein and Redfield 2010; Hopgood 2013.

80. See Goodale 2013.

81. As implied by Soysal's pioneering work (1994), discussed in Chapter 3. On the recognition of migrants' rights within the UN human rights system, see Grant 2011b.

82. Hollenbach 2010 explores such a normative question from multiple vantage points, including Catholic social teachings.

83. On the intersections of charity and hospitality see Albahari forthcoming; Rozakou 2012.

84. In this work (especially in Chapter 6) I bring together politics, moral propriety, and aesthetics building on Falasca-Zamponi 1997; Chambers 2008; Herzfeld 2009; Rancière 2010.

85. As Feldman would critically put it (2012:19).

86. *Euronews.com*, August 27, 2014, "EU 'Frontex Plus' agency to replace Italy migrant sea rescue," http://www.euronews.com/2014/08/27/eu-frontex-plus-agency -to-replace-italy-migrant-sea-rescue/, accessed August 27, 2014.

87. Personal communication, director of nongovernmental Italy-based agency, September 13, 2014.

88. European Council 2014:19.

89. As illustrated by Feldman 2012:150–79.

90. European Council 2014:19.

91. *Official Journal of the European Union* 2013:1.

92. In this work I borrow the phrase "the drowned and the saved" (*i sommersi e i salvati*) from Primo Levi, the Jewish Italian anti-Fascist World War II partisan and writer (Levi 1997 [1958]:79–90). While Levi uses the phrase as relevant to the Shoah, I do not imply a priori any historical parallelism. I simply intend to convey that survival, death, and salvation are at the center of politics that routinely become biopolitics; and that maritime migrants are exposed to the contradictions of morality, power, subsistence, agency, and resistance, whether they manage to survive their journey or not. Levi's reflections on "the gray area" he lived through also inform some of my reflections in Chapter 6.

93. Donen 1974.

Chapter 1. Genealogies of Care and Confinement

1. Unless otherwise noted, the account of early 1990s events in Albania and Italy (Apulia) given in the following chapters is based on my cross-check of multiple sources, including my own notes and experiences as a resident of coastal Apulia; on conversations, spanning several years, with a number of Albanian-born residents of Italy (in the cities of Florence, Bari, Brindisi, and Lecce) who prefer anonymity; on information provided at the time by the Apulian regional newspaper *La Gazzetta del Mezzogiorno* and national newspapers; and on video footage available through the

television channels Telenorba and TG3 Puglia and through documentaries by Eshja and Soranzo 2004; Vicari 2012; and Sejko 2013.

2. Dal Lago 2004:182.

3. Perrone 1996:33.

4. I borrow "America" here from Gianni Amelio's fictional movie account of Albanian emigration, titled *Lamerica* (1994). See Pajo (2008) for a detailed analysis of Albanian articulations of belonging and longing to travel "west," and in particular to Greece and Italy. See Todorova (2009) for a critical account of the complicated but ultimately orientalist perceptions and self-designations of "the Balkans."

5. Leogrande 2011:152.

6. See Leogrande 2010:56.

7. Small fishing boats also reached Sicily and Lampedusa in the 1980s. But these arrivals were largely ignored by national policymakers, and were not framed as an immigration issue to be methodically addressed.

8. On a larger scale, Holmes (2000:28) credits the solidarism of Catholic social doctrine as having imparted "a moral perspective, organizational theory, and technocratic practice" to the construction of the EU.

9. *Prefetto*, operating locally on behalf of the Ministry of the Interior, and under its authority.

10. Don Giuseppe, personal interview, August 11, 2004.

11. *La Repubblica*, March 7, 1991.

12. His real name.

13. Anna Dalfino, qtd. in Maria Grazia Rongo, "L'arrivo della Vlora nel '91: 'Il mio Enrico, il sindaco che disse no al lager,'" *La Gazzetta del Mezzogiorno*, August 4, 2011, http://www.lagazzettadelmezzogiorno.it/homepage/l-arrivo-della-vlora-nel-91-il-mio-enrico-il-sindaco-che-no446365/, accessed August 12, 2014.

14. Perrone 1996:35.

15. Dal Lago 2004:183.

16. Pietro, personal interview, January 14, 2005.

17. For a theoretical foundation of my ethnographically grounded statement, see Simmel 1971 [1908]; Mauss 1990 [1950]; Bornstein 2012. James's edited volume (forthcoming) speaks to global reconfigurations of charity, faith, and security in an age of terrorism and counterterrorism.

18. Ministry of the Interior, "Interventi e interviste: L'emergenza immigrazione: l'intervento del prefetto Michele Lepri Gallerano," Erice, November 22, 2002.

19. Personal interview, July 14, 2013.

20. Personal interview, January 15, 2005.

21. Albania is a religiously pluralistic country, and includes Muslims, Catholics, and Christian Orthodox, among others. At that time, in Italian smaller locales very few volunteers would have been initially aware of the need to attend to Islamic dietary practices.

22. Don Geremia, personal interview, October 23, 2004.

23. Personal interview, February 2, 2005.

24. As I describe in the next chapter.

25. Don Giuseppe, personal interview, August 11, 2004.

26. See Albahari forthcoming.

27. Don Cesare, personal interview, September 22, 2004.

28. Personal interview with lawyer, September 24, 2004. The high rate of successful appeals shows the weak legal basis of expulsion decrees in the first place. This lawyer's appeal procedure is paid for by individual migrants, or by the state if the latter loses the case.

29. Don Cesare, personal interview, September 22, 2004.

30. Padre Ampelio, personal interview, October 13, 2004.

31. Don Cesare, personal interview, September 22, 2004.

32. Archbishop Cosmo Francesco Ruppi, "Movimento Cristiano Lavoratori" Conference, Lecce, January 21, 2005.

33. Don Cesare qtd. in *La Gazzetta del Mezzogiorno*, August 19, 2004.

34. The focus of Chapter 5.

35. Don Cesare, "Movimento Cristiano Lavoratori" Conference, Lecce, January 21, 2005.

36. On immigrant holding facilities in Italy, see Sciurba 2009; MEDU 2013.

37. The relationship of (moral) propriety and aesthetics has been noted by Rancière 2010, for example.

38. As understood by Muehlebach 2012, most recently.

39. On the medicalization of immigration and its management (in France), see Ticktin 2011. On the global economy of salvation, see Comaroff and Comaroff 2000; Bornstein 2012.

40. See De Genova and Peutz 2010; and in particular Cornelisse 2010.

41. Initiated and supported by associations such as Democratic Jurists, Class Action Procedimentale, and A Buon Diritto. A group of journalists has established the LasciateCIEntrare (Let us in) network, seeking not only access to CIEs (for documentary and humanitarian purposes), but also their dismantling.

42. Qtd. in Tiziana Colluto, "Bari, il giudice: 'Migranti più garantiti in carcere che nel Cie,'" *Il Fatto Quotidiano*, January 11, 2014, http://www.ilfattoquotidiano.it/ 2014/01/11/bari-il-giudice-migranti-piu-garantiti-in-carcere-che-nel-cie/839160/, accessed January 16, 2014.

43. Qtd. in Raffaella Cosentino, "Crotone: chiuso Cie, devastato da una rivolta dopo la morte di un immigrato," *La Repubblica*, August 19, http://www.repubblica.it/ solidarieta/immigrazione/2013/08/19/news/chiuso_il_cie_di_crotone_devastato_da_ una_rivolta_dopo_la_morte_di_un_immigrato-64989177, accessed August 20, 2013.

44. For a recent report in English, see MEDU 2013.

Chapter 2. Genealogies of Rescue and Pushbacks

1. On the methodological and analytical problems of mapping and interpreting "routes" of unauthorized migration, see Coutin 2005. Additionally, Coutin effectively

problematizes spatialized conceptions of "arrival" that do not take into account migrants' legal status.

2. The volume edited by Hage (2009) provides insightful examples of the many challenges and opportunities of different kinds of "waiting." In Chapter 4, in particular, I pursue waiting as it intersects with "boredom" for migrants in administrative detention.

3. Giovanni Maria Bellu, "Il nuovo schiaffo dell'Italia alle vittime del naufragio," *La Repubblica*, April 13, 2005, http://www.repubblica.it/2005/b/rubriche/glialtrinoi/schia/schia.html, accessed September 19, 2014.

4. Rory Carroll, John Hooper and David Rose, "Fishermen's nets haul in secrets of immigrant 'ship of death,'" *Guardian*, June 9, 2001, http://www.theguardian.com/world/2001/jun/10/davidrose.rorycarroll, accessed August 16, 2014.

5. *Il Manifesto*, "Chi si ricorda della Iohan?" December 17, 2006.

6. In compiling the dynamics leading to the shipwreck I draw primarily on Frisullo 1997.

7. Ibid.

8. Ibid.

9. Ibid.

10. Livio Quagliata, "Imprigionati nella stiva," *Il Manifesto*, January 11, 1997.

11. Including Balwant Singh Khera and Zabiullah Bacha; and Shabir Mohammed Khan, leader of the Pakistani Workers' Association in Italy.

12. Including Livio Quagliata (*Il Manifesto*), Jesmond Bonello (*Malta Independent*), Tejinder Singh (*Link Canada*), John Hooper (*Observer*), Panos Sobolos (*Ethnos*), and the Telecolor Catania local television channel.

13. Domenico Castellaneta, "Blocco navale per fermare i clandestini," *La Repubblica*, March 25, 1997.

14. Respectively in *La Repubblica*, March 15, 1997; *La Repubblica*, March 16, 1997; *Corriere della Sera*, March 18, 1997.

15. R.C., "Diluvio di telefonate anti profughi per Pinocchio," *Corriere della Sera*, April 3, 1997.

16. Footage available in Sejko 2013.

17. For an overview of the Northern League ideology, see Cento Bull 2000.

18. Reported in Giovanni Maria Bellu, "Il naufragio degli albanesi e la giornalista Pivetti," *La Repubblica*, April 1, 2007, http://www.repubblica.it/2005/b/rubriche/glialtrinoi/naufragio-albanesi/naufragio-albanesi.html, accessed September 12, 2014.

19. Leogrande 2011:20.

20. For an exhaustive account of Italian "politics of proximity" with Albania, see Perlmutter 1998.

21. Stefano Citati, "Polemica tra l'Onu e l'Italia. L'Alto commissario per i profughi: Il blocco navale è illegale," *La Repubblica*, March 28, 1997.

22. Because the list of the *Kater i Radës* passengers is in public records, passengers' real names are given.

23. Leogrande 2011:130.

24. Ibid.:35.

25. On the Italian navy's role in combating unauthorized migration, and for its own statements and position on the *Kater i Radës*, see Caffio 2003.

26. Ratzel (1844–1904) was a German geographer.

27. In addition to the allusion to "skin" and living organisms here, in a variety of languages the common use of botanical metaphors (e.g., "roots") suggests that "each nation is a grand genealogical tree, rooted in the soil that nourishes it," and contributes to territorialized political assertions (Malkki 1992:28). Peasants, wild nature, sequoias, and eagles are among the naturalistic metaphors used around the world to essentialize the relationship between the natural spatial domain and the national one (Alonso 1994:383).

28. See, in particular, Dunn 1996; Andreas 2000.

29. Italian army, "Operazione Salento," http://www.esercito.difesa.it/root/atti vita/op_salento.asp, accessed July 10, 2012.

30. Lutterbeck 2006:65.

31. Italian Ministry of Defense, "Missione," http://www.difesa.it/OperazioniMili tari/op_int_concluse/Albania28GNavale/Pagine/Missione.aspx, accessed July 14, 2014.

32. Qtd. in Paolo Salom, "La battaglia segreta della Finanza in Albania," *Corriere della Sera*, February 10, 2011.

33. Cinzia Gubbini, "Strage nel Canale d'Otranto," *Il Manifesto*, January 11, 2004.

34. Some Romanian citizens (like others from mostly eastern European and African countries) do become the objects of excruciating and predatory working conditions, especially in agriculture (including women) and construction.

35. Sociologist Devi Sacchetto, personal communication, September 24, 2004.

36. More specifically, the Council of the European Union.

37. This, in turn, has provided them the possibility of staying longer than three months.

38. In recent years, an increasing number of Italian citizens—medical students, professionals, real estate developers, restaurant owners, and manual workers—have traveled to Albania to pursue profits, degrees, or a steady income.

39. Delle Donne 2004:146–47.

40. On the Kosovo war, see Fassin and Pandolfi 2010; and see Pandolfi 2010 for a discussion of the "permanent state of emergency" in the Balkan Peninsula.

41. Stefano Mencherini, "Gente di Valona: Vita quotidiana nella quarta città d'Albania: In attesa di una via di fuga," October 2002, http://www.stefanomencherini.org/ita/index.php?option = com_content&task = view&id = 48&Itemid = 28, accessed September 23, 2014.

42. Roberto Bonavoglia, "Si spari agli scafisti quando fuggono," *Corriere della Sera*, January 28, 1999.

43. Roberto Bonavoglia, "Il governo del Montenegro: 'Un centinaio i Rom annegati nell' Adriatico," *Corriere della Sera*, August 25, 1999.

44. Ibid.

45. *Il Messaggero*, "Scafisti-killer, morti due finanzieri," July 25, 2000.

46. Leogrande 2010:83.

47. *Corriere della Sera*, "Morti due finanzieri speronati dagli scafisti," July 25, 2000.

48. ANSA, "Nasce il drone 'made in Ue', c'è anche Finmeccanica," November 20, 2013, http://www.ansa.it/europa/notizie/rubriche/economia/2013/11/20/Nasce-drone -made-Ue-e-anche-Finmeccanica_9650143.html, accessed November 21, 2013.

49. Lutterbeck 2006:66.

50. Steffen Leidel, "Europe's Invisible Walls," Deutsche Welle, July 16, 2004, http://dw.de/p/5Ju8, accessed September 1, 2014.

51. Carling 2007.

52. Personal interview, December 21, 2005.

53. Umberto Bossi qtd. in Fabio Cavalera, "Basta rinvii, cacciare i clandestini con la forza," *Corriere della Sera*, June 16, 2003.

54. Roberto Calderoli, interview, Telegiornale (News) TG3, 7 P.M., August 17, 2004.

55. Giannicola Sinisi, qtd. in *La Repubblica*, "Sicilia: emergenza clandestini: Più di 800 immigrati in 2 giorni," July 19, 2005.

56. A phrase coined in Andreas 2000.

57. See Feldman 2012:101–4; Andersson 2014:80–84.

58. Coluccello and Massey 2007:81–82.

59. A pseudonym.

60. Human Rights Watch 2014.

61. Bureau of Democracy, Human Rights and Labor 2012.

62. Human Rights Watch 2013.

63. Patrick Maigua, "4,000 Eritreans fleeing human rights violations every month," United Nations Radio, June 5, 2013, http://www.unmultimedia.org/radio/en glish/2013/06/4000-eritreans-fleeing-human-rights-violations-every-month/, accessed July 17, 2014.

64. Personal communication, July 2, 2013. On the Eritrean diaspora, see Bernal 2014. Journalist Fabrizio Gatti has researched the ties between the government of Eritrea and certain Italian politicians and businessmen. His investigation is available at *L'Espresso*, "Speciale Eritrea," http://speciali.espresso.repubblica.it/interattivi/speciale -eritrea/, accessed September 1, 2014.

65. Human Rights Watch 2014.

66. On such technological and institutional arrangements, and how people try to navigate them, see Lucht 2012; Andersson 2014.

67. Cassarino 2005:6.

68. Del Grande 2013:57.

69. For a comprehensive account (and statistics) of smuggling and migrants' arrival in Europe from North Africa, see UNODC 2010; on smuggling and migrants' arrivals from West Africa, see UNODC 2011.

70. Sabratha doctor, personal communication, July 6, 2014.

71. Del Grande 2007:125.

72. Lucht 2012:160–76; See also Laura Smith-Spark and Arwa Damon, "Sahara desert deaths: 92 migrants perish in Niger after vehicle breakdowns," *CNN*, October 31, 2013, http://www.cnn.com/2013/10/31/world/africa/niger-bodies/, accessed September 17, 2014.

73. Fabrizio Gatti, "Le nuove rotte dei disperati," *L'Espresso*, May 15, 2009, http://espresso.repubblica.it/internazionale/2009/05/15/news/le-nuove-rotte-dei-disperati-1.13584, accessed September 17, 2014.

74. Claudia Fusani, "Gheddafi leader della libertà," *La Repubblica*, October 8, 2004.

75. In its General Affairs and External Relations configuration.

76. Council of the European Union 2004.

77. European Commission 2005:14.

78. Ibid., 61–62.

79. Del Grande 2007:127.

80. Gatti, "Le nuove rotte dei disperati."

81. Amnesty International EU Office, "Immigration Cooperation with Libya: The Human Rights Perspective," April 12, 2005, http://www.amnesty.eu/static/documents/2005/JHA_Libya_april12.pdf, accessed September 15, 2014.

82. Ministero dell'Interno 2005:43.

83. European Commission 2005:59.

84. Ibid., 60.

85. European Parliament 2005.

86. IOM, "Press Briefing Notes: Geneva–IOM and Libya Sign Agreement," August 9, 2005.

87. *Official Journal of the European Union* 2011.

88. Pastore 2008:1.

89. Hein 2013:26.

90. Ibid., 27.

91. "Trattato di Amicizia, Partenariato e Cooperazione tra la Repubblica Italiana e la Grande Giamahiria Araba Libica Popolare Socialista," *Gazzetta Ufficiale della Repubblica Italiana*, February 18, 2009, p. 5, http://www.interno.gov.it/mininterno/export/sites/default/it/assets/files/16/0769_trattato_libia_2.pdf, accessed September 18, 2014.

92. Finmeccanica, "SELEX Sistemi Integrati signed an agreement with Libya, worth EUR 300 million, for Border Security and Control," October 7, 2009, http://www.finmeccanica.com/en/-/selex-sistemi-integrati-firma-accordo-da-300-milioni-di-euro-con-la-libia-per-la-protezione-e-sicurezza-dei-confini, accessed June 23, 2014.

93. The news conference was broadcast by TG Nord, the news program of the Northern League's television channel, *TelePadania*.

94. Note that the Treaty of Friendship, Partnership, and Cooperation does not specifically include the possibility of such operations.

95. Del Grande 2010:91.

96. Navy sailors and other armed forces soldiers refer to gloves, overalls, and masks as *dispositivi di protezione individuale*.

97. I provide an additional example of pushback modalities in Chapter 3.

98. Hein 2013:28–29.

99. As Dembour 2012 explains.

100. Ben-Yehoyada 2011 offers an ethnographic account centered on Mazara. In particular, he illuminates the identitarian configurations and transnational aspirations of the Italian-born children of Tunisian migrants working in Mazara's fishing industry.

101. Maroni qtd. in *Corriere della Sera*, "Peschereccio mitragliato dai libici: Con loro anche sei militari italiani," September 13, 2010, http://www.corriere.it/cronache/ 10_settembre_13/peschereccio-mitragliato-libici_4a713790-bf18-11df-8975-00144f02 aabe.shtml, accessed September 2, 2014.

102. Lutterbeck 2006:64.

103. ECRE, "Carrier Sanctions," http://ecre.org/topics/areas-of-work/access-to -europe/7.html, accessed June 1, 2014.

104. For example, when proposing bilateral agreements, EU signatories fail to consider whether countries and regions *neighboring* signatory non-EU countries might subsequently become transit regions.

105. The author of the study (June 2006) is lawyer Claire Rodier, who provides a comprehensive analysis of the emerging externalization of EU asylum and immigration. See also Feldman 2012.

106. Lahav and Guiraudon 2000:59.

Chapter 3. Sovereignty as Salvation

1. Enver, personal interview, January 15, 2006.

2. As argued, among others, by Thielemann 2004:47.

3. As suggested more generally by Cornelius 2005.

4. See, for example, Lucht 2012:xvii; Feldman 2012:80.

5. Carnimeo 2014:66.

6. Qtd. in Di Nicola and Musumeci 2014:21.

7. Frisullo 1997.

8. Bellu 2004:186.

9. Qtd. in Giovanni Maria Bellu, "Non sarò il solo a pagare per i 283 morti del naufragio," *La Repubblica*, May 19, 2003, http://www.repubblica.it/online/cronaca/ palo/pagare/pagare.html, accessed September 10, 2014.

10. Dajti, personal interview, April 6, 2006.

11. Sali, personal interview, July 14, 2013. In addition to relying on his information and on several conversations with southern Albanian migrants in Italy, here I also draw from Barjaba and Perrone 1996:138–46; and Leogrande 2010:114–30.

12. The quality of the fuel is fundamental to the success of the smuggling enterprise, as low-quality fuels may cause hazardous engine problems.

13. Also in June 2001, Italian Nobel laureates Rita Levi Montalcini, Renato Dulbecco, Carlo Rubbia, and Dario Fo wrote to the Italian government, supporting the relatives of the drowned in requesting once again the recovery of the wreckage and the remains. A few years later, in February 2007, center-left prime minister Romano Prodi (second cabinet, 2006–8) announced to Member of Parliament Tania de Zulueta that the technical details for the recovery were being worked out, drawing on funds made available by his cabinet. Later that year, Don Palacino, the parish priest of Portopalo, at Sicily's southern tip, sent the Italian Senate a petition with a thousand signatures, again asking for the recovery. To this day, the wreckage lies at a depth of 108 meters (356 feet) in international waters off the coast of Portopalo. It is located beyond Italian jurisdiction. In order to keep working on this case, Italian judges had to press charges for multiple aggravated murder. Only the captain and owner of the *Yiohan*, Youssef El Hallal and Sheik Thourab respectively, could be prosecuted for such a grave accusation. El Hallal was eventually convicted in 2008, and sentenced to thirty years. In 2009, Maltese-Pakistani citizen Sheik Ahmed Thourab was also convicted and sentenced to thirty years, in absentia.

14. Fisherman qtd. in Bellu 2004:33.

15. Fisherman qtd. in Bellu 2004:35.

16. As nicely articulated by Ratcliffe 1966.

17. Claudia Fusani, "'Sono scafisti.' 'No, pescatori.' Tensione Roma-Bruxelles-Tunisi," *La Repubblica*, September 6, 2007, http://www.repubblica.it/2007/07/sezioni/cronaca/immigrati/tensione-italia-tunisia/tensione-italia-tunisia.html, accessed September 6, 2014.

18. Fulvio Vassallo Paleologo, "Agrigento—processo ai pescatori Tunisini: Una sentenza contraddittoria," Progetto Melting Pot Europa, November 18, 2009, http://www.meltingpot.org/Agrigento-Processo-ai-pescatori-tunisini-Una-sentenza.html#.VBsuq1ZSaVg, accessed September 18, 2014.

19. Germana Graceffo, "Pescatori d'uomini (Italia, 2007–2008)," Storie Migranti, January 2008, http://www.storiemigranti.org/spip.php?rubrique47, accessed September 18, 2014.

20. But in a logical twist, it found them guilty of resisting the coast guard officers' order to return to Tunisia.

21. Their real names. Gabriele Del Grande, "Delitto di solidarietà: Il processo ai pescatori Tunisini visto da Teboulbah," *Fortress Europe*, November 16, 2009, http://fortresseurope.blogspot.com/2009/11/delitto-di-solidarieta-il-processo-ai.html, accessed September 18, 2014.

22. Some of them suggest that the high-tech instruments increasingly used to locate the catch have something to do with the depletion.

23. Qtd. in RaiNews24, "Immigrazione. Peschereccio affondato in Libia. Pisanu: una tragica realtà, l'Europa deve intervenire." December 1, 2002. http://www.rainews24.it/Notizia.asp?NewsID=29652, accessed December 20, 2005.

24. Qtd. in Alfio Sciacca, "Pisanu, traffico di clandestini: 1.167 morti al largo della Sicilia," *Corriere della Sera*, August 17, 2004.

25. In 2004, Greek authorities started to clear their 24,751 mines (Del Grande 2007:138).

26. ICMPD 2004:8.

27. A detailed list is available at UNITED for Intercultural Action, "List of 13824 documented refugee deaths through Fortress Europe," June 17, 2010, http://www.stor iemigranti.org/IMG/pdf/List_of_13824_documented_refugee_deaths_through_Fort ress_Europe.pdf, accessed September 15, 2014.

28. Gabriele Del Grande, *Fortress Europe*, http://fortresseurope.blogspot.com/, accessed October 13, 2013.

29. UNHCR *News Stories*, "UNHCR alarmed at death toll from boat sinkings in the Mediterranean," September 16, 2014, http://www.unhcr.org/54184ae76.html, accessed September 16, 2014.

30. IOM 2014.

31. IOM *Press Briefing Notes*, "Migrants risking lives in Mediterranean topped 45,000 in 2013: IOM," January 28, 2014, http://www.iom.int/cms/en/sites/iom/home/ news-and-views/press-briefing-notes/pbn-2014/pbn-listing/migrants-risking-lives-in -medite.html, accessed January 28, 2014.

32. The Migrants' Files project is partially funded by the European nonprofit Journalismfund.eu. The media analysis (not confined to migration) developed by PULS was commissioned by the Joint Research Center of the European Commission.

33. Migrants' Files, https://www.detective.io/detective/the-migrants-files/, ac-cessed September 20, 2014.

34. Ibid.

35. On "distant suffering," especially as perceived through the media, see Boltan-ski 1999 [1993]; on more active forms of "denial," including through the media, see Mutman 1992; Cohen 2001.

36. *AgrigentoFlash.it*, "Lampedusa, gommone con immigrati in navigazione verso l'isola," November 21, 2009, http://www.agrigentoflash.it/2009/11/21/lampedusa-gom mone-con-immigrati-in-navigazione-verso-lisola/, accessed April 19, 2014.

37. Gabriele Del Grande, "Nuovo Respingimento. Motovedette Libiche Insegu-ono 80 Rifugiati in Acque Maltesi," *Fortress Europe*, November 24, 2009, http://fortress europe.blogspot.com/2009/11/respingimento-nelle-acque-maltesi.html, accessed Jan-uary 15, 2014.

38. For a more comprehensive survey of national and EU citizenship, see Hansen and Hager 2010.

39. I would also add differences in legal rights and protections shaped by geopoli-tics, or by membership in more or less powerful states of origin. For a thorough discussion of Carens's work, see Albahari 2014.

40. See also Balibar 2004:119.

41. *Mensile Polizia di Stato* (independent magazine), February 18, 2012, http://www.mensilepoliziadistato.it/nasce-a-roma-il-centro-nazionale-di-coordinamento-per-limmigrazione/, accessed January 16, 2014.

42. See Andersson 2014 for further details.

43. Frontex, "Hera: Archive of Operations," July 2–December 15, 2012, http://frontex.europa.eu/operations/archive-of-operations/LtmVSR, accessed January 18, 2014.

44. Frontex, "Hera: Archive of Operations," February 4–December 14, 2008, http://frontex.europa.eu/operations/archive-of-operations/XrEThw, accessed January 18, 2014.

45. Ilkka Laitinen, "Frontex Five Years On: A Short Discussion of the Agency's Key Activities and Outcomes to Date," *EurAsylum Monthly Policy Interviews*, September 2010, http://www.eurasylum.org/092010-gen-brig-ilkka-laitinen/, accessed December 2, 2013.

46. Lieutenant Antonio Morana (his real name), personal interview, June 20, 2011.

47. On such performative aspects of the border spectacle, see Rosaldo 1997; Chavez 2008; Brown 2010.

48. As suggested more generally by Debord 1995 [1967].

49. Italian Ministry of Defense, "Mare Nostrum," http://www.marina.difesa.it/attivita/operativa/Pagine/MareNostrum.aspx, accessed September 2, 2014.

50. Italian Government, "Immigrazione: al via 'Operazione Mare Nostrum,'" October 14, 2013, http://www.governo.it/Notizie/Palazzo%20Chigi/dettaglio.asp?d =73282, accessed September 2, 2014.

51. See, e.g., Foucault 1979 [1975].

52. Slavery, in its current forms, can perhaps be understood as loss of a "home," loss of rights over one's own body, and loss of political status (Mbembe 2003). But if we take "slavery" seriously, then we also need to ask: who are the traffickers, the profiteers, the masters, the exploiters, the employers, and ultimately the beneficiaries?

53. For a similar dilemma regarding the death penalty (in the United States), see Kaufman-Osborn 2002; more generally, see Dean 2002.

54. To borrow and adapt Ngai's phrase (2004).

Chapter 4. Sovereignty as Preemption

1. January 13, 2005. My tasks included assisting with translations, with meals, and with the routine maintenance of communal spaces.

2. Within the center, the finance guard has no investigative role in matters of immigration.

3. I was permitted access after becoming a member of the only independent organization allowed to send volunteers to the center at that time.

4. As of 2014, the center was classified by the Ministry of the Interior as a center of first assistance and reception. It provides basic refreshments and a temporary shelter

while the police collect information (including photographs and fingerprints), before migrants are escorted to other detention, identification, and processing facilities. The center was shut down and the facility abandoned at the end of December 2005. During summer 2007 it was used by the local waste-management company as an unauthorized rubbish dump for "recycled" paper and plastic, causing outrage among Otranto's citizens. The facility is owned by the local municipality, which, in cooperation with the Italian Red Cross, reopened it in summer 2010 to cope with maritime immigration to the area. For bibliographic references on such facilities, see Chapter 1.

5. Owing to their status as asylum seekers waiting for their applications to be examined. Unless such a temporary permit was granted, the norm required migrants to leave the country within five days, except in the case of an appeal.

6. As southern Slavic languages, Serbian and Bulgarian—with effort and good will—are partly mutually intelligible. At the time of this incident (January 2005) Bulgaria was a EU candidate, not a member.

7. As routinely happens with migrants. See Arendt 1958 [1951]:296–97; Malkki 1996.

8. They have in fact entered the EU through Hungary. Austria is instead the country where they entered the Schengen Area, which as of 2014 did not include EU members Croatia, Bulgaria, and Romania.

9. Echoing Arendt 1958 [1951]:296; see also Albahari 2014.

10. My phrasing here adapts Ngai's "impossible subjects" (2004).

11. For a more comprehensive account of the EU's digital identification infrastructure, see Feldman 2012.

12. The Bulgarian citizens' own minibus will be towed to Austria. These costs, together with the fuel for the Jeeps and the overtime to be paid to the police agents traveling to the Austrian border, result in a great expense for the police.

13. Malkki 1992; see also several contributors to Basaglia and Basaglia Ongaro 2013a [1975].

14. See Ngai 2004; Inda 2005.

15. See also Collier, Maurer, and Suárez-Navaz 1997.

16. Tundjel seems to be appropriating the sovereign logic that routinely demands "papers" of travelers (residence permits, birth certificates, visas, passports). On the authoritativeness of papers, see Yngvesson and Coutin 2006; Hull 2012.

17. They asked for their real names to be given.

18. One could also explicate larger tensions among law, modernism, and nationalism underpinning what I document in this ethnographic context. See Borneman 1998 and Fitzpatrick 2001.

19. Rosen 1995:5 reminds us that concern with "intentions" (in our case of travelers as well as of institutional actors) must include attention to the distribution of power, the representation of events, the interplay between trust and deception, the social assigning of moral responsibility, and in essence attention to the formation of truth.

20. In such combination with "knowledge," I use "preemptive" as qualifying actions generally based on "speculative concerns" about "possible future actions" (O'Connell 2002:21), such as in the phrase and doctrine of "preemptive strikes." In such a doctrine, a preemptive attack is warranted by the presumed "knowledge" of the opponent's "intention" to attack.

21. Even if it may be hesitant to acknowledge that undocumentedness.

22. Such expansion calls attention to the discretionary power embedded in actuarial justice (i.e., informed by algorithms and statistics) and to its reliance on indicators such as race, religion, and nationality (Leun and Van der Woude 2012).

23. Ferguson 2012 also notes that predictive policing raises issues of class-based and race-based targeting, among many others. He acknowledges that current predictive policing systems (i.e., in Los Angeles) "are being conducted in a careful, reflective, and scientific manner" (317). And yet as a growing number of police departments worldwide adopt the technology, it is unclear whether this discretionary caution will remain.

24. "Data-driven" assessments and "personal" hunches are not dichotomous, then.

25. As explained by Feldman 2012:136–46.

26. On the significance of writing practices for the legitimation of institutional authorities, see Messick 1993; Gupta 2005; Hull 2012.

27. On transparency, see Sanders and West 2003; on absolute meaning, see Herzfeld 1992:110; on rationality, see Gramsci 1971:247; and on certain belief, see Asad 2004.

28. Oberweis and Musheno 2001:6.

29. Scott 1998:311.

30. As explored by Ferguson and Gupta 2002.

31. See also Taussig 1997.

32. On rule of law, see Sarat, Douglas, and Merrill Umphrey 2005:10; on illegality, see De Genova 2002:436.

33. See Haney 1996, especially 774–76.

34. Possibly reflecting their frustration with everything "Italian" (laws, staff, food, guards, and police), these Bulgarian travelers used the language I spoke with them (Serbian), the complexity of my ancestry, and the woman I married to make me an honorary Slav (even as they see themselves as non-Slavic Turks of Bulgaria). They fully understood my position within the logics of the facility and my role as an anthropologist.

35. I borrow the phrase, in this context, from Amoore and de Goede 2008, who focus on the "war on terror" and the everyday face of its "preemptive strikes" based on registering, mining, and connecting credit card transactions, travel data, and so on.

36. Also because we are never extraneous to larger power relations (Greenhouse 2002:29).

37. See Bateson 1958:287.

Chapter 5. Spring Uprisings, Fall Drownings

1. On such complicated constructions of place and belonging, see Albahari 2008; Ben-Yehoyada 2011.

2. Personal interview, June 11, 2011.

3. On this facility in relation to deportation, see also Andrijasevic 2010.

4. Carlo Chianura, "L'Italia dietro il Golpe in Tunisia," *La Repubblica*, October 10, 1999.

5. See the essay by Hassan Boubakri (2013).

6. Del Grande 2010:57.

7. Boubakri 2013:8.

8. Del Grande 2010:66.

9. Boubakri 2013:6.

10. "Lampedusa, Clandestino Fugge dal Cpa e si Nasconde su un Aereo," *Il Messaggero*, January 28, 2009.

11. Sanfilippo and Scialoja 2010:16.

12. Francesco Viviano, "Lampedusa, Rivolta nel Centro di Accoglienza. Violenti Scontri tra i Migranti e la Polizia," *La Repubblica*, February 18, 2009.

13. Tunisia achieved independence from France in 1956.

14. Alexander Smoltczyk, "The Streets of the Revolution: North Africa, One Year Later," *Spiegel Online*, December 22, 2011, http://www.spiegel.de/international/world/the-streets-of-the-revolution-north-africa-one-year-later-a-805190-8.html, accessed December 23, 2011.

15. To ground my account of 2011 events in Lampedusa, I spoke with Tunisian persons on the island; with young Tunisian males I met in Milan who transited from Lampedusa; and with local residents, both in May–June 2011 (in person) and at later dates (electronically).

16. Personal interview, June 16, 2011.

17. Personal interview, June 16, 2011.

18. The Council of Europe is the international organization, *distinct from the EU* and its bodies, promoting pan-European cooperation on issues including human rights, rule of law, and democracy.

19. Chope 2011:11.

20. See, for such figures, UNHCR 2014, "Country Operations Profile—Europe," http://www.unhcr.org/pages/4a02d9346.html, accessed September 15, 2014.

21. Personal interview, June 20, 2011.

22. Lampedusa used to host NATO (specifically U.S.) military personnel in its long range navigation "LORAN" radar station; the facility is currently under Italian armed forces' responsibility. The Italian coast guard, finance guard, and air force have a permanent presence in Lampedusa. Since 2008, army soldiers have been conspicuously dispatched to the island, throughout Italian cities, and outside CIE facilities as part of Operation Safe Streets. Most of the army soldiers on the island reside in local hotels.

23. Giovanna, personal interview, June 13, 2011.

24. Giorgio, personal interview, June 5, 2013. Giorgio, together with other local residents and Tunisian citizens in Milan (June 2011), has helped me understand the Manduria and Oria events from the spring months of 2011.

25. I learned his story from a young resident of Oria, June 2011, and from a Tunisian person (in Milan, June 2011) who was hosted in Manduria.

26. Nick Squires, "Libya: Italy Fears 300,000 Refugees," *Telegraph*, February 23, 2011, http://www.telegraph.co.uk/news/worldnews/africaandindianocean/libya/8343 963/Libya-Italy-fears-300000-refugees.html, accessed September 11, 2014.

27. "L'Onu all'Italia: Accogliete i Rifugiati '200–300 Mila Migranti in Arrivo'," *Corriere della Sera*, February 22, 2011, http://www.corriere.it/esteri/11_febbraio_22/evacuazione-italiani-libia_13f156fc-3e78-11e0-a025-f4888ad76c86.shtml, accessed September 11, 2014.

28. "Libia: Navi Mimbelli e San Giorgio in rada a Misurata per l'evacuazione. Martino, la Nato Intervenga Subito," *GrNet*, February 25, 2011, http://www.grnet.it/news/95-news/2491-libia-navi-mimbelli-e-san-giorgio-in-rada-a-misurata-per-levac uazione-martino-la-nato-intervenga-subito, accessed September 11, 2014.

29. Kelly and Wadud 2012:6.

30. "Libia: è Caccia agli Immigrati Africani," *Corriere della Sera*, February 22, 2011, http://www.corriere.it/esteri/11_febbraio_22/libia-africani-perseguitati_d48bf 1cc-3e84-11e0-a025-f4888ad76c86.shtml, accessed September 11, 2014.

31. Human Rights Watch, "Libya: Stranded Foreign Workers Need Urgent Evacu-ation," March 3, 2011, http://www.hrw.org/news/2011/03/02/libya-stranded-foreign -workers-need-urgent-evacuation, accessed September 11, 2014.

32. "Africa/Libya—Appeal by Bishop Martinelli for the Eritrians in Libya: 'Yester-day 2,000 Came Back to Our Church and Buildings Asking for Help'," *Agenzia Fides*, February 28, 2011, http://www.fides.org/en/news/28440?idnews = 28440&lan = eng# .VBMnDlZSaVg, accessed September 12, 2014.

33. UNHCR, *News Stories*, "UNHCR Urges Evacuation of People Trying to Leave Libya," February 28, 2011, http://www.unhcr.org/4d6bc1629.html, accessed Septem-ber 1, 2014.

34. Ibid.

35. "Libya's Humanitarian Crisis," *Al Jazeera*, February 28, 2011, http://www.alja zeera.com/programmes/insidestory/2011/02/20112289513477110.html, accessed Sep-tember 12, 2014.

36. Human Rights Watch, "Libya."

37. Ibid.; my emphasis.

38. Amnesty International, "Fears Grow for Libya Migrants as Thousands Flee," March 2, 2011, http://www.amnesty.org/en/news-and-updates/fears-grow-libya-mi grants-thousands-flee-2011-03-02, accessed September 12, 2014.

39. Qtd. in Strik 2012:19.

40. NATO, "Operation Active Endeavour," August 20, 2014, http://www.nato.int/cps/en/natolive/topics_7932.htm, accessed July 16, 2014.

41. Ibid.

42. Gianluca di Feo, "Lampedusa e Spese Militari Quella Missione Nato Inutilizzata," *L'Espresso*, October 14, 2013, http://espresso.repubblica.it/inchieste/2013/10/14/news/lampedusa-altro-che-nuove-spese-militari-lo-scandalo-della-missione-nato-in utilizzata-1.137540, accessed September 12, 2014.

43. De Giorgi 2014.

44. Qtd. in Strik 2012:5.

45. Qtd. in ibid.:7.

46. Jack Shenker, "Aircraft Carrier Left Us to Die, Say Migrants," *Guardian*, May 8, 2011, http://www.theguardian.com/world/2011/may/08/nato-ship-libyan-migrants, accessed September 12, 2014.

47. Angelique Chrisafis, "African Migrants 'Left to Die' in Dinghy Sue Spanish and French Military," *Guardian*, June 18, 2013, http://www.theguardian.com/world/2013/jun/18/boat-tragedy-migrants-sue-france-spain, accessed September 12, 2014.

48. Shenker, "Aircraft Carrier Left Us to Die, Say Migrants."

49. Strik 2012:9.

50. Chrisafis, "African Migrants 'Left to Die.'"

51. Jack Shenker, "Survivor of Migrant Boat Tragedy Arrested in Netherlands," *Guardian*, March 29, 2012, http://www.theguardian.com/world/2012/mar/29/survi vor-migrant-boat-arrested-netherlands, accessed September 12, 2014.

52. Radio Netherlands Worldwide, "Council of State Suspends Deportation Order," April 3, 2012, http://www.rnw.nl/english/bulletin/council-state-suspends-de portation-order, accessed September 12, 2014.

53. Strik 2012:13.

54. Ibid.:1; my emphasis.

55. Nima Elbagir and Jomana Karadsheh, "Hundreds missing after overcrowded boat from Libya capsizes," *CNN.com*, May 10, 2011, http://www.cnn.com/2011/WORLD/africa/05/10/libya.boat.capsize/index.html, accessed May 15, 2011.

56. Peter Mayer, "UN says up to 1,200 fleeing Libya dead at sea," UNHCR, *Refugees Daily*, May 15, 2011, http://www.unhcr.org/cgi-bin/texis/vtx/refdaily?pass = 463 ef21123&id = 4dd0c45c5, accessed May 16, 2011.

57. See, for example, Mencherini 2013.

58. See Albahari 2010.

59. Since 2011, Article 603bis of the Penal Code has subjected convicted exploiters and recruiters, including migrants, to harsh punishment.

60. *Lettera 43*, "Tunisia, Barcone in Avaria: 270 Dispersi Due i Morti. L'Imbarcazione si è Guastata. Salvi 570 Migranti," June 2, 2011, http://www.lettera43.it/attualita/17738/270-migranti-dispersi-al-largo-della-tunisia.htm, accessed September 12, 2014.

61. Emily Parker, "The Life Cycle of a Refugee Camp Along the Tunisia-Libya Border," *Tunisia-live.net*, October 5, 2011, http://www.tunisia-live.net/2011/10/05/

the-life-cycle-of-a-refugee-camp-along-the-tunisia-libya-border/, accessed October 6, 2011.

62. Rai Giornale Radio, "Maroni Chiede il Blocco Navale della Libia," June 17, 2011, http://www.grr.rai.it/dl/grr/notizie/ContentItem-567622db-f9f2-4375-aab9-f84 2aa170957.html?refresh_ce, accessed September 12, 2014.

63. "Migranti Soffocati Nella Stiva 'Gridavano per Uscire'," *Corriere della Sera*, August 1, 2011, http://www.corriere.it/cronache/11_agosto_01/sbarchi-lampedusa -vittime_19261206-bc00-11e0-9ecf-692ab361efb9.shtml, accessed September 12, 2014.

64. Francesco Viviano, "Un Sopravvissuto: 'Ho Gettato in Acqua il Corpo di Mio Cugino'," *La Repubblica*, August 6, 2011, http://www.repubblica.it/cronaca/2011/08/ 06/news/testimonianze_immigrati-20092803/, accessed September 12, 2014.

65. Ibid.
66. Ibid.
67. IOM 2012.
68. Amnesty International 2011.

69. UNHCR, "More Than 1,500 Drown or Go Missing Trying to Cross the Mediterranean in 2011," January 31, 2012, http://www.unhcr.org/4f2803949.html, accessed September 13, 2014.

70. Gabriele Del Grande, *Fortress Europe*, http://fortresseurope.blogspot.com/ 2006/02/nel-canale-di-sicilia.html, accessed June 1, 2014.

71. Nobel Committee, "The Nobel Peace Prize 2012 to the European Union (EU)—Press Release," October 12, 2012, http://www.nobelprize.org/nobel_prizes/ peace/laureates/2012/press.html, accessed September 13, 2014.

72. Stefano Montefiori, "Francia-Italia, è Scontro sui Migranti," *Corriere della Sera*, April 7, 2011, http://www.corriere.it/esteri/11_aprile_07/montefiori-francia-cin que-punti-per-respingere_025219d4-60f3-11e0-9e67-aae4bf36a1a3.shtml, accessed September 13, 2014.

73. Carlo Bonini and Vladimiro Polchi, "Operazione Ventimiglia—Operazione Maglie Larghe. Nessun Controllo nei Cie Così si Aiuta la Fuga all' Estero," *La Repubblica*, March 30, 2011.

74. Ibid.

75. Member of Parliament Luigi Vitali, qtd. in *La Gazzetta del Mezzogiorno*, "A Manduria 1.716, a Potenza 483,"April 2, 2011, http://www.lagazzettadelmezzogiorno .it/GdM_traduci_notizia.php?IDNotizia = 416549&IDCategotia = 2699, accessed April 3, 2011.

76. UNHCR, "More Refugees Flee Western Libya, New Aid Reaches the East," April 26, 2011, http://www.unhcr.org/4db6b51c9.html, accessed September 13, 2014.

77. "Berlusconi a Lampedusa: Isola Svuotata 'L'Ue sia Concreta o è Meglio Dividerci'," *Corriere della Sera*, April 9, 2011, http://www.corriere.it/cronache/11_aprile_09/ lampe-sbarchi_31c26e04-62b9-11e0-9ac7-6bfe8e040bf1.shtml, accessed September 13, 2014.

78. Crépeau 2013:13.

79. Monti, a renowned economist, led a "technical" (politically moderate) government between 2011 and 2013, following Berlusconi's fourth cabinet.

80. Italian Ministry of the Interior, "Cancellieri a Tripoli: Prima Visita di un Ministro dell'Interno Ue Dopo la Rivoluzione," April 3, 2012, http://www.interno.gov.it/mininterno/export/sites/default/it/sezioni/sala_stampa/notizie/rapporti_internazionali/00000039_2012_04_03_Cancellieri_a_Tripoli.html, accessed September 13, 2014.

81. Amnesty International 2012:10.

82. IntegrA/Azione 2012.

83. UNHCR, "Libya—Global Report," 2012, http://www.unhcr.org/51b1d639a.html, accessed July 1, 2014.

84. See the many institutional and nongovernmental sources in Human Rights Watch 2014.

85. On Israel's complicated asylum policies and practices of "ordered disorder," see Paz 2011.

86. Human Rights Watch 2014:67.

87. Batsheva Sobelman, "Israel completes most of Egypt border fence," *Los Angeles Times*, January 2, 2013, http://articles.latimes.com/2013/jan/02/world/la-fg-israel-africa-immigration-20130103, accessed July 4, 2014.

88. See EUBAM-Libya, "Missions and Operations," http://eeas.europa.eu/csdp/missions-and-operations/eubam-libya/, accessed July 29, 2014.

89. Mohamed Najah, "Malta Bins Plans to Fly Arriving Migrants Straight Back to Libya," *Libya Herald*, July 12, 2013, http://www.libyaherald.com/2013/07/12/malta-bins-plans-to-fly-arriving-migrants-straight-back-to-libya/#axzz3QhQq9yk4, accessed September 13, 2014.

90. UNHCR, "Libya: External Update," August 30, 2013, http://reliefweb.int/sites/reliefweb.int/files/resources/UNHCR%20Libya%20-%20External%20update%20-%20August%202013.pdf, accessed September 15, 2014.

91. UNHCR, "Libya: External Update," September 30, 2013, http://reliefweb.int/sites/reliefweb.int/files/resources/UNHCR%20Libya%20-%20External%20update%20-%20September%202013.pdf, accessed September 15, 2014.

92. Tom Westcott and Ashraf Abdul Wahab, "Inside Tripoli Zoo's Prison for Illegal Immigrants," *Libya Herald*, August 26, 2013, http://www.libyaherald.com/2013/08/26/inside-tripoli-zoos-prison-for-illegal-immigrants/#axzz3DDoMpvn4, accessed September 13, 2014.

93. International Federation for Human Rights, "Egypt: Hostile environment for Syrian refugees. How long will the international community remain indifferent?," September 24, 2013, http://www.refworld.org/docid/526102b8d.html, accessed September 25, 2013.

94. Zeinab el Gundy, "Two Palestinian Refugees Killed in Emigration Attempt from Egypt," *Ahram Online*, September 18, 2013, http://english.ahram.org.eg/NewsContent/1/64/81934/Egypt/Politics-/Two-Palestinian-refugees-killed-in-emigration-atte.aspx, accessed September 13, 2014.

95. UNHCR, "UNHCR Highlights Dangers Facing Syrians in Transit, Urges Countries to Keep Borders Open," October 18, 2013, http://www.unhcr.org/5261 14299.html, accessed September 13, 2014.

96. "Syrian Asylum Seekers: Lost at Sea, Barred from Land," *Ahram Online*, November 2, 2013, http://english.ahram.org.eg/News/85381.aspx, accessed January 20, 2014.

97. "Napolitano: 'Immigrati, Riflettere su Integrazione e Sicurezza sul Lavoro,'" *La Repubblica*, August 8, 2013, http://www.repubblica.it/politica/2013/08/08/news/ napolitano_affermare_piena_integrazione_immigrati-64466392/?ref=search, accessed September 13, 2014.

98. It is plausible smugglers in Libya confiscated cell phones, and that the boat driver threw his own satellite phone into the sea upon approaching Lampedusa, to prevent being identified as a smuggler.

99. "Lampedusa: Diretta web 4 ottobre," *Unità.it*, October 4, 2013, http://www .unita.it/italia/lampedusa-diretta-web-4-ottobre-1.5252 52?page=3, accessed January 9, 2014.

100. European Commission, "Tragic Accident Outside Lampedusa: Statement by European Commissioner for Home Affairs, Cecilia Malmström," October 3, 2013, http://europa.eu/rapid/press-release_MEMO-13-849_en.htm, accessed October 3, 2013.

101. Charges are dropped if temporary protection or refugee status is recognized. Otherwise people receive the order to leave or are deported, unless they appeal (the 5,000 euro fine they should pay is routinely not collected).

102. Salvo Palazzolo, "'Noi Eritree Violentate dai Miliziani.' I Racconti dell'-Orrore nel Deserto," *La Repubblica—Palermo*, November 8, 2013, http://palermo.re pubblica.it/cronaca/2013/11/08/news/noi_eritree_violentate_dai_miliziani_i_raccon ti_dell_orrore_nel_deserto-70502272/, accessed September 14, 2014.

103. Paolo Lambruschi, "'La Mia Fuga dall'Inferno dell'Eritrea'," *Avvenire*, October 8, 2013, http://www.avvenire.it/Cronaca/Pagine/la-mia-figlia-inferno-eritrea.aspx, accessed September 14, 2014. Here and below, I opt for pseudonyms when referring to Eritrean nationals.

104. Ibid.

105. "Tra i Corpi una Puerpera con il Figlio appena Partorito," *Avvenire*, October 9, 2013, http://www.avvenire.it/Cronaca/Pagine/lampedusa-partorisce-durante-nau fragio-morti-.aspx, accessed September 14, 2014.

106. Mayy el Sheikh and Kareem Fahim, "Dozens Are Killed in Street Violence Across Egypt," *New York Times*, October 7, 2013, http://www.nytimes.com/2013/10/ 07/world/middleeast/clashes-in-egypt-leave-at-least-15-dead.html, accessed September 14, 2014.

107. European Commission, "Commissioner Malmström's intervention on Lampedusa during the Home Affairs Council press conference," October 8, 2013,

http://europa.eu/rapid/press-release_MEMO-13-864_en.htm, accessed September 14, 2014.

108. Frontex, "FRONTEX Budget 2013," http://frontex.europa.eu/assets/About_Frontex/Governance_documents/Budget/Budget_2013.pdf, accessed May 5, 2014.

109. European Commission, "Commissioner Malmström's Intervention on Lampedusa."

110. Fiorenza Sarzanini, "Pronti 1.500 uomini e la San Marco per la missione contro gli scafisti," *Corriere della Sera*, October 14, 2013, http://www.corriere.it/cronache/13_ottobre_14/pronti-1500-uomini-san-marco-la-missione-contro-scafisti-4f9905a0-3494-11e3-b0aa-c50e06d40e68.shtml, accessed September 2, 2014.

111. Francesco Viviano, "Lampedusa, Cittadini: 'Assassini, Vergogna' Proteste all'Arrivo di Letta, Alfano e Barroso," *La Repubblica—Palermo*, October 9, 2013, http://palermo.repubblica.it/cronaca/2013/10/09/news/lampedusa_cittadini_assassini_vergogna_proteste_all_arrivo_di_letta_alfano_e_barroso-68221335/, accessed September 14, 2014.

112. Paolo Lambruschi, "Lampedusa, Letta: 'L'Italia Chiede Scusa'," *Avvenire*, October 10, 2013, http://www.avvenire.it/Cronaca/Pagine/barroso-a-lampedusa.aspx, accessed September 14, 2014.

113. Steve Scherer, "Migrant Disaster Survivors Protest at Exclusion from Funeral Ceremony," *Reuters*, October 21, 2013, http://www.reuters.com/article/2013/10/21/us-italy-migrants-idUSBRE99K0M620131021, accessed September 14, 2014.

114. European Commission, "EUROSUR: New Tools to Save Migrants' Lives at Sea and Fight Cross-Border Crime," June 19, 2013, http://europa.eu/rapid/press-release_MEMO-13-578_en.htm, accessed June 20, 2014. See also *Official Journal of the European Union* 2013.

115. Hayes and Vermeulen 2012:8.

116. I explain the principle of nonrefoulement in Chapter 3.

117. As Crépeau 2013 systematically argues.

118. Hayes and Vermeulen 2012:8.

119. Qtd. in Nikolaj Nielsen, "EU border surveillance system not helping to save lives," *EUobserver.com*, May 14, 2014, https://euobserver.com/justice/124136, accessed May 15, 2014.

120. Fabrizio Gatti, "The Children Who Drowned on October 11th Lie Under the Sea, Forgotten. While Europe Postpones the Issue," *L'Espresso*, October 30, 2013, http://espresso.repubblica.it/attualita/2013/10/30/news/names-and-photographs-of-the-children-who-drowned-on-october-11th-while-europe-postpones-the-issue-1.139493, accessed September 14, 2014.

121. Still to be determined is whether this was the act of a Libyan patrol boat intending to discourage the unauthorized departure, of militias, or of common criminals attempting to steal from passengers. It is important to note that Libyan patrols, like their Egyptian colleagues, have routinely rescued migrants at sea. This happens both in search-and-rescue operations and as part of interceptions to prevent departures.

122. "Lasciati Affogare, Ecco le Prove La Mappa che Conferma le Accuse," *L'Espresso*, November 11, 2013, http://espresso.repubblica.it/attualita/2013/11/11/news/ecco-la-mappa-che-conferma-le-accuse-1.140560, accessed September 14, 2014.

123. Neil Camilleri, "PM Hints at Hesitation to Save Migrants Due to International Laws," *Malta Independent*, December 31, 2013, http://www.independent.com.mt/articles/2013-12-31/news/pm-hints-at-hesitation-to-save-migrants-due-to-international-laws-3568566272/, accessed September 14, 2014.

124. Fabrizio Gatti, "Italia e Malta litigano sul naufragio," *L'Espresso*, January 24, 2014, http://gatti.blogautore.espresso.repubblica.it/2014/01/24/italia-e-malta-litigano-sul-naufragio/, accessed January 24, 2014.

125. Neil Camilleri, "Lampedusa Tragedy: 'My Wife and Daughter Did Not Die For Nothing,'" *Malta Independent*, July 20, 2014, http://www.independent.com.mt/articles/2014-07-20/news/they-tried-to-help-us-and-made-a-big-mistake-but-i-forgive-them-5900992513/, accessed July 21, 2014.

126. Neil Camilleri, "Lampedusa Tragedy: Did Italy Let Migrant Boat Enter Maltese SAR Zone to Avoid Responsibility?" *Malta Independent,* January 5, 2014, http://www.independent.com.mt/articles/2014-01-05/news/lampedusa-tragedy-did-italy-let-migrant-boat-enter-maltese-sar-zone-to-avoid-responsibility-3602710528/, accessed September 14, 2014.

127. Neil Camilleri, "Lampedusa Tragedy: 'My Wife and Daughter Did Not Die For Nothing.'"

128. Neil Camilleri and Stephen Calleja, "27 Dead, More Than 200 Rescued off Lampedusa," *Malta Independent*, October 11, 2013, http://www.independent.com.mt/articles/2013-10-11/news/afm-in-migrant-rescue-operation-2862284800/, accessed September 14, 2014.

129. The Italian navy could visually inspect the wreckage with its remotely operated underwater vehicle *Pluto Plus*. This could be helpful in assessing the damage caused by gunshots and in investigating responsibilities in Libya.

130. Gatti, "Italia e Malta litigano sul naufragio."

131. Camilleri, "PM Hints at Hesitation."

132. Gatti, "Italia e Malta litigano sul naufragio." This is also the argument put forward, in a letter to *L'Espresso*, by the head of the coast guard, admiral Angrisano. The letter is available at "Lampedusa, il ritardo nei soccorsi: ecco i documenti," *L'Espresso*, November 28, 2013, http://espresso.repubblica.it/internazionale/2013/11/28/news/lampedusa-i-soccorsi-in-ritardo-ecco-i-documenti-1.143247, accessed September 16, 2014.

133. Lieutenant Antonio Morana, personal interview, June 20, 2011.

134. Qtd. in Herman Grech and Kurt Sansone, "Shrinking Malta's Search and Rescue Area Is 'Not an Option'," *Times of Malta*, April 26, 2009, http://www.timesofmalta.com/articles/view/20090426/local/shrinking-maltas-search-and-rescue-area-is-not-an-option.254380, accessed September 14, 2014.

135. Ibid.

136. Ashraf A. Wahab, "Libyan Vessel Picks Up Syrian Migrants in International Waters," *Libya Herald*, October 13, 2013, http://www.libyaherald.com/2013/10/13/li byan-vessel-picks-up-syrian-migrants-in-international-waters/, accessed September 14, 2014.

137. "Libya Investigating Migrants' Claims They Were Shot At, But Libyan PM Zidan Says Military Not Involved," *Tripoli Post*, October 14, 2013, http://www.tripoli post.com/articledetail.asp?c = 1&i = 10724, accessed September 14, 2014.

138. Wahab, "Libyan Vessel Picks Up Syrian Migrants."

139. Steve Scherer, "Italy Rescues 370 Migrants, Steps Up Naval Patrols," *Reuters*, October 15, 2013, http://www.reuters.com/article/2013/10/15/us-italy-migrants-idUS BRE99C04K20131015, accessed September 14, 2014.

140. Steve Scherer, personal communication, October 23, 2013.

141. Marco Ludovico, "Alfano Contestato Dagli Immigrati," *Il Sole 24 ORE*, October 22, 2013, http://www.ilsole24ore.com/art/notizie/2013-10-22/alfano-contest ato-immigrati-065431.shtml?uuid = AbifwVwI, accessed September 14, 2014.

142. Sami Zaptia, "Italy to Commence Aerial and Electronic Border Surveillance—Zeidan," *Libya Herald*, November 3, 2013, http://www.libyaherald.com/2013/11/03/italy-to-commence-aerial-and-electronic-border-surveillance-zeidan/#axzz3DDoM pvn4, accessed September 14, 2014.

143. It features an average of five navy vessels per day in the central Mediterranean, plus two submarines, helicopters, and the support of other Italian armed forces, with a total of almost 1,000 sailors at sea every day.

144. Giovanni Pinto, "Audizione del direttore centrale dell'immigrazione e della polizia delle frontiere presso il Ministero dell'Interno," Parliament of the Italian Republic (Lower Chamber), Rome, December 10, 2013.

145. Dan Bilefsky, "Give Malta Your Tired and Huddled, and Rich," *New York Times*, February 1, 2014, http://www.nytimes.com/2014/02/01/world/europe/give-malta -your-tired-and-huddled-and-rich.html?_r = 1, accessed September 14, 2014.

146. *Novinite.com*, "Bulgaria's Border Fence Operation Going as Planned— Defense Min.," November 28, 2013, http://www.novinite.com/articles/155962/Bulgar ia%27s + Border + Fence + Operation + Going + as + Planned + - + Defense + Min, accessed September 14, 2014.

147. *Hürriyet Daily News*, "Greek, Bulgarian Fences Along Turkish Border Draw Criticism," January 21, 2011, http://www.hurriyetdailynews.com/default.aspx?pag eid = 438&n = greek-bulgarian-fence-plans-along-turkish-border-draws-criticism-20 11-01-21, accessed September 14, 2014.

148. *Ekathimerini.com*, "Greece Completes Anti-Migrant Fence at Turkish Border," December 17, 2012, http://www.ekathimerini.com/4dcgi/_w_articles_wsite1_1 _17/12/2012_474782, accessed September 14, 2014.

149. Constanze Letsch, "Turkey's New Border Wall Angers Kurds on Both Sides of Syrian Divide," *Guardian*, November 8, 2013, http://www.theguardian.com/world/2013/nov/08/turkey-new-border-wall-kurds-syria, accessed September 14, 2014.

150. Sobelman, "Israel Completes Most of Egypt Border Fence."

151. Ilan Lior, "For One Eritrean Asylum Seeker in Israel, Hope for a New Life," *Haaretz*, February 2, 2014, http://www.haaretz.com/news/national/.premium-1.571871, accessed July 2, 2014. On detention, see UNHCR *Briefing Notes*, "UNHCR is concerned at new Amendment to Israel's Law on the Prevention of Infiltration," January 10, 2014, http://www.unhcr.org/52cfe2a09.html, accessed January 11, 2014.

152. Yaakov Katz, "India, US Learning from Israel's Border Security," *Jerusalem Post*, July 30, 2012, http://www.jpost.com/Defense/India-US-learning-from-Israels-border-security, accessed July 29, 2014.

153. *Ansamed.info*, "Italy: Migrant Landings on the Rise in 2013," February 4, 2013, http://www.ansamed.info/ansamed/en/news/sections/generalnews/2014/02/04/Italy-migrant-landings-the-rise-2013_10014784.html, accessed September 14, 2014.

154. Reported in Antonello Mangano, " 'Non vogliamo essere buoni? Cerchiamo di essere intelligenti'. Nel 2013 nessuna emergenza sbarchi," *Terrelibere.org*, November 18, 2013, http://www.terrelibere.org/4713-non-vogliamo-essere-buoni-cerchiamo-di-essere-intelligenti-nel-2013-nessuna-emergenza-sbarchi, accessed July 1, 2014.

155. De Giorgi 2014.

156. Ministero del Lavoro 2011. For a more systematic discussion of labor, law, and migration in Italy, see Calavita 2005.

157. Italian Ministry of the Interior, "Flussi d'Ingresso 2013 per Lavoratori Non Stagionali: le Domande Possono Essere Inviate dalle Ore 9 del 20 Dicembre per Via Telematica," December 19, 2013, http://www.interno.gov.it/mininterno/site/it/sezioni/sala_stampa/notizie/immigrazione/2013_12_19_domande_flussi2013.html, accessed September 14, 2014. The average total of EU and non-EU workers admitted yearly is about 43,000 people.

158. IDOS 2013:2.

159. As defined by Cornelius in his discussion of the U.S. labor market and immigration laws (2005).

160. UNHCR 2013.

161. De Wet 2005.

162. Nicolini with Bellingreri 2013.

163. European Council 2013.

164. For the full list of proposals articulated by the task force, see European Commission 2013.

Chapter 6. Public Aesthetics Amid Seas

1. Qtd. in Barbara Minafra, "Per non 'rottamare' la Memoria: a Otranto la Kater I Rades diventa un monumento all'Umanità migrante," *Albania News*, January 30, 2012, http://www.albanianews.it/italia/2319-kater-rades-monumento-umanita, accessed July 18, 2014.

2. Qtd. in Tiziana Colluto, *Il Fatto Quotidiano*, January 29, 2012, http://www.ilfattoquotidiano.it/2012/01/29/rivive-nave-kater-rades-relitto-tragedia-opera-allumanita-migrante/187484/, accessed July 18, 2014.

3. On the complications of such Mediterranean and southern heritage, see Albahari 2008.

4. On the many aspects of memory and memorialization, see Levi 1997 [1958]; Boyarin 1994; Bernal 2014.

5. Qtd. in Minafra, "Per non 'rottamare' la Memoria."

6. Between its launch in October 2013 and mid-September 2014 (De Giorgi 2014).

7. *BBC News*, "UN urges refugee 'solidarity' within European Union," June 19, 2011, http://www.bbc.co.uk/news/world-europe-13826315, accessed July 4, 2014.

8. Working primarily with street children in Kenya, Zambia, and Sudan.

9. Salvatore, personal interview, June 20, 2011.

10. Qtd. in Leonardo Servadio, "L'artista Paladino: 'Nobel a Lampedusa? Svolta sulla via di una nuova umanità,'" *Avvenire*, July 23, 2013. http://www.avvenire.it/Cronaca/Pagine/nobel-lampedusa-svolta-via-nuova-umanita.aspx, accessed July 4, 2014.

11. Qtd. in Attilio Bolzoni, "La porta che guarda l''Africa in ricordo di chi non è mai arrivato," *La Repubblica*, June 26, 2008.

12. This was made possible by stationing police agents on board. Admiral De Giorgi (2014) acknowledged that most Syrian refugees have refused such identification (at least while on navy vessels), as they hope to reach other EU countries (see Albahari forthcoming on their reception in Milan on the way to northern Europe).

13. *Rainews.it*, "Immigrazione, Ue risponde ad Alfano: 'Scioccati da tragedie, grazie Italia. Pronti ad intervenire,'" August 24, 2014, http://www.rainews.it/dl/rainews/articoli/Immigrazione-Ue-risponde-ad-Alfano-Scioccati-da-tragedie-grazie-Italia-65a67130-199b-42c8-b5e6-51acefded01b.html, accessed August 24, 2014.

14. Together with NATO vessels, a variety of non-European navies including China's and India's, and European non-EU navies. This is in accordance with relevant international laws and UN Security Council Resolutions. See, for more details, EU Naval Force, "Mission," http://eunavfor.eu/mission/, accessed August 10, 2014.

15. To be noted that former prime minister Letta has continued to express support for the operation, conceived during his tenure.

16. See Cunliffe 2011; Reinold 2013; Glanville 2014.

17. Personal communication, officer of international organization, December 7, 2012.

18. Comprising the twenty-eight EU heads of state or government, plus the president of the Council, Herman Van Rompuy, and the president of the EU Commission, José Manuel Barroso.

19. Here writer Jean-Claude Izzo (2007 [1997]:207) reminded me that the Greek language deploys several words to refer to the "sea," including *hals, pelagos, pontos, thalassa,* and *kolpos.*

20. See Pojmann 2008 and Reed-Danahay and Brettell 2008 for examples of forms of citizenship and political engagement that transcend ethnonational and state boundaries.

21. Detailed information on his biography is to be credited to two organizations: Centro Siciliano di Documentazione 'Giuseppe Impastato' ("Giuseppe Impastato: l'attività, il delitto, l'inchiesta e il depistaggio, le condanne dei mandanti," http://www .centroimpastato.it/conoscere/peppino.php3, accessed September 15, 2014) and Associazione Culturale Peppino Impastato-Casa Memoria ("Biografia di Giuseppe Impastato," http://www.peppinoimpastato.com/biografia.htm, accessed September 15, 2014).

22. *I Cento Passi* is the title of a movie (2000) on the life of Peppino Impastato, directed by Marco Tullio Giordana.

23. Franca, personal interview, June 16, 2011.

24. Lunaria 2013.

25. "New Norms on Citizenship," Law No. 91, Parliament of Italy, Rome, February 5, 1992.

26. Judith Gleitze, "Gli Eritrei del 3 Ottobre 2013 vengono trasferiti da Lampedusa dopo 101 giorni," *Siciliamigranti*, January 12, 2014, http://siciliami granti.blogspot.com/2014/01/gli-eritrei-del-3-ottobre-2013-vengono.html, accessed January 19, 2014.

27. For the October 3, 2013, shipwreck, Italian police authorities have compiled a collection of photographs and other identifying information from the retrieved bodies. These images, stored on DVD, are intended for members of the Eritrean diaspora, especially in northern Europe, to possibly recognize relatives, mostly buried in Sicily. DNA matching for relatives in Eritrea is also being considered, but the political framework there makes it difficult for potential relatives of unauthorized emigrants (refugees) to come forward.

28. Sanfilippo and Scialoja 2010:115.

29. His real name.

30. City Council Deliberation, Comune di Lampedusa e Linosa, "Originale di deliberazione della Giunta Municipale: Oggetto: Costituzione Museo delle Migrazione," December 19, 2012.

31. Basile died on July 30, 2013. *Giuseppebasile.org*, "Museo delle Migrazioni di Lampedusa e Linosa, primo appuntamento con il nuovo archivio e centro di documentazione," http://www.giuseppebasile.org/index.php/incontri-conferenze-seminari -convegni/48-museo-delle-migrazioni-di-lampedusa-e-linosa-primo-appuntamento -con-il-nuovo-archivio-e-centro-di-documentazione, accessed September 20, 2014.

Bibliography

Agamben, Giorgio. 2009 [1993]. *The Coming Community*. Trans. Michael Hardt. Minneapolis: University of Minnesota Press.

———. 1998. *Homo Sacer: Sovereign Power and Bare Life*. Stanford, CA: Stanford University Press.

Agnew, John A. 2002. *Place and Politics in Modern Italy*. Chicago: University of Chicago Press.

Albahari, Maurizio. 2007. "Religious Symbols: Made in Italy." *ISIM Review* 19: 30–31. Available at https://openaccess.leidenuniv.nl/handle/1887/17124. Accessed July 15, 2014.

———. 2008. "Between Mediterranean Centrality and European Periphery: Migration and Heritage in Southern Italy." *International Journal of Euro-Mediterranean Studies* 1(2): 141–62. Available at http://www.emuni.si/press/ISSN/1855-3362/1_141-162.pdf. Accessed July 15, 2014.

———. 2010. "Guest Editor's Note: Al Confine della Primavera." *Italian Culture* 28(2): 82–84.

———. 2014. "Review of Joseph H. Carens, *The Ethics of Immigration*." *Human Rights Quarterly* 36(4): 949–55.

———. Forthcoming. "I Was a Stranger: Catholic Charity on the Edge of Justice." In *Faith, Charity, and the Security State*, ed. Erica C. James. Santa Fe, NM: School for Advanced Research Press.

———. N.d. "'Statistically Undetectable': Depleted Uranium and NATO's Kosovo War." Unpublished manuscript.

Allievi, Stefano. 2010. "Immigration and Cultural Pluralism in Italy: Multiculturalism as a Missing Model." *Italian Culture* 28(2): 84–103.

Alonso, Anna Maria. 1994. "The Politics of Space, Time and Substance: State Formation, Nationalism and Ethnicity." *Annual Review of Anthropology* 23: 379–405.

Amelio, Gianni, dir. 1994. *Lamerica*. Gecchi Gori Home Video, Italy.

Amnesty International. 2011. *Detention Abuses Staining the New Libya*. London: Amnesty International.

———. 2012. *S.O.S. Europe—Human Rights and Migration Control*. London: Amnesty International.

Amoore, Louise and Marieke de Goede, eds. 2008. *Risk and the War on Terror*. New York: Routledge.

Andersson, Ruben. 2014. *Illegality, Inc.: Clandestine Migration and the Business of Bordering Europe*. Berkeley: University of California Press.

Andreas, Peter. 2000. *Border Games: Policing the U.S.-Mexico Divide*. Ithaca, NY: Cornell University Press.

Andrijasevic, Rutvica. 2010. "From Exception to Excess: Detention and Deportations Across the Mediterranean Space." In *The Deportation Regime: Sovereignty, Space, and the Freedom of Movement*, ed. Nicholas De Genova and Nathalie Peutz, 147–65. Durham, NC: Duke University Press.

Angel-Ajani, Asale. 2004. "Expert Witness: Notes Toward Revisiting the Politics of Listening." *Anthropology and Humanism* 29(2): 133–44.

Arendt, Hannah. 1958 [1951]. *The Origins of Totalitarianism*. New York: Meridian Books.

Aronson, Jay D. 2010. "The Law's Use of Brain Evidence." *Annual Review of Law and Social Science* 6: 93–108.

Asad, Talal. 1983. "Anthropological Conceptions of Religion: Reflections on Geertz." *Man*, n.s., 18: 237–59.

———. 1994. "Ethnographic Representation, Statistics and Modern Power." *Social Research* 61(1): 55–88.

———. 2004. "Where Are the Margins of the State?" In *Anthropology in the Margins of the State*, ed. Veena Das and Deborah Poole, 279–88. Santa Fe, NM: School of American Research Press.

Austin, John Langshaw. 1962. *How to Do Things with Words*. Cambridge, MA: Harvard University Press.

Balibar, Etienne. 2004. *We, the People of Europe? Reflections on Transnational Citizenship*. Princeton, NJ: Princeton University Press.

Barjaba, Kosta and Luigi Perrone. 1996. "Forme e grado di adattamento dei migranti di cultura Albanese in Europa (Italia, Grecia, Germania): 1992–1995." In *Naufragi Albanesi: Studi, ricerche e riflessioni sull'Albania*, ed. Luigi Perrone, 123–53. Rome: Sensibili alle Foglie.

Basaglia, Franco and Franca Basaglia Ongaro, eds. 2013a [1975]. *Crimini di Pace: Ricerche sugli intellettuali e sui tecnici come addetti all'oppressione*. Milan: Baldini e Castoldi.

———. 2013b [1975]. "Crimini di Pace." In *Crimini di Pace: Ricerche sugli intellettuali e sui tecnici come addetti all'oppressione*, ed. Franco Basaglia and Franca Basaglia Ongaro, 11–106. Milan: Baldini e Castoldi.

Bateson, Gregory. 1958. "Epilogue." In *Naven: A Survey of the Problems Suggested by a Composite Picture of the Culture of a New Guinea Tribe Drawn from Three Points of View*, 280–303. Stanford, CA: Stanford University Press.

Bauman, Zygmunt. 2000. *Liquid Modernity*. Malden, MA: Blackwell.

Bayat, Asef. 2013. *Life as Politics: How Ordinary People Change the Middle East*. 2nd ed. Stanford, CA: Stanford University Press.

Beck, Charlie and Colleen McCue. 2009. "Predictive Policing: What Can We Learn from Wal-Mart and Amazon About Fighting Crime in a Recession?" *Police Chief* 76(11): 18–24.

Bellu, Giovanni Maria. 2004. *I fantasmi di Portopalo: Natale 1996: La morte di 300 clandestini e il silenzio dell'Italia*. Milan: Arnoldo Mondatori.

Benasayag, Miguel. 2005 [2004]. *Contro il niente: Abc dell'impegno*. Trans. Guendalina Sartorio. Milan: Feltrinelli.

Ben-Ghiat, Ruth and Mia Fuller, eds. 2005. *Italian Colonialism*. New York: Palgrave Macmillan.

Benhabib, Seyla. 2001. *Transformations of Citizenship: Dilemmas of the Nation State in the Era of Globalization*. Assen: Koninklijke Van Gorcum.

———. 2006. *Another Cosmopolitanism: The Tanner Lectures*. Ed. Robert Post. New York: Oxford University Press.

Benjamin, Walter. 1968 [1955]. "Theses on the Philosphy of History." In *Illuminations: Essays and Reflections*, ed. Hannah Arendt, Trans. Harry Zohn, 253–64. New York: Schocken.

Ben-Yehoyada, Naor. 2011. "The Moral Perils of Mediterraneanism: Second Generation Immigrants Practicing Personhood Between Sicily and Tunisia." *Journal of Modern Italian Studies* 16(3): 386–403.

Bernal, Victoria. 2014. *Nation as Network: Diaspora, Cyberspace, and Citizenship*. Chicago: University of Chicago Press.

Biehl, João. 2013. *Vita: Life in a Zone of Social Abandonment*. 2nd ed. Berkeley: University of California Press.

Boltanski, Luc. 1999 [1993]. *Distant Suffering: Morality, Media, and Politics*. Trans. Graham Burchell. Cambridge: Cambridge University Press.

Borneman, John. 1998. *Subversions of International Order: Studies in the Political Anthropology of Culture*. Albany: State University of New York Press.

Bornstein, Erica. 2012. *Disquieting Gifts: Humanitarianism in New Delhi*. Stanford, CA: Stanford University Press.

Bornstein, Erica and Peter Redfield, eds. 2010. *Forces of Compassion: Humanitarianism Between Ethics and Politics*. Santa Fe, NM: School for Advanced Research Press.

Boubakri, Hassan. 2013. *Revolution and International Migration in Tunisia*. MPC Research Reports 2013/04, Robert Schuman Centre for Advanced Studies. San Domenico di Fiesole, Italy: European University Institute.

Bowen, John R. 2007. *Why the French Don't Like Headscarves: Islam, the State, and Public Space*. Princeton, NJ: Princeton University Press.

Boyarin, Jonathan. 1994. "Space, Time, and the Politics of Memory." In *Remapping Memory: The Politics of TimeSpace*, 1–37. Minneapolis: University of Minnesota Press.

Braidotti, Rosi. 2011. *Nomadic Subjects: Embodiment and Sexual Difference in Contemporary Feminist Theory*. 2nd ed. New York: Columbia University Press.

Brennan, Denise. 2014. *Life Interrupted: Trafficking into Forced Labor in the United States*. Durham, NC: Duke University Press.

Brown, Wendy. 2010. *Walled States, Waning Sovereignty*. New York: Zone Books.

Brubaker, Rogers W. 1992. *Citizenship and Nationhood in France and Germany*. Cambridge, MA: Harvard University Press.

Brysk, Alison, and Austin Choi-Fitzpatrick, eds. 2012. *From Human Trafficking to Human Rights: Reframing Contemporary Slavery*. Philadelphia: University of Pennsylvania Press.

Bureau of Democracy, Human Rights and Labor. 2012. *Eritrea—Country Reports on Human Rights Practices for 2012*. Washington, DC: U.S. Department of State.

Butler, Judith. 2003. "Violence, Mourning, Politics." *Studies in Gender and Sexuality* 4(1): 9–37.

Cabot, Heath. 2014. *On the Doorstep of Europe: Asylum and Citizenship in Greece*. Philadelphia: University of Pennsylvania Press.

Caffio, Fabio. 2003. *Immigrazione Clandestina Via Mare: L'esperienza italiana nella vigilanza, prevenzione e contrasto*. Supplement to *Rivista Marittima* 10. Rome: Marina Militare Italiana.

Calavita, Kitty. 2005. *Immigrants at the Margins: Law, Race, and Exclusion in Southern Europe*. Cambridge: Cambridge University Press.

Calhoun, Greg. 2010. "The Idea of Emergency: Humanitarian Action and Global (Dis)Order." In *Contemporary States of Emergency: The Politics of Military and Humanitarian Interventions*, ed. Didier Fassin and Mariella Pandolfi, 29–58. New York: Zone Books.

Candea, Matei and Giovanni Da Col. 2012. "The Return to Hospitality." *Journal of the Royal Anthropological Institute* 18(S1): 1–19.

Caneva, Elena. 2014. *The Integration of Migrants in Italy: An Overview of Policy Instruments and Actors*. INTERACT RR 2014/05, Robert Schuman Centre for Advanced Studies. San Domenico di Fiesole, Italy: European University Institute.

Capussotti, Enrica. 2010. "*Nordisti contro Sudisti*: Internal Migration and Racism in Turin, Italy: 1950s and 1960s." *Italian Culture* 28(2): 121–38.

Carens, Joseph H. 2013. *The Ethics of Immigration*. New York: Oxford University Press.

Carling, Jørgen. 2007. "The Merits and Limitations of Spain's High-Tech Border Control." Migration Policy Institute, June 7. Available at http://www.migrationpolicy.org/article/merits-and-limitations-spains-high-tech-border-control/. Accessed September 17, 2014.

Carnimeo, Nicolò. 2014. *Come è profondo il mare: Dal nostro inviato nella più grande discarica del pianeta: La plastica, il mercurio, il tritolo e il pesce che mangiamo*. Milan: Chiarelettere.

Carter, Donald M. 1997. *States of Grace: Senegalese in Italy and the New European Immigration*. Minneapolis: University of Minnesota Press.

Cassarino, Jean-Pierre. 2005. "I negoziati relativi alla riammissione nell'ambito del Processo di Barcellona." September. Servizio Studi/Servizio Affari Internazionali, Senate of the Italian Republic, Rome.

Cento Bull, Anna. 2000. *Social Identities and Political Cultures in Italy: Catholic, Communist and Leghist Communities Between Civicness and Localism.* New York: Berghahn Books.

Chambers, Ian. 2008. *Mediterranean Crossings: The Politics of Interrupted Modernity.* Durham, NC: Duke University Press.

———. 2010. "Maritime Criticism and Theoretical Shipwrecks." *PMLA* 125(3): 678–84.

Chavez, Leo R. 2001. *Covering Immigration: Popular Images and the Politics of the Nation.* Berkeley: University of California Press.

———. 2008. *The Latino Threat: Constructing Immigrants, Citizens, and the Nation.* Stanford, CA: Stanford University Press.

Chebel d'Appollonia, Ariane. 2012. *Frontiers of Fear: Immigration and Insecurity in the United States and Europe.* Ithaca, NY: Cornell University Press.

Chope, Christopher. 2011. "The Arrival of Mixed Migratory Flows in Italian Coastal Areas." Report. October 31. Committee on Migration, Refugees and Displaced Persons, Parliamentary Assembly, Council of Europe.

Cohen, Stanley. 2001. *States of Denial: Knowing About Atrocities and Suffering.* Malden, MA: Blackwell.

Cole, Jeffrey. 1997. *The New Racism in Europe: A Sicilian Ethnography.* Cambridge: Cambridge University Press.

Collier, Jane F., Bill Maurer, and Liliana Suárez-Navaz. 1997. "Sanctioned Identities: Legal Constructions of Modern Personhood." *Identities* 2(1–2): 1–27.

Coluccello, Salvatore and Simon Massey. 2007. "Out of Africa: The Human Trade Between Libya and Lampedusa." *Trends in Organized Crime* 10: 77–90.

Comaroff, Jean and John L. Comaroff . 2000. "Millennial Capitalism: First Thoughts on a Second Coming." *Public Culture* 12(2): 291–343.

Connolly, William E. 2005. *Pluralism.* Durham, NC: Duke University Press.

Cornelisse, Galina. 2010. "Immigration Detention and the Territoriality of Universal Rights." In *The Deportation Regime: Sovereignty, Space, and the Freedom of Movement,* ed. Nicholas De Genova and Nathalie Peutz, 101–22. Durham, NC: Duke University Press.

Cornelius, Wayne A. 2005. "Controlling 'Unwanted' Immigration: Lessons from the United States, 1993–2004." *Journal of Ethnic and Migration Studies* 31(4): 775–94.

Cornelius, Wayne A. and Marc R. Rosenblum. 2004. "Immigration and Politics." Working Paper 105, Center for Comparative Immigration Studies, UC San Diego, October.

Council of the European Union. 2004. "2609th Council Meeting, General Affairs and External Relations, External Relations." News release, October 11.

Coutin, Susan Bibler. 2000. *Legalizing Moves: Salvadoran Immigrants' Struggle for U.S. Residency*. Ann Arbor: University of Michigan Press.

———. 2005. "Being En Route." *American Anthropologist* 107(2): 195–206.

Crépeau, François. 2013. "Regional Study: Management of the External Borders of the European Union and Its Impact on the Human Rights of Migrants." April 24. UN General Assembly. Human Rights Council.

Cunliffe, Philip, ed. 2011. *Critical Perspectives on the Responsibility to Protect: Interrogating Theory and Practice*. London: Routledge.

Dainotto, Roberto M. 2007. *Europe (in Theory)*. Durham, NC: Duke University Press.

Dal Lago, Alessandro. 2004. *Non-Persone: L'esclusione dei migranti in una societa' globale*. Milan: Feltrinelli.

Dalla Chiesa, Nando. 2014. *Manifesto dell'Antimafia*. Turin: Einaudi.

Darian-Smith, Eve. 1999. *Bridging Divides: The Channel Tunnel and English Legal Identity in the New Europe*. Berkeley: University of California Press.

De Bruycker, Philippe. 2014. "The Missed Opportunity of the 'Ypres Guidelines' of the European Council Regarding Immigration and Asylum." Available at http://blogs.eui.eu/migrationpolicycentre/the-missed-opportunity-of-the-ypres-guidelines-of-the-european-council-regarding-immigration-and-asylum/. Accessed July 30, 2014.

De Genova, Nicholas P. 2002. "Migrant 'Illegality' and Deportability in Everyday Life." *Annual Review of Anthropology* 31:419–47.

———. 2010. "The Deportation Regime: Sovereignty, Space, and the Freedom of Movement." In *The Deportation Regime: Sovereignty, Space, and the Freedom of Movement*, ed. Nicholas De Genova and Nathalie Peutz, 33–65. Durham, NC: Duke University Press.

De Genova, Nicholas and Nathalie Peutz, eds. 2010. *The Deportation Regime: Sovereignty, Space, and the Freedom of Movement*. Durham, NC: Duke University Press.

De Giorgi, Giuseppe. 2014. "Operation 'Mare Nostrum': Hearing by Admiral De Giorgi, Italian Navy Chief of Staff." September 24. Senate of the Italian Republic, Human Rights Committee, Rome.

De Martino, Ernesto. 1996 [1961]. *La Terra del Rimorso*. Milan: Il Saggiatore.

De Wet, Chris. 2005. *Development-Induced Displacement: Problems, Policies and People*. New York: Berghahn.

Dean, Jodi. 2009. *Democracy and Other Neoliberal Fantasies: Communicative Capitalism and Left Politics*. Durham, NC: Duke University Press.

Dean, Mitchell. 2002. "Powers of Life and Death Beyond Governmentality." *Cultural Values* 6(1–2): 119–38.

Debono, Daniela. 2011. "'Not Our Problem': Why the Detention of Irregular Migrants Is Not Considered a Human Rights Issue in Malta." In *Are Human Rights for Migrants? Critical Reflections on the Status of Irregular Migrants in Europe and the United States*, ed. Marie-Bénédicte Dembour and Tobias Kelly, 146–62. New York: Routledge.

Debord, Guy. 1995 [1967]. *The Society of the Spectacle*. Trans. Donald Nicholson-Smith. New York: Zone Books.

Del Grande, Gabriele. 2007. *Mamadou va a morire: La strage dei clandestini nel Mediterraneo*. Rome: Infinito.

———. 2010. *Il mare di mezzo, al tempo dei respingimenti*. Rome: Infinito.

———. 2013. "Ma l'Europa non è più il Paradiso." In *Mare Chiuso*, ed. Stefano Liberti, 55–62. Rome: Minimum Fax.

Delle Donne, Marcella. 2004. *Un cimitero chiamato Mediterraneo: Per una storia del diritto d'asilo nell'Unione Europea*. Rome: DeriveApprodi.

Dembour, Marie-Bénédicte. 1996. "Human Rights Talk and the Anthropological Ambivalence: The Particular Context of Universal Claims." In *Inside and Outside the Law: Anthropological Studies of Authority and Ambiguity*, ed. Olivia Harris, 19–40. London: Routledge University Press.

———. 2012. "Interception-at-Sea: Illegal as Currently Practiced—Hirsi and Others v. Italy." *Strasbourg Observers*, March 1. Available at http://strasbourgobservers .com/2012/03/01/interception-at-sea-illegal-as-currently-practiced-hirsi-and-oth ers-v-italy/. Accessed June 1, 2014.

Dembour, Marie-Bénédicte and Tobias Kelly, eds. 2011. *Are Human Rights for Migrants? Critical Reflections on the Status of Irregular Migrants in Europe and the United States*. New York: Routledge.

Di Nicola, Andrea and Gianpaolo Musumeci. 2014. *Confessioni di un trafficante di uomini*. Milan: Chiarelettere.

Donen, Stanley, dir. 1974. *The Little Prince*. Based on *The Little Prince* by Antoine de Saint-Exupéry. Hollywood, CA: Paramount Pictures.

Donnan, Hastings and Thomas M. Wilson. 1999. *Borders: Frontiers of Identity, Nation and State*. Oxford: Berg.

Douglas, Mary. 1966. *Purity and Danger: An Analysis of Concepts of Pollution and Taboo*. New York: Praeger.

Dunn, Timothy J. 1996. *The Militarization of the U.S.-Mexico Border, 1978–1992: Low-Intensity Conflict Doctrine Comes Home*. Austin, TX: Center for Mexican American Studies Books.

Duranti, Alessandro. 1993. "Truth and Intentionality: Towards an Ethnographic Critique." *Cultural Anthropology* 8(2): 214–45.

ECRE (European Council on Refugees and Exiles). 2014. "Mind the Gap: Annual Report 2013/2014. An NGO Perspective on Challenges to Accessing Protection in the Common European Asylum System." Brussels: European Council on Refugees and Exiles. Available at http://www.cir-onlus.org/images/pdf/2014_09%20AIDA %20Annual%20Report%202013-2014.pdf. Accessed September 15, 2014.

Eliade, Mircea. 1959. *The Sacred and the Profane: The Nature of Religion: The Significance of Religious Myth, Symbolism, and Ritual Within Life and Culture*. Trans. William R. Trask. New York: Harcourt Brace Jovanovich.

Eshja, Ervis and Mattia Soranzo, dirs. 2004. *Jetoj—Vivo*. Cavallino, Italy: Muud Film.

European Commission. 2005. *Technical Mission to Libya in Illegal Immigration 27 Nov–6 Dec 2004*. Report 7753/05. Brussels: European Commission.

———. 2013. "Communication from the Commission to the European Parliament and the Council on the Work of the Task Force Mediterranean." December 4.

European Council. 2013. "European Council 19/20 December 2013: Conclusions."

———. 2014. "June 26/27 2014: Conclusions."

European Parliament. 2005. "The Resolution on Lampedusa (Number P6_TA (2005)0138)." April 14.

Falasca-Zamponi, Simonetta. 1997. *Fascist Spectacle: The Aesthetics of Power in Mussolini's Italy*. Berkeley: University of California Press.

Farmer, Paul. 2003. *Pathologies of Power: Health, Human Rights, and the New War on the Poor*. Berkeley: University of California Press.

Fassin, Didier. 2005. "Compassion and Repression: The Moral Economy of Immigration Policies in France." *Cultural Anthropology* 20(3): 362–87.

———. 2011. "Policing Borders, Producing Boundaries: The Governmentality of Immigration in Dark Times." *Annual Review of Anthropology* 40: 213–26.

———. 2012. *Humanitarian Reason: A Moral History of the Present*. Trans. Rachel Gomme. Berkeley: University of California Press.

Fassin, Didier and Estelle D'Halluin. 2005. "The Truth from the Body: Medical Certificates as Ultimate Evidence for Asylum Seekers." *American Anthropologist* 107(4): 597–608.

Fassin, Didier and Mariella Pandolfi, eds. 2010a. *Contemporary States of Emergency: The Politics of Military and Humanitarian Interventions*. New York: Zone Books.

———. 2010b. "Military and Humanitarian Government in the Age of Intervention." Introduction to *Contemporary States of Emergency: The Politics of Military and Humanitarian Interventions*, ed. Didier Fassin and Mariella Pandolfi, 9–25. New York: Zone Books.

Feldman, Allen. 1991. *Formations of Violence: The Narrative of the Body and Political Terror in Northern Ireland*. Chicago: University of Chicago Press.

Feldman, Gregory. 2012. *The Migration Apparatus: Security, Labor, and Policymaking in the European Union*. Stanford, CA: Stanford University Press.

Ferguson, Andrew Guthrie. 2012. "Predictive Policing: The Future of Reasonable Suspicion." *Emory Law Journal* 62: 259–325.

Ferguson, James and Akhil Gupta. 2002. "Spatializing States: Toward an Ethnography of Neoliberal Governmentality." *American Ethnologist* 29(4): 981–1002.

Fitzpatrick, Peter. 2001. *Modernism and the Grounds of Law*. Cambridge: Cambridge University Press.

Forgacs, David. 2014. *Italy's Margins: Social Exclusion and Nation Formation Since 1861*. Cambridge: Cambridge University Press.

Fortun, Kim. 2001. *Advocacy After Bhopal: Environmentalism, Disaster, New Global Orders*. Chicago: University of Chicago Press.

Foucault, Michel. 1979 [1975]. *Discipline and Punish: The Birth of the Prison.* Trans. Alan Sheridan. New York: Vintage Books.

———. 2003 [1997]. *"Society Must Be Defended": Lectures at the College de France, 1975–76.* Trans. David Macey. New York: Picador.

Fraser, Nancy. 1992. "Rethinking the Public Sphere: A Contribution to the Critique of Actually Existing Democracy." In *Habermas and the Public Sphere,* ed. Craig Calhoun, 109–42. Cambridge, MA: MIT Press.

Frisullo, Dino. 1997. "Buon Natale, clandestino." *Narcomafie* 5(9):3–5.

Geertz, Clifford. 2004. "What Is a State if It Is Not a Sovereign? Reflections on Politics in Complicated Places." *Current Anthropology* 45(5): 577–93.

Ginzburg, Carlo. 2003. "On the Dark Side of history." Interview by T. R. Gundersen. Trans. J. Basil Cowlishaw. Available at http://www.eurozine.com/articles/2003-07 -11-ginzburg-en.html. Accessed August 25, 2014.

Giordana, Marco Tullio, dir. 2000. *I Cento Passi.* Rome: Rai Cinemafiction.

Giordano, Cristiana. 2014. *Migrants in Translation: Caring and the Logics of Difference in Contemporary Italy.* Berkeley: University of California Press.

Giordano, Daniela et al. 2009. "An Automatic System for Skeletal Bone Age Measurement by Robust Processing of Carpal and Epiphysial/Metaphysial Bones." *IEEE Transactions on Instrumentation and Measurement* 59(10): 2539–53.

Glanville, Luke. 2014. *Sovereignty and the Responsibility to Protect: A New History.* Chicago: University of Chicago Press.

Gramsci, Antonio. 1957. *The Modern Prince and Other Writings.* New York: International.

———. 1971. *Selection from the Prison Notebooks.* Ed. and trans. Quintin Hoare and Geoffrey Nowell Smith. New York: International.

Grant, Stephanie. 2011a. "Recording and identifying European frontier deaths." *European Journal of Migration and Law* 13(2):135–56.

———. 2011b. "The Recognition of Migrants' Rights Within the UN Human Rights System." In *Are Human Rights for Migrants? Critical Reflections on the Status of Irregular Migrants in Europe and the United States,* ed. Marie-Bénédicte Dembour and Tobias Kelly, 25–47. New York: Routledge.

Green, Sarah. 2013. "Borders and the Relocation of Europe." *Annual Review of Anthropology* 42: 345–61.

Greenhouse, Carol J. 2002. "Altered States, Altered Lives." Introduction to *Ethnography in Unstable Places: Everyday Lives in Contexts of Dramatic Political Change,* ed. Carol J. Greenhouse, Elizabeth Mertz, and Kay B. Warren, 1–34. Durham, NC: Duke University Press.

Gupta, Akhil. 2005. "Narratives of Corruption: Anthropological and Fictional Accounts of the Indian State." *Ethnography* 6(1): 5–34.

Gupta, Akhil and James Ferguson. 1992. "Beyond 'Culture': Space, Identity, and the Politics of Difference." *Cultural Anthropology* 7(1): 6–23.

———. 1997. "Discipline and Practice: 'The Field' as Site, Method and Location in Anthropology." In *Anthropological Locations: Boundaries and Grounds of a Field Science*, ed. Akhil Gupta and James Ferguson, 1–46. Berkeley: University of California Press.

Hage, Ghassan, ed. 2009. *Waiting*. Melbourne: Melbourne University Press.

Haney, Lynne. 1996. "Homeboys, Babies, Men in Suits: The State and the Reproduction of Male Dominance." *American Sociological Review* 61(5): 759–78.

Hansen, Peo and Sandy Brian Hager. 2010. *The Politics of European Citizenship: Deepening Contradictions in Social Rights and Migration Policy*. New York: Berghahn.

Hansen, Thomas Blom and Finn Stepputat, eds. 2005. *Sovereign Bodies: Citizens, Migrants, and States in the Postcolonial World*. Princeton, NJ: Princeton University Press.

Harris, Olivia, ed. 1996. *Inside and Outside the Law: Anthropological Studies of Authority and Ambiguity*. New York: Routledge.

Harvey, John H. and Gifford Weary, eds. 1985. *Attribution: Basic Issues and Applications*. Orlando, FL: Academic Press.

Hastrup, Kirsten. 2004. "Getting It Right: Knowledge and Evidence in Anthropology." *Anthropological Theory* 4(4): 455–72.

Hayes, Ben and Mathias Vermeulen. 2012. *Borderline: The EU's New Border Surveillance Initiatives. Assessing the Costs and Fundamental Rights Implications of EUROSUR and the 'Smart Borders' Proposals*. Berlin: Heinrich Böll Foundation.

Heidbrink, Lauren. 2014. *Migrant Youth, Transnational Families, and the State: Care and Contested Interests*. Philadelphia: University of Pennsylvania Press.

Hein, Christopher. 2013. "Come il Mediterraneo e' Diventato una Barriera." In *Mare Chiuso*, ed. Stefano Liberti, 23–31. Rome: Minimum Fax.

Herzfeld, Michael. 1992. *The Social Production of Indifference: Exploring the Symbolic Roots of Western Bureaucracy*. New York: Berg.

———. 2004. *The Body Impolitic: Artisans and Artifice in the Global Hierarchy of Value*. Chicago: University of Chicago Press.

———. 2007. "Small-Mindedness Writ Large: On the Migrations and Manners of Prejudice." *Journal of Ethnic and Migration Studies* 33(2): 255–74.

———. 2009. *Evicted from Eternity: The Restructuring of Modern Rome*. Chicago: University of Chicago Press.

———. 2012. "Afterword: Reciprocating the Hospitality of These Pages." *Journal of the Royal Anthropological Institute* 18(S1): 210–17.

Heyman, Josiah M. 2000. "Respect for Outsiders? Respect for the Law? The Moral Evaluation of High-Scale Issues by US Immigration Officers." *Journal of the Royal Anthropological Institute* 6(4): 635–52.

Hollenbach, David, ed. 2010. *Driven from Home: Protecting the Rights of Forced Migrants*. Washington, DC: Georgetown University Press.

Holmes, Douglas R. 2000. *Integral Europe: Fast-Capitalism, Multiculturalism, Neofascism*. Princeton, NJ: Princeton University Press.

Holmes, Seth M. 2013. *Fresh Fruit, Broken Bodies: Indigenous Mexican Farmworkers in the United States.* Berkeley: University of California Press.

Honig, Bonnie. 2009. *Emergency Politics: Paradox, Law, Democracy.* Princeton, NJ: Princeton University Press.

Hopgood, Stephen. 2013. *The Endtimes of Human Rights.* Ithaca, NY: Cornell University Press.

Hull, Matthew S. 2012. "Documents and Bureaucracy". *Annual Review of Anthropology* 41:251–67.

Human Rights Watch. 2013. *Hear No Evil: Forced Labor and Corporate Responsibility in Eritrea's Mining Sector.* New York: Human Rights Watch.

———. 2014. *"I Wanted to Lie Down and Die": Trafficking and Torture of Eritreans in Sudan and Egypt.* New York: Human Rights Watch.

ICMPD (International Centre for Migration Policy Development). 2004. *Irregular Transit Migration in the Mediterranean—Some Facts, Futures and Insights.* Vienna: International Centre for Migration Policy Development.

IDOS (Centro Studi e Ricerche IDOS). 2013. *Immigrazione Dossier Statistico 2013.* Rome: Centro Studi e Ricerche IDOS.

Illich, Ivan. 1987. "Hospitality and Pain." Paper presented at McCormick Theological Seminary, Chicago. Available at http://www.pudel.uni-bremen.de/pdf/Illich_1423 id.pdf. Accessed June 25, 2014.

Inda, Jonathan X. 2005. *Targeting Immigrants: Government, Technology, and Ethics.* Malden, MA: Blackwell.

IntegrA/Azione. 2012. *Fronte Libico.* Rome: Fondazione IntegrA/Azione.

IOM (International Organization for Migration). 2012. *Migrants Caught in Crisis: The IOM Experience in Libya.* Ed. Christine Aghazarm, Patrice Quesada, and Sarah Tishler. Geneva: International Organization for Migration.

———. 2014. *Fatal Journeys: Tracking Lives Lost During Migration.* Ed. Tara Brian and Frank Laczko. Geneva: International Organization for Migration.

Izzo, Jean-Claude. 2007 [1997]. *The Lost Sailors.* Trans. Howard Curtis. New York: Europa.

James, Erica C. 2010. *Democratic Insecurities: Violence, Trauma, and Intervention in Haiti.* Berkeley: University of California Press.

———, ed. Forthcoming. *Faith, Charity, and the Security State.* Santa Fe, NM: School for Advanced Research Press.

Jesuit Refugee Service Malta. 2014. *Beyond Imagination: Asylum Seekers Testify to Life in Libya.* Birkirkara, Malta: Jesuit Refugee Service Malta.

Joppke, Christian. 1998. "Immigration Challenges the Nation State." In *Challenge to the Nation-State: Immigration in Western Europe and the United States,* ed. Christian Joppke, 5–46. New York: Oxford University Press.

Kantorowicz, Ernst H. 1997 [1957]. *The King's Two Bodies: A Study in Medieval Political Theology.* Princeton, NJ: Princeton University Press.

Karakayali, Serhat and Enrica Rigo. 2010. "Mapping the European Space of Circulation." In *The Deportation Regime: Sovereignty, Space, and the Freedom of Movement*, ed. Nicholas De Genova and Nathalie Peutz, 123–44. Durham, NC: Duke University Press.

Kaufman-Osborn, Timothy V. 2002. *From Noose to Needle: Capital Punishment and the Late Liberal State.* Ann Arbor: University of Michigan Press.

Kelly, Brian and Anita Jawadurovna Wadud. 2012 "Asian Labour Migrants and Humanitarian Crises: Lessons from Libya." *Issue in Brief* 3 (July). Bangkok: International Organization for Migration; Washington, DC: Migration Policy Institute.

Lahav, Gallya and Virginie Guiraudon. 2000. "Comparative Perspectives on Border Control: Away from the Border and Outside the State." In *The Wall Around the West: State Borders and Immigration Controls in North America and Europe*, ed. Peter Andreas and Timothy Snider, 55–77. Oxford: Rowman and Littlefield.

Latour, Bruno. 1999. *Pandora's Hope: Essays on the Reality of Science Studies.* Cambridge, MA: Harvard University Press.

———. 2005. *Reassembling the Social: An Introduction to Actor-Network-Theory.* New York: Oxford University Press.

Lauth Bacas, Jutta and William Kavanagh, eds. 2013. *Border Encounters: Asymmetry and Proximity at Europe's Frontiers.* New York: Berghahn Books.

Leogrande, Alessandro. 2010. *Le male vite: Storie di contrabbando e di multinazionali.* Rome: Fandango.

———. 2011. *Il naufragio: Morte nel Mediterraneo.* Milan: Feltrinelli.

Leun, Joanne P. van der and Maartje A.H. van der Woude. 2012. "Ethnic Profiling in the Netherlands? A Reflection on Expanding Preventive Powers, Ethnic Profiling and a Changing Social and Political Context." *Policing and Society* 4(21): 444–55.

Levi, Primo. 1997 [1958]. *Se questo e' un uomo: La tregua.* Turin: Einaudi.

Lucht, Hans. 2012. *Darkness Before Daybreak: African Migrants Living on the Margins in Southern Italy Today.* Berkeley: University of California Press.

Lunaria. 2013. *Rights Are Not An "Expense"—Immigration, Welfare, and Public Finance: A Report by Lunaria.* Rome: Lunaria.

Lutterbeck, Derek. 2006. "Policing Migration in the Mediterranean." *Mediterranean Politics* 11(1): 59–82.

Malkki, Liisa. 1992. "National Geographic: The Rooting of Peoples and the Territorialization of National Identity Among Scholars and Refugees." *Cultural Anthropology* 7(1): 24–44.

———. 1995. "Refugees and Exile: From 'Refugee Studies' to the National Order of Things." *Annual Review of Anthropology* 24: 495–523.

———. 1996. "Speechless Emissaries: Refugees, Humanitarianism, and Dehistoricization." *Cultural Anthropology* 11(3): 377–404.

Marcus, George. 1995. "Ethnography in/of the World System: The Emergence of Multi-Sited Ethnography." *Annual Review of Anthropology* 24: 95–117.

Maurer, Bill. 2005. *Mutual Life, Limited: Islamic Banking, Alternative Currencies, Lateral Reason*. Princeton, NJ: Princeton University Press.

Mauss, Marcel. 1990 [1950]. *The Gift: The Form and Reason for Exchange in Archaic Societies*. Trans. W. D. Halls. London: Routledge.

Mbembe, Achille. 2003. "Necropolitics." Trans. Libby Meintjes. *Public Culture* 15(1): 11–40.

MEDU (Medici per i Diritti Umani). 2013. "The CIE Archipelago: Inquiry into the Italian Centres for Identification and Expulsion (Synthesis)." Rome: Medici per i Diritti Umani onlus.

Mellah, Fawzi. 2001. *Clandestino nel Mediterraneo*. Trans. Antonella Furlan. Trieste, Italy: Asterios.

Mencherini, Stefano, dir. 2013. *Schiavi: Le rotte di nuove forme di sfruttamento*. Less Onlus and Flai CGIL, Naples, Italy.

Merry, Sally Engle. 2005. "Anthropology and Activism: Researching Human Rights Across Porous Boundaries." *PoLAR* 28(2): 240–57.

Mertz, Elizabeth. 1994. "Legal Language: Pragmatics, Poetics, and Social Power." *Annual Review of Anthropology* 23: 435–55.

———. 2002. "The Perfidy of Gaze and the Pain of Uncertainty: Anthropological Theory and the Search for Closure." In *Ethnography in Unstable Places: Everyday Lives in Contexts of Dramatic Political Change*, ed. Carol J. Greenhouse, Elizabeth Mertz, and Kay B. Warren, 355–78. Durham, NC: Duke University Press.

Messick, Brinkley M. 1993. *The Calligraphic State: Textual Domination and History in a Muslim Society*. Berkeley: University of California Press.

Mezzadra, Sandro and Brett Neilson. 2014. *Confini e frontiere: La moltiplicazione del lavoro nel mondo globale*. Bologna: il Mulino.

Ministero Del Lavoro e Delle Politiche Sociali. 2011. *L'Immigrazione per Lavoro in Italia: Evoluzione e prospettive—sintesi rapporto 2011*. Rome: Italia Lavoro.

Ministero dell'Interno. 2005. *Rapporto annuale: Lo stato della sicurezza in Italia*. Rome: Ministero dell'Interno.

Mitchell, Timothy. 1991. "The Limits of the State: Beyond Statist Approaches and Their Critics." *American Political Science Review* 85(1): 77–96.

Mouffe, Chantal. 2005. *On the Political*. New York: Routledge.

Mountz, Alison. 2010. *Seeking Asylum: Human Smuggling and Bureaucracy at the Border*. Minneapolis: University of Minnesota Press.

Muehlebach, Andrea. 2012. *The Moral Neoliberal: Welfare and Citizenship in Italy*. Chicago: University of Chicago Press.

Murray, Nancy. 2010. "Profiling in the Age of Total Information Awareness." *Race and Class* 52(2): 3–24.

Mutman, Mahmut. 1992. "Pictures from Afar: Shooting the Middle East." In *Orientalism and Cultural Differences*, ed. Mahmut Mutman and Meyda Yegenoglu, 1–44. Santa Cruz, CA: Center for Cultural Studies.

Ngai, Mae N. 2004. *Impossible Subjects: Illegal Aliens and the Making of Modern America, 1924–1965.* Princeton, NJ: Princeton University Press.

Nicolini, Giusi with Marta Bellingreri. 2013. *Lampedusa: Conversazioni su isole, politica, migranti.* Turin: Gruppo Abele.

Nordstrom, Carolyn. 2007. *Global Outlaws: Crime, Money, and Power in the Contemporary World.* Berkeley: University of California Press.

Oberweis, Trish and Michael Musheno. 2001. *Knowing Rights: State Actors' Stories of Power, Identity and Morality.* Aldershot: Ashgate.

O'Connell, Mary Ellen. 2002. "The Myth of Preemptive Self-Defense." Task Force on Terrorism Papers. Presented at American Society of International Law, August, Washington, D.C.

Official Journal of the European Union. 2011. "Twelfth Annual Report According to Article 8(2) of Council Common Position 2008/944/CFSP Defining Common Rules Governing Control of Exports of Military Technology and Equipment (2011/C 9/01)." January 13.

———. 2013. "Regulation (EU) No 1052/2013 of the European Parliament and of the Council of 22 October 2013 establishing the European Border Surveillance System (Eurosur)." November 6.

Olson, J. M. and M. Ross. 1985. "Attribution Research: Past Contributions, Current Trends, and Future Prospects." In *Attribution: Basic Issues and Applications*, ed. John H. Harvey and Gifford Weary, 283–311. Orlando, FL: Academic Press.

Ong, Aihwa. 2003. *Buddha Is Hiding: Refugees, Citizenship, the New America.* Berkeley: University of California Press.

Pagden, Anthony, ed. 2002. *The Idea of Europe: From Antiquity to the European Union.* New York: Cambridge University Press.

Pajo, Erind. 2008. *International Migration, Social Demotion, and Imagined Advancement: An Ethnography of Socioglobal Mobility.* New York: Springer.

Palumbo, Patrizia, ed. 2003. *A Place in the Sun: Africa in Italian Colonial Culture from Post-unification to the Present.* Berkeley: University of California Press.

Pandolfi, Mariella. 2010. "From Paradox to Paradigm: The Permanent State of Emergency in the Balkans." In *Contemporary States of Emergency: The Politics of Military and Humanitarian Interventions*, ed. Didier Fassin and Mariella Pandolfi, 153–72. New York: Zone Books.

Pastore, Ferruccio. 2008. *Migrazioni e relazioni Italo-Libiche: Come uscire da questa impasse.* Rome: CeSPI, Centro Studi di Politica Internazionale.

Paz, Yonathan. 2011. "Ordered Disorder: African Asylum Seekers in Israel and Discursive Challenges to an Emerging Refugee Regime." New Issues in Refugee Research Research Paper No. 205, UN Refugee Agency Policy Development and Evaluation Service, Geneva.

Perlmutter, Ted. 1998. "The Politics of Proximity: The Italian Response to the Albanian Crisis." *International Migration Review* 32(1): 203–22.

Però, Davide. 2005. "Immigrants and the Politics of Governance in Barcelona." Center for Migration, Policy and Society Working Paper 19/2005, Oxford.

Perrone, Luigi, ed. 1996. *Naufragi Albanesi: Studi, ricerche e riflessioni sull'Albania.* Rome: Sensibili alle Foglie.

Pojmann, Wendy, ed. 2008. *Migration and Activism in Europe since 1945.* New York: Palgrave MacMillan.

Pottage, Alain. 2004. "Introduction: The Fabrication of Persons and Things." In *Law, Anthropology, and the Constitution of the Social,* ed. Alain Pottage and Martha Mundy, 1–39. Cambridge: Cambridge University Press.

Prescott, J. R.V. 1978. *Boundaries and Frontiers.* London: Croom Helm.

Rabinow, Paul. 1999. *French DNA: Trouble in Purgatory.* Chicago: University of Chicago Press.

———. 2003. *Anthropos Today: Reflections on Modern Equipment.* Princeton, NJ: Princeton University Press.

Rancière, Jacques. 2010. *Dissensus: On Politics and Aesthetics.* Ed. and trans. Steven Corcoran. New York: Continuum.

Ratcliffe, James M. 1966. *The Good Samaritan and the Law.* Garden City, NY: Anchor.

Reed-Danahay, Deborah and Caroline B. Brettell, eds. 2008. *Citizenship, Political Engagement, and Belonging: Immigrants in Europe and the United States.* New Brunswick, NJ: Rutgers University Press.

Reinold, Theresa. 2013. *Sovereignty and the Responsibility to Protect: The Power of Norms and the Norms of the Powerful.* London: Routledge.

Riles, Annelise, ed. 2006. *Documents: Artifacts of Modern Knowledge.* Ann Arbor: University of Michigan Press.

Rodier, Claire. 2006. *Analysis of the External Dimension of the EU's Asylum and Immigration Policies—Summary and Recommendations for the European Parliament.* Brussels: European Parliament.

Rosaldo, Renato. 1997. "Cultural Citizenship, Inequality, and Multiculturalism." In *Latino Cultural Citizenship,* ed. William V. Flores and Rina Benmayor, 27–38. Boston: Beacon Press.

Rosen, Lawrence. 1995. "The Cultural Analysis of Others' Inner States." Introduction to *Other Intentions: Cultural Contexts and the Attribution of Inner States,* ed. Lawrence Rosen, 3–11. Santa Fe, NM: School of American Research Press.

Rouse, Roger. 1991. "Mexican Migration and the Social Space of Postmodernism." *Diaspora* 1(1): 8–23.

Rozakou, Katerina. 2012. "The Biopolitics of Hospitality in Greece: Humanitarianism and the Management of Refugees." *American Ethnologist* 39(3): 562–77.

Rudzinski, Aleksander W. 1966. "The Duty to Rescue: A Comparative Analysis." In *The Good Samaritan and the Law,* ed. James M. Ratcliffe, 91–134. Garden City, NY: Anchor.

Sanders, Todd and Harry G. West, eds. 2003. *Transparency and Conspiracy: Ethnographies of Suspicion in the New World Order.* Durham, NC: Duke University Press.

Sanfilippo, Fabio and Alice Scialoja. 2010. *A Lampedusa: Affari, malaffari, rivolta e sconfitta dell'isola che voleva diventare la porta d'Europa*. Rome: Infinito.

Sarat, Austin. 2014. *Gruesome Spectacles: Botched Executions and America's Death Penalty*. Stanford, CA: Stanford University Press.

Sarat, Austin, Douglas Lawrence, and Martha Merrill Umphrey. 2005. "At the Limits of Law: An Introduction." In *The Limits of Law*, ed. Austin Sarat, Lawrence Douglas, and Martha Merrill Umphrey, 1- 20. Stanford, CA: Stanford University Press.

Sassen, Saskia. 1996. *Losing Control? Sovereignty in an Age of Globalization*. New York: Columbia University Press.

———. 2006. *Territory, Authority, Rights: From Medieval to Global Assemblages*. Princeton, NJ: Princeton University Press.

Save the Children. 2014. *Piccoli schiavi invisibili: I volti della tratta e dello sfruttamento*. Rome: Save the Children.

Saviano, Roberto. 2007. *Gomorrah: A Personal Journey into the Violent International Empire of Naples' Organized Crime System*. Trans. Virginia Jewiss. New York: Picador.

Sayad, Abdelmalek. 2004 [1999]. *The Suffering of the Immigrant*. Preface by Pierre Bourdieu. Trans. David Macey. Malden, MA: Polity Press.

Scheper-Hughes, Nancy. 1993. *Death Without Weeping: The Violence of Everyday Life in Brazil*. Berkeley: University of California Press.

Schlesinger, Philip and François Foret. 2006. "Political Roof and Sacred Canopy? Religion and the EU Constitution." *European Journal of Social Theory* 9(1): 59–81.

Schneider, Jane, ed. 1998. *Italy's "Southern Question": Orientalism in One Country*. Oxford: Berg.

Sciurba, Alessandra. 2009. *Campi di forza: Percorsi confinati di migranti in Europa*. Verona: Ombre Corte.

Scott, James C. 1998. *Seeing like a State: How Certain Schemes to Improve the Human Condition Have Failed*. New Haven, CT: Yale University Press.

Sejko, Roland, dir. 2013. *Anija: La nave*. Luce Cinecittà, Rome.

Shamir, Ronen. 2005. "Without Borders? Notes on Globalization as a Mobility Regime." *Sociological Theory* 23(2): 197–217.

Shryock, Andrew. 2012. "Breaking Hospitality Apart: Bad Hosts, Bad Guests, and the Problem of Sovereignty." *Journal of the Royal Anthropological Institute* 18(S1): 20–33.

Simmel, Georg. 1971 [1908]. "The Poor." In *On Individuality and Social Forms*, ed. Donald N. Levine, 150–78. Chicago: University of Chicago Press.

Sniderman, Paul M., et al. 2000. *The Outsider: Prejudice and Politics in Italy*. Princeton, NJ: Princeton University Press.

Soysal, Yasemin N. 1994. *Limits of Citizenship: Migrants and Postnational Membership in Europe*. Chicago: University of Chicago Press.

Strik, Tineke. 2012. "Lives Lost in the Mediterranean Sea: Who Is Responsible? Committee on Migration, Refugees and Displaced Persons," Parliamentary Assembly of the Council of Europe, April 5, Strasbourg.

Stolcke, Verena. 1995. "Talking Culture: New Boundaries, New Rhetorics of Exclusion in Europe." *Current Anthropology* 36(1): 1–24.

Suárez-Navaz, Liliana. 2004. *Rebordering the Mediterranean: Boundaries and Citizenship in Southern Europe*. New York: Berghahn Books.

Sweeney, James A. 2009. "Credibility, Proof and Refugee Law." *International Journal of Refugee Law* 21(4): 700–726.

Taussig, Michael T. 1997. *The Magic of the State*. New York: Routledge.

Thielemann, Eiko. 2004. "Why European Policy Harmonization Undermines Refugee Burden-Sharing." *European Journal of Migration and Law* 6(1): 43–61.

Ticktin, Miriam I. 2011. *Casualties of Care: Immigration and the Politics of Humanitarianism in France*. Berkeley: University of California Press.

Todorova, Maria N. 2009. *Imagining the Balkans*. 2nd ed. Oxford: Oxford University Press.

Torpey, John. 2000. *The Invention of the Passport: Surveillance, Citizenship and the State*. Cambridge: Cambridge University Press.

Tsing, Anna Lowenhaupt. 2005. *Friction: An Ethnography of Global Connection*. Princeton, NJ: Princeton University Press.

UNHCR (United Nations High Commissioner for Refugees). 2013. *Displacement, the New 21st Century Challenge—UNHCR Global Trends 2012*. Geneva: UNHCR.

———. 2014. *Asylum Trends 2013: Levels and Trends in Industrialized Countries*. Geneva: UNHCR.

UNODC (United Nations Office on Drugs and Crime). 2010. *Smuggling of Migrants into, Through and from North Africa: A Thematic Review and Annotated Bibliography of Recent Publications*. New York: United Nations.

———. 2011. *The Role of Organized Crime in the Smuggling of Migrants from West Africa to the European Union*. New York: United Nations.

Urbinati, Nadia. 2014. *Democracy Disfigured: Opinion, Truth, and the People*. Cambridge, MA: Harvard University Press.

Urla, Jacqueline. 1993. "Cultural Politics in an Age of Statistics: Numbers, Nations, and the Making of Basque Identity." *American Ethnologist* 20(4): 818–43.

Vicari, Daniele, dir. 2012. *La nave dolce*. Indigo Film, Apulia Film Commission, Rai Cinema, and Albanian Central State Archive, Italy.

Walters, William. 2002. "Mapping Schengenland: Denaturalizing the Border." *Environment and Planning D: Society and Space* 20: 561–80.

Waterston, Alisse. 2014. *My Father's Wars: Migration, Memory, and the Violence of a Century*. New York: Routledge.

Weber, Max. 1998 [1948]. *From Max Weber: Essays in Sociology*. Trans., ed., and with an intro. by H. H. Gerth and C. Wright Mills. Oxford: Oxford University Press.

Wolf, Eric. 1982. *Europe and the People Without History*. Berkeley: University of California Press.

Yngvesson, Barbara and Susan Bibler Coutin. 2006. "Backed by Papers: Undoing Persons, Histories, and Return." *American Ethnologist* 33(2): 177–90.

Zammit, David E. 2007. "Migration in the Mediterranean: Equalising Strategies and
    Social Hierarchies in Migrant Integration." *Journal of Mediterranean Studies* 17(2):
    169–84.
Zincone, Giovanna. 2006. "The Making of Policies: Immigration and Immigrants in
    Italy." *Journal of Ethnic and Migration Studies* 32(3): 347–75.
Žižek, Slavoj. 1989. *Sublime Object of Ideology.* New York: Verso.
———. 2009. *First as Tragedy, Then as Farce.* New York: Verso.

Index

Acknowledgments

This book expresses a decade of professional research and a personal journey, bound in paper and ink. An interdisciplinary work such as this can only be written with the assistance and support of many people—scholars, research participants, friends, and family around the Mediterranean and in the United States. Naming everyone to record my sincere gratitude would be impossible, and I regret any omissions.

Several persons and institutions have directly enabled me to research and write the book I have always wanted to write. Pennsylvania Studies in Human Rights series editor Bert Lockwood and Penn Press editor Peter Agree have courageously believed in this project and supported it with enthusiasm, professionalism, and countless examples of a job well done, in their respective fields. Speaking of a job well done, my patient copyeditor, and Penn Press staff in acquisitions, design, editing, and promotion receive my thanks and admiration for their perceptive and detailed work on this project. I am grateful to my anonymous reviewer for generous, thorough, and insightful comments, and to David FitzGerald, Anthony Messina, Carolyn Nordstrom, and Takeyuki Tsuda for equally helpful comments on earlier chapters.

My central preoccupation with human rights, maritime migration, and the rule of law emerged during my time at the University of California, Irvine (Anthropology), and at the Center for Comparative Immigration Studies (CCIS), University of California, San Diego. At Irvine, supported by brilliant colleagues and friends, I had the privilege of working with scholars who shaped the contentious field I participate in: Victoria Bernal, Leo Chavez, Jim Ferguson, and Bill Maurer were crucial mentors and read substantial portions of this work. Liisa Malkki and Adriana Petryna encouraged rigorous research open to the challenges and opportunities of existential anthropology. Kitty Calavita, Susan Coutin, Robert Garfias, George Marcus, Michael Montoya, and Mei Zhan provided beautiful examples of how culturally complex and embodied legal and political issues can be empirically studied and rendered. At UC Irvine, my research trajectory also intersected with the availability of Talal Asad, Étienne Balibar, Jacques Derrida, and Philomena Essed. At CCIS, I was generously offered the time, facilities, and expertise to start writing about the relationships between migrant deaths and sovereignty. For that, I am particularly grateful to Wayne Cornelius and Takeyuki Tsuda, and to David FitzGerald and Eiko Thielemann for our conversations.

The Erasmus Institute at the University of Notre Dame provided the unique opportunity to think and write about the intersections of religion, democracy, and humanitarianism. The example of the Institute's eponym, humanist Desiderius Erasmus of Rotterdam, reminded me that it is possible to write about people, power, and politics with grace, desire, and even love. I am deeply grateful to Dianne Phillips and to Robert Sullivan.

At Notre Dame, I have the daily pleasure of working in what is a most supportive and engaging department, Anthropology. I have greatly benefited from such an environment and from conversations with each one of my colleagues, ranging from the minutiae of x-ray imaging to our aspirations as a discipline. Regarding this book in particular, I need to acknowledge Susan Blum, Agustín Fuentes, Patrick Gaffney, Tala Jarjour, Ian Kuijt, Jim McKenna, Carolyn Nordstrom, Mark Schurr, and Susan Sheridan. Teaching talented students has also contributed to sharpening these materials. Indeed I did "test" portions of the book on students Jennifer Heil, Kerry Pecho, Emily Salvaterra, Erin Scott, and Marianinna Villavicencio. My research assistant Megan McCormick, in particular, closely read the manuscript, and provided invaluable help also with bibliographic formatting; Jude Wafai helped with Arabic translations. Within the supportive environment at Notre Dame, the Nanovic Institute for European Studies, the Center for Civil and Human Rights, the Kellogg Working Group on Migrants' Political Transnationalism, the Office of Media Relations, and the Program in Italian Studies have allowed for consequential venues where some of these pages have been written, debated, and made better. This engagement was made possible, most directly, by Thomas Burish, Joseph Buttigieg, Paolo Carozza, Ted Cachey, Chris Cervenak, Shannon Chapla, Anthony Monta, and Karen Richman.

Research and writing were made possible through the generosity of several institutions: travel grants from the Institute for Scholarship in the Liberal Arts (ISLA, College of Arts and Letters, University of Notre Dame) and the Nanovic Institute for European Studies, Notre Dame; a Carey Postdoctoral Fellowship at the Erasmus Institute, Notre Dame; a Visiting Research Fellowship at CCIS, UC San Diego; two University of California Regents' Fellowships; multiple grants from the School of Social Sciences and the Department of Anthropology at UC Irvine; and a grant from the Institute of European Studies at UC Berkeley. This publication is made possible in part by support from ISLA. My appreciation goes to the work of the directors, staff, and board members of these institutions.

Some of the materials hereby expanded and revised were originally presented at international conferences, and have benefited from ensuing conversations. Thanks are due to conveners and respondents including Stefano Allievi, Asef Bayat, Eileen Botting, Fiona Bowie, Marina Calloni, William Chandler, Aurora Donzelli, Alessandro Duranti, Didier Fassin, Patricia Fernández–Kelly, Joseph Francese, Erica James, Cynthia Mahmood, Giovanni Ruggiero, Kamal Sadiq, Martin van Bruinessen, David Zammit, and Sami Zubaida.

Christian Bonatesta, Stefano Mencherini, and Bledar Toroci made available some of the video materials informing this work. Tonica Hunter and Daria Huss granted permission to adapt the i-map. Now substantially revised portions of Chapters 1 and 2 originally appeared in my contribution "The Birth of a Border: Policing by Charity on the Italian Maritime Edge" in *Border Encounters: Asymmetry and Proximity at Europe's Frontiers* (2013), edited by Jutta Lauth Bacas and the late William Kavanagh. I am grateful to Jutta Lauth Bacas and to Berghahn Books for permission to expand my chapter here.

This book is grounded in a decade of research in coastal southern Italy, in Lampedusa, in maritime travel around these locations, and in shorter trips to Malta, to coastal Libya, Tunisia, Greece and Montenegro, and to Serbia. In all these places, and at sea, my research and my life benefited from the quest and the existence of people who shared with me a sweet glass of tea, a communal couscous, a clay pot of *sarma*, a huge tray of sea urchins, or their daily meal from the workplace cafeteria. It is more than food we shared: knowledge, stories, glances, relations, pain, frustration, and worldviews. I am grateful to each person who participated in this work; this is their book too. Most need their anonymity to be preserved; others may share their names in this text.

Loved ones resist being thanked, but they still need my public recognition, as it is our relationships that allow these pages to exist, from the most ambitious theoretical insight down to the shortest syllable. I shared most of my adult life, and this book's personal and professional journey, with my better half, Tamara Stojanović. Dario and Lorenzo: don't fence in your curiosity and your imagination, as you grow tall and generous like your uncles Daniele and Vladimir. And please read everything, don't just look at the pictures!

It is hard to accept that many of the people at the center of this book—and my mother-in-law, uncles, aunts, and mom and dad Divina and Giuseppe—will not be able to read it as it is written in English. But this also means that there is no closure, that our relationship remains open and suspended, and that we have an excuse to meet and talk more. In the meantime, please accept this book, and a *caffè sospeso*, as a token of my admiration, respect, gratitude.